Acknowledgments

The research reported in this book was made possible by the generous interest and assistance of many people. We are first indebted to F. W. Taussig and C. S. Joslyn whose earlier study of American business leaders provided a basis for the conception and much of the methodology of the present research. We must express also our debt to the many American businessmen whose response to our inquiries made the study possible.

We wish to thank the following men, who by their sponsorship of the research and advice in its formulation aided in the presentation of the study to the American business community:

> Lawrence A. Appley, New York City
> John Cowles, Minneapolis
> Clarence B. Randall, Chicago
> Frank Stanton, New York City
> General Robert E. Wood, Chicago

Advice and counsel in the execution of the study was provided by the following men, to whom we wish to express our appreciation:

> W. G. Caples, Chicago
> L. H. Fisher, St. Paul
> Howard Goodman, Chicago
> James C. Worthy, Washington, D.C.

Chancellor Lawrence A. Kimpton of the University of Chicago lent the study his active support, as did also George Watkins and Brinton Stone of the University of Chicago.

For assistance in the design of the study, we are grateful to Professors Garfield V. Cox, Philip Hauser, and Theodore W. Schultz of the University of Chicago. We wish to thank Mildred Hall Warner for her invaluable editorial assistance. Important research assistance was provided by Alice Chandler.

T0338415

Occupational Mobility

Primary financial support for the project was contributed by the Louis W. and Maud Hill Foundation, and we are indebted to the Foundation for critical and understanding support of the project's purpose and significance.

We would like to thank the following for their early appreciation of the study and generous financial assistance:

E. B. Busby, R. R. Donnelley and Sons Company, Chicago
Marshall Field, New York City
Goodman Manufacturing Company, Chicago
Inland Steel Company, Chicago
Sears, Roebuck and Company, Chicago

Special acknowledgment is owed three individuals. By their early interest in the problem of social mobility in American business, Howard Goodman and James C. Worthy encouraged us to undertake this research. A. A. Heckman, through his understanding of the scientific and practical import of the study and his continuing advice and encouragement, played a central part in the execution of the study.

W. L. W.
J. C. A.

University of Chicago
June 30, 1955

OCCUPATIONAL MOBILITY

in American Business and Industry

OCCUPATIONAL MOBILITY

in American Business and
Industry

1928 〰〰〰〰〰〰〰〰〰〰〰〰〰〰 1952

W. Lloyd Warner
James C. Abegglen

UNIVERSITY OF MINNESOTA PRESS, Minneapolis

PRINTED AT THE LUND PRESS, INC., MINNEAPOLIS

Library of Congress Catalog Card Number: 55-9372

PUBLISHED IN GREAT BRITAIN, INDIA, AND PAKISTAN BY
GEOFFREY CUMBERLEGE: OXFORD UNIVERSITY PRESS, LONDON, BOMBAY, AND KARACHI

TO THE MEMORY OF

WALLACE B. DONHAM

Table of Contents

List of Tables

TEXT TABLES

x

List of Tables

xi

Occupational Mobility

List of Tables

Occupational Mobility

List of Tables

Occupational Mobility

List of Tables

Occupational Mobility

APPENDIX TABLES

List of Tables

IV. The Education of the Business Elite, page 266

V. The Business Career, page 271

Time Factors in the Career

Occupational Mobility

List of Tables

OCCUPATIONAL MOBILITY
in American Business and Industry

CHAPTER I

The American Business Elite

This volume is concerned with American business leadership, that powerful, prestigeful, and important occupational elite concentrated at the high levels of business enterprise. It presents the findings of extensive research on all varieties of leaders of business and industry from every region of the United States. Mining and manufacturing, finance, construction, and all other types of business and industrial enterprise are represented by the 8000 leaders studied. All levels of top management, from chairman of the board and large owner to secretary and treasurer, are included.

The principal purpose of the research on the business elite was to learn about vertical occupational mobility — how fluid and flexible our society is in this important area. Are the top-status levels increasingly open and accessible to those born at lower levels, or less open, and accessible only to the sons of top-status fathers? What factors are principally responsible for occupational mobility from lower to higher levels and what forces operate to prevent more mobility? Is more or less movement represented by this than by previous generations of business leaders? We wanted to know whether hereditary and aristocratic principles operate to hold families at the top or whether the competitive forces which emphasize individual achievement determine who will be a leader.

It is first necessary to set forth the theoretical and methodological framework in which the study was conceived, and within which the data from the study have been analyzed. Following this, some of the previous work dealing with occupational mobility in America is reviewed and discussed in the light of the objectives of this research. This chapter concludes with a brief summary and discussion of the

3

principal findings of the study. The summary serves both as an introduction and as a guide to the detailed statement of findings in succeeding chapters.

Occupational Succession: Theory and Method

A major theoretical and methodological interest was in what we have called *occupational succession*. We shall term *occupational succession* the ordered process by which individuals succeed each other in occupations. The study of occupational succession, therefore, consists of examining the circulation and movement of personnel through positions, and of determining the regularities and uniformities which have to do with entering, holding, and leaving a given status. In the present discussion we are concerned with a *type* of status, the big business owner and manager, and with but one kind of elite, the business and owning class. More particularly, this investigation of occupational succession is concerned with how this society orders and determines which men, through the changing generations of individuals, shall occupy certain occupational statuses.

To found our investigation soundly, it is necessary to relate occupational theory, particularly that of occupational succession, to theory of family structure, for the two are interdependent. Men are born to fathers who are at given occupational levels, they grow to maturity, learn and follow a particular profession in life, marry, sire sons who are reared to maturity and work at their own trades or professions. We shall extend our view back to the preceding generation so that the fathers of the present business elite are also related to their fathers; thus we shall be examining three generations. At the level of fact and evidence we shall be examining a particular man, and at times his paternal grandfather and his father, and their occupations.

Meanwhile we will expand our evidence by studying occupational succession throughout all industries and all regions of the United States. Broad as well as limited generalizations are thus possible and can be scientifically formed about occupational succession and the activities of the ambitious. We can thus place a particular man or a particular occupation into a more general category, such as a generation or region; we can see the individual in his appropriate universe and compare his occupational level with that of other individuals; or we can move to more abstract levels and relate any of the facts about

4

a particular man to the whole occupational structure of the United States. This, of course, is always in terms of the limitations set up by the research, the study of occupational succession and the American business elite.

What has just been said needs more theoretical and technical treatment. The kinship dimension does not change through life; the position of fathers and sons or of wives' fathers and their daughters remains structurally the same. Although their behavior through the years changes, their positions are fixed by a biological base socially recognized in the kinship structure. No matter how great the occupational or social distance may become, they always remain a birth cycle [1] apart. A birth cycle is a unit of *time* between one's own birth and one's procreation of another individual. Consequently the movement or lack of movement among occupations can be measured timewise by use of the birth cycle. The type of occupational status of each son will be the same as, or different from, his father's. Each man marries a woman who is the daughter of a man of either the same or different status.

If there is no difference between the positions of the son and father, and they hold occupations at the same level, there has been no movement and no occupational distance separates them. If there has been movement, the distance and its direction (up, down, or across) can be identified and measured. The men who moved from the working class of their fathers to the business elite, and thus in one birth cycle moved upward through several loosely defined occupational strata, were mobile at a far more rapid rate than those who rose to the business elite from the white-collar class of their fathers after the fathers had risen from the laboring group. The distance covered was the same, the direction taken the same, but the time involved was cut in half and the velocity accordingly doubled.

Since the occupational movement of fathers and sons can be identified and measured, it is possible to measure the amount of movement from different occupational distances into the elite. This is accomplished by equating all business leaders as sons (in the family universe) of one generation and their fathers as the generation "above" in occupational succession. This being operationally feasible, the amount

[1] Kingsley Davis and W. Lloyd Warner, "Structural Analysis of Kinship," *American Anthropologist*, Vol. 39, No. 2 (April–June 1937), pp. 291–313.

of movement from each occupational level into the elite can be measured, as well as the time it took in terms of one or two generations (or of the years within a lifetime). Equally important, the immobility of occupational succession in the business elite can be determined.

At further levels of generalization we will be able to speak of the characteristics of the top occupational status and of kinds of movement out of it and into it from the rest of the occupational universe.

Children are born to the social and economic position of their parents; it is therefore possible, by ascertaining the parents' status, to learn whether men of the elite are all from families of similar positions or from families of different positions. Since a family's socioeconomic position is largely dependent on the father's occupational place in the economic order, it is possible to examine the life careers of the men of the elite and to trace their present status back through their occupational history to the time when they were children and still dependent on, and identified with, the status of their fathers and their families.[2]

The biological level, composed of parents and children, more particularly fathers and sons, provides a consistent unit of measurement for the occupational nearness and distance, closure and access, existing between two or more generations. When this unit of measurement is combined with a time unit such as the age of the business leader when he achieved a position in the elite, the velocity of movement as well as the direction and amount may be determined and the degree of occupational *dispersal* measured. The occupational *dispersal* of three generations of fathers and sons may be confined to one occupational level, to two, or spread from the top to the bottom. The velocity may be spoken of as measurable by one, two, or three generations of time for any occupational movement. The *direction* of movement of fathers and sons may be *all* upward, or up and down. But all of it will always be seen from the position of those who belong *now* to the present business elite. We will see their lives and the generations out of which they come from the perspective of their present position. Consequently our study is limited. It does not try to examine the careers

---

[2] The problem involved is occupational mobility and, more generally, occupational succession. However, when occupational mobility takes place usually social mobility takes place too; consequently we have sometimes referred to this as social mobility, following general practice. The reader, however, can determine by context when we are referring quite specifically to one or the other. For example, in the later chapters on the family and marriage, it is more likely that social mobility will usually be involved whenever occupational change takes place.

of the men who are presently at other levels. It does not present, for example, the social backgrounds or careers of white-collar men or workers who have or have not tried to advance themselves to the business elite. Nor can it say whether all the sons of professional men would or would not welcome the opportunity to acquire the prestige, the honor, and the power of status in the elite.

Another way by which the relation of the occupations of one generation to those of the succeeding ones may be examined is to learn the occupation of the wife's father. The fathers of the wives of the present elite (and the mothers of the sons of the elite) provided the occupational origins of the women who greatly influenced the occupational careers of the men studied. A study of the women these men marry also helps determine whether the men (1) move into the elite by marriage and possibly acquire their high position without earning it; (2) achieve elite position and then marry a woman at their newly acquired rank; or (3) marry either at their level of origin, or someone along the route to high position. Hence the study of the occupational succession of males to the elite must also be a research on the women who marry them. Some women from the lower occupational origins marry men born to the elite, others marry men of low origins, and some women of the elite marry men of their own occupational class.

Occupation, marriage, and descent are inextricably interwoven into *one* status-giving system since all members of the family are classified as similar or the same for basic purposes of social identification. Should the sons and daughters inherit their family's occupational rank, should the rules of marriage require that they mate with those of the same occupational level, and should these occupational orders be ranked, the combination of endogamy and occupational inheritance would conform to one type of caste system. There would be no movement from one level to another. Such a system would be closed. No occupational status would be open to those above or below it. There would be no vertical *status* movement.

At the other pole would be a system in which there were no formal or informal rules, beliefs, or values separating those who wish to marry or preventing men at any level and occupation from moving to any other. There is no such system existing in the world. Our own system of marriage and occupational succession falls between these two extremes.

Occupational Mobility

From these considerations, we can distinguish (and validate empirically) several types and varieties of elite in the American business world. Each type may be re-divided, according to scientific purpose, into subcategories based upon kind of industry, region, ethnic group, education, and other such factors.

From the point of view of personnel at the elite level, there are two major types: the birth elite and the mobile elite. The birth elite is divided into two major types: recent, of one generation; and old, of two or more generations. The mobile elite includes those men who achieved the position by movement into it from positions outside it, usually but not always from occupations lower than the present one. Men coming to the elite from the laboring, white-collar, and small business classes rise of course to this higher level; most men coming from the farming classes also rise to the status.

But some men, possibly a minority, from the professional classes move laterally, not vertically, into the business elite. This is so because sons of men in high-ranking professions and government positions and sons of a small percentage of farmers are by the judgments of our culture ranked equally with those of the business elite. The son or daughter of a banker or of the president of a great business enterprise, when marrying the daughter or son of a prominent lawyer or government official or high military officer, does not necessarily marry beneath him; *socially* he may be marrying above himself.

Since marriage may be important in the rise of the mobile man, several subtypes of *mobile* elite in terms of marriage need to be distinguished. They are (1) those who rose from the lowest level to the top of the business world and who (a) married women of their own level, (b) married women from levels between their own and the top, or (c) married women after they arrived (or when they achieved top status); (2) men from the white-collar, (3) small business, and (4) farming classes who climbed to the elite and who married women below them, at their own, at an intervening, or at the elite level; (5) men from the professional group (including, among others, government officers, military men, doctors, and lawyers) and a few farmers who moved *across* and into (or up to) the business elite and married women at the top or at some lower level.

Those statuses which are impossible, or almost so, for those outside to enter we shall call closed. Those not so limited we shall call open and free. The status of a person may be fixed in one position. When an individual can move he is comparatively free — that is, his position is not fixed.

The movement up we shall call *achieved status* or *achieved occupation*.[3] Occupational succession of the business elite means either continuance of sons at their fathers' positions in the elite or a movement of men from outside into such positions. The continuation in the same position may be accompanied by marriage to someone at the same level (endogamy) or to someone outside it.[4] If the latter, it may be to one equivalent to, or below, the elite.

Occupational Status in Time and Flux

It is possible to study the short-term variations and fluctuations in the social system within a generation, and not learn about the deep, ongoing changes in the system or the direction of these changes. For this purpose in this study we compare the occupations of the leaders in the present generation with those of their fathers and paternal grandfathers. To examine the long-term trends in the society a more critical test requires the comparison of the elites and of movement into the elites at two separate points in time.

The research method and evidence for such a test should allow comparison between the occupational structure and the kinds of personnel in the several statuses over an interval of no less than one full generation. From a theoretical examination of the interaction between structure and personnel, it is possible to derive several important and socially significant principles of cultural transmission between generations. Further generalizations having to do with social structure and its changing personnel,[5] occupational and social ranks, and movement in and out of them also appear. These generalizations are stated below and provide theoretical guidance for the research and tests of the meaning of the empirically derived results.

[3] Ralph Linton, *The Study of Man* (New York: D. Appleton-Century Co., 1936).

[4] The term "same," which we have frequently used, needs further scrutiny, for it has two meanings in this context. It may mean that a son inherits or acquires the identical position in the same firm so that, for example, when his father retires from that position, the son becomes president and owner of the A.B.C. Shoe Manufacturing Company. It also can mean that the son acquires the same *kind* (category) of position as the father. He may become a business executive in another large firm and thus achieve a similar position in the same ranked category.

[5] Georg Simmel, *The Sociology of Georg Simmel*, translated by Kurt H. Wolff (Glencoe, Ill.: The Free Press, 1950).

Occupational Mobility

When one generation (or more) has successfully transmitted its social structure (from an older to a younger biological generation) and thus succeeded in continuing its own system so that the *same kinds of personnel* occupy the same kinds of positions, such an unchanging order of stable relations results in a closed system of occupational rank, a castelike system.

Or it may be that there has been drastic modification of the system of change to the point where there is little or no similarity between two generations either in structure or personnel. Such a condition is only theoretically possible. Revolutions happen, but not total ones.

It may be that the social structure has *changed* from one generation to another, but that the *same kinds* of people occupy the same relative positions in the new social structure; there is thus created a self-perpetuating elite. The characteristics of the top status change, but the people who occupy it come from the same kind of families and the same kind of background as previously.

It may be demonstrated that the social structure has remained unchanged from one generation to another, but that the older elite generation has not been succeeded by its offspring and has not been successful in putting the same kinds of people into the elite positions in the following generation. The top positions, once filled with old Americans, may now be filled by men newly arrived in the society — immigrants or sons of immigrants — or by men from economic origins outside the elite ranks.

It may be that the older generation has only partly succeeded in transmitting the social structure to succeeding generations and in putting the same kinds of people into the various positions in the structure: this is adaptive continuity in a larger world of social and technological change.

These and other propositions raise major questions of both practical and theoretical significance. To learn whether our system is more or less static, less or more flexible than it was a generation ago, and to do this with precision, the data from this study of American business leaders of 1952 are compared with those of an earlier study of American businessmen.[6] The previous study, conducted in 1928, one generation ago, examined the origins and backgrounds of the business

[6] F. W. Taussig and C. S. Joslyn, *American Business Leaders* (New York: The Macmillan Co., 1932).

leaders of that time. The authors of the earlier study stated their purposes as follows:

(1) To ascertain from what social classes American business leaders are recruited;
(2) To determine whether the proportionate contribution of each social class to the supply of business leaders is less than, equal to, or greater than the proportion of that class in the population at large;
(3) To throw light, so far as possible, on the relative influence of hereditary and environmental factors in causing such disparities as may exist between the representation of the several classes among business leaders and their representation in the population at large.[7]

It will be seen that their study bears directly on a portion of the problems considered in this research. There were several reasons why this original project should be repeated at the present. Firstly, our knowledge of social class in America, and thus of the basic framework into which such data would fit, has vastly increased. Secondly, we are more than two decades, or roughly one generation, removed in time from the original investigation. The interval, in addition to its intrinsic significance, has included a major depression, a major war, and a major industrial boom, all leaving deep marks on our society.

This early research provided a technique of demonstrated effectiveness for the investigation of problems related to those considered here as well as a partial basis for the study of trends through time. Accordingly, comparable data (see Chapter VIII) were obtained for contemporary business leaders, and this made it possible to compare in important respects the business leaders of two generations.

It must be said that the basic conception underlying our thinking was that the American society of 1952 is essentially the same society as that of 1928; a generation has passed, and there have been social changes, but there has been ordered continuity.

Since the whole business universe has expanded (productivity, technology, etc.) the top now is far more powerful than in 1928. It controls more. In this sense the two universes (1928 and 1952) are different, but relatively the grades (occupational levels) are very similar. The similarities may be due to the fact that no hierarchy can be-

[7] *Ibid.*, p. 1.

come too extended vertically, despite today's expanded industrial and business universe. To care for the increased complexity, the horizontal structure of the business system has been elaborated. The hierarchy has in the interval not been greatly extended vertically, but it has been differentiated horizontally. To a considerable degree there are now approximately the same named positions in the hierarchy as formerly.

The number of steps in the occupational hierarchy is relatively the same (the same type of differentiation) so that the mobile man now probably takes no more steps than in 1928. But the volume of business (index of power) has changed, so the mobile man is in a more complex area of decision, and the steps he takes are somewhat different, for the larger system around him is more complex.

Many trends and forces, which were only beginning to be evident in 1928 and earlier, reached full strength and influence in the next two decades. Some major trends in the business and industrial structure that were concomitant with the broad social and political changes over these years, subsequent on booms, busts, wars and quasi-wars, can be noted here: The impact of taxation has changed income distribution. There has been a separation of ownership and management. The distribution of education in the total society has changed. There has been a tremendous advance of technology resulting in the introduction of highly specialized personnel into the hierarchy as well as in the establishment and expansion of some industries (e.g., communications, chemicals, service industries) and contraction of others (e.g., mining). There have been changes in the corporate structure and in the relations of business to local communities and to government.

Despite these differences, it is important to remember that we are comparing the business system at two points of extreme expansion. Despite all the changes (the intensification of technological change, the impersonalization of the business structure, etc.), the scalar structure [8] in most business enterprises in terms of positions and statuses remains very similar.

The implications of these similarities and changes for the mobile man in the two generations (1928 and 1952) may be stated as a question with its possible answers:

[8] Chester Barnard, "Functions and Pathology of Status Systems in Formal Organizations," in William F. Whyte, ed., *Industry and Society* (New York: McGraw-Hill Book Co., Inc., 1946), pp. 46–83.

How may the mobile man in the present structure be different from the mobile man in the earlier structure?

1. The routes and methods may be different.

2. The routes to the top may tap different social "territories" so that different people use them.

3. More of some territories, less of others, might be tapped.

4. Certain routes may be no longer readily available.

The use of the 1928 business leaders for comparative purposes, although raising further problems, greatly expanded the scope of our investigation. Taussig and Joslyn studied not only the American business leaders of that time but the fathers and paternal grandfathers of these men. These three generations of occupational succession carried their study back from 1928 well into the last century. Our own study, some twenty-four years (a generation of business leaders) later, when combined with theirs provides knowledge about an entire century of American business leaders. During that time the United States went through a civil war, expanded to the Pacific, fought several foreign wars, suffered the ravages of a number of panics, changed from what was largely an agricultural to an industrial society, and increased in world power and influence from an isolated and withdrawn country of only moderate significance to a great world power, now involved in the affairs of the greatest and least nations and regions. Meanwhile the rest of the world has changed drastically. Revolutions of major magnitude have reordered the social structures and economies of other countries and secondarily influenced us; empires have come and gone. A great technological revolution has greatly changed us and all other countries.

Some of the Issues Involved: Selected Literature

In the discussion above, the term *occupational succession* has been used to designate the several types of occupational movement under study. By generation, occupational succession refers to the relationship between the occupation of the father and the occupation of his son; by status, to the movement into and out of any occupational position. Occupational mobility may also refer to movement within the individual's own occupational career. Such mobility may include changes from one job to another within a community, from one job to another between communities, and from one type of job to another within or between communities. On the whole, these latter types of movement have not been closely studied, and are treated only as peripheral factors in this study of the business elite.

Much of the research on occupational mobility or occupational succession is a product of the past two decades of sociological investigation. Subsequent to the analysis of earlier work by Sorokin,[9] studies dealing with movement at all points in the occupational hierarchy have been conducted by a number of investigators, chief among them Davidson and Anderson[10] in San Jose in the mid-thirties, Centers[11] and the National Opinion Research Center[12] on national samples in the mid-forties, and Rogoff[13] in Indianapolis in two time periods, the more recent about 1940. The general conclusions of these studies are similar: sons are engaged in the occupation of their fathers more often than in any other single occupation; mobility is most frequent into those occupations whose status evaluation is most like the father's; approximately two thirds of the populations under study are found to be engaged in different occupations from the father. Davidson and Anderson summarize their results as follows: "The preponderance of sons did not move far from their father's level. Nevertheless sons of fathers on any level are found distributed along the entire series of levels. Real 'climbers' and those seriously degraded in comparison with their fathers apparently constitute a minor fraction."[14] Rogoff, reviewing her results in the light of these other studies, states: "These findings are, for the most part, consistent with those of previous mobility research. In both time periods, about 70 per cent of the men were in occupations different from those of their fathers; this proportion is about the same as that found by [others]. As in these studies, the father's occupation is the most likely destination of his son."[15]

The convergence of data and interpretation from these studies provides a measure of the degree of openness of our society, and substan-

---

[9] Pitirim A. Sorokin, *Social Mobility* (New York: Harper and Brothers, 1927).

[10] Percy E. Davidson and H. Dewey Anderson, *Occupational Mobility in an American Community* (Stanford University: Stanford University Press, 1937).

[11] Richard Centers, "Occupational Mobility of Urban Occupational Strata," *American Sociological Review*, Vol. 13 (April 1948), pp. 197–203.

[12] "Jobs and Occupations: A Popular Evaluation," *Opinion News*, Vol. 9 (September 1, 1947), pp. 3–13.

[13] Natalie Rogoff, *Recent Trends in Occupational Mobility* (Glencoe, Ill.: The Free Press, 1953).

[14] Davidson and Anderson, *op. cit.*, pp. 164–65.

[15] Rogoff, *op. cit.*, p. 107.

tial mobility is found to take place in terms of occupational succession. At the same time, these studies demonstrate the limited range and amount of such mobility. These results bring into relief the underlying question for research: can it be assumed that vertical occupational mobility is increasing or decreasing?

On this problem of time trends evidence is not available comparable in scope and detail to that cited above concerning mobility incident at a single point in time. In general, however, while there has been dissent,[16] the present consensus of opinion may be fairly concluded to hold that occupational mobility in particular and status mobility in general are and have been decreasing in American society.

As an illustration of what appears to be the prevailing view, the following summary remarks from several studies and commentaries may be cited:

It seems probable that our class system is becoming less open and mobility increasingly difficult for those at the bottom of the social heap.[17]

The long-existing favorable balance of vertical circulation of individuals in American society, i.e., the excess of upward over downward moves, has diminished and seems likely to be further reduced.[18]

"Success" in America has been a widespread fact, an engaging image, a driving motive and a way of life. In the middle of the twentieth century, it has become less widespread as a fact, more confused as an image, often dubious as a motive, and soured as a way of life.[19]

In terms of class structure there seems to be a marked trend toward lessened interclass mobility, and a consequent increasing fixation of boundaries. While upward mobility is still permissive, it is becoming more difficult; rigidities are developing. . . . In general there is evidence that the American Dream is becoming less real for many people.[20]

The bases for this general conclusion are diverse and may be seen in four groups: one, the assumption of substantial widespread and far-ranging mobility in the American past; two, conclusions derived from

---

[16] See, for example, Gideon Sjoberg, "Are Social Classes Becoming More Rigid?" *American Sociological Review*, Vol. 16 (December 1951), pp. 775–83.

[17] W. Lloyd Warner and J. O. Low, *The Social System of the Modern Factory* (New Haven: Yale University Press, 1947), p. 185.

[18] Elbridge Sibley, "Some Demographic Clues to Stratification," *American Sociological Review*, Vol. 7 (June 1942), p. 322.

[19] C. Wright Mills, *White Collar* (New York: Oxford University Press, 1931), p. 259.

[20] J. O. Hertzler, "Some Tendencies toward a Closed Class System in the United States," *Social Forces*, Vol. 30 (March 1952), pp. 313–14.

studies of the social structure of small communities; three, conclusions derived from studies of occupational mobility from which projections into the future have been made; four, conclusions from the analysis of factors (immigration, education, and the like) demonstrated or presumed to have an important influence on mobility.

It will be noted that each of the authors quoted states or implies that some considerable degree of occupational mobility existed at an earlier point in the history of American society. Undoubtedly at all times in our history mobility has been widespread in our society, as compared to most other societies. The extent of such mobility, however, the number of persons participating, and the actual social distances traversed, have not been well established. Legend has it, and some historians seem to agree,[21] that particularly in the business elite of the American past almost all recruitment took place from substantially lower status levels. Recent studies challenge this proposition. A series of examinations of American business leaders of the late nineteenth and early twentieth centuries, conducted by William Miller, indicate that in general business leaders were recruited from backgrounds which in most cases represented the upper and upper-middle classes of their time. One of the studies concludes:

Was the typical industrial leader of the 1870's then a "new man," an escapee from the slums of Europe or from the paternal farm? Did he rise by his own efforts from a boyhood of poverty? Was he as innocent of education and of formal training as has often been alleged? He seems to have been none of these things. American by birth, of a New England father, English in national origin, Congregational, Presbyterian or Episcopal in religion, urban in early environment, he was rather born and bred in an atmosphere in which business and a relatively high social standing were intimately associated with his family life.[22]

Another historical study, using less intensive data but covering the period 1570 through 1879, concludes:

For the whole of United States history: the typical member of the American business elite is of Northeastern origin. . . . He did not

[21] See, for example, Arthur M. Schlesinger, *The Political and Social Growth of the American People* (New York: The Macmillan Co., 1941); Charles A. and Mary R. Beard, *The Rise of American Civilization* (New York: The Macmillan Co., 1930).

[22] Frances W. Gregory and Irene D. Neu, "The American Industrial Elite in the 1870's," in *Men in Business*, edited by William Miller (Cambridge: Harvard University Press, 1952), p. 204.

migrate westward to success. He was definitely of the upper classes by birth . . . and was educated well above the level of the general population. . . . The father of the business elite has typically been a business man.[23]

While the history of the American business elite is not at issue in this study, it is important to recall that few empirical studies of occupational mobility have in fact dealt with past generations; rather, studies of occupational mobility for the present have been made, and a condition of limited mobility observed. The conclusion of diminished occupational mobility then derived is no doubt in part a result of a comparison of these present-day data with a hypothetical, "open" past — a past which was in fact "open" only to a limited extent.

Important sources of generalization about status and mobility in American society have been the community studies, chief among these the reports of the Lynds and of Warner.[24] Several characteristics of these studies are relevant to the question of time trends in American society in occupational mobility. These researches have concluded that the mobility functions of a number of institutions believed important in the mobility process are increasingly limited; they cite chiefly the credit structure, the business and industrial organizations, and the educational institutions.

It is difficult to estimate the relevance of these studies to the problem of increasing or diminishing mobility in the total society for several reasons. One, most of these community researches were carried out during the 1929–39 depression period, an era during which both the atmosphere and the economic reality of the social milieu probably made optimistic projection of mobility estimates difficult. Two, these researches were of necessity conducted in small towns or cities. As the data of the present study of the business elite make clear, the small cities of America are not important sources of the business elite, and it is in terms of business mobility that time trends have most often been examined. Further, these community studies were concerned with the

[23] C. Wright Mills, "The American Business Elite: A Collective Portrait," in "The Tasks of Economic History," *Journal of Economic History*, Supplement V (December 1945), p. 44.

[24] R. S. Lynd and H. M. Lynd, *Middletown: A Study in Contemporary American Culture* (New York: Harcourt Brace and Co., 1929); and *Middletown in Transition* (New York: Harcourt Brace and Co., 1937); W. Lloyd Warner *et al.*, *Yankee City Series* (New Haven: Yale University Press, 1941–47); W. Lloyd Warner and associates, *Democracy in Jonesville* (New York: Harper and Brothers, 1949).

problems of the ongoing social structure as seen in a specific locale. Examination of emigration and the subsequent careers of emigrees from these communities were not included in the research designs. It is likely that much of the mobile or potentially mobile populations of these communities was not available to the researchers.

In general, it may be concluded that the studies of communities have accurately and insightfully delineated much of the nature of the mobility process and the functions of community institutions in this process. These studies have further analyzed the sources of rigidity in the social system and their historical development. But they have not dealt with the direction of our social system, as regards mobility, with the precision that would warrant substantial generalization.

Another source of conclusions regarding increasing or decreasing occupational mobility is found in those studies of specific occupations which have dealt directly with the problem of time trends. Inadequate research methods have made the conclusions from some of these studies dubious. For example, in a study of nine hundred members of the business elite *Fortune* stated: "In short, new members of the Nine Hundred are tending to come increasingly from economically comfortable families." [25] In this study the time dimension was examined by means of a comparison of the younger with the older men of the group as to fathers' occupations. Inevitably, larger proportions of the younger men were found to be from higher status occupations. While *Fortune* concluded that this reflects increased occupational inheritance, the more accurate conclusion is of course that men from higher status backgrounds, advantaged in both tangible and intangible ways by education, money, friends, and way of life, attain these positions at an earlier age.

Another kind of error is illustrated by another study of occupational inheritance: "In the general polarization of the middle-sized city's stratification, the top and the bottom are becoming more rigid: 73 per cent of the upper half of the income-occupation scale is descended from the upper half." [26] In this instance, the observed rate of inheritance in no way permits a conclusion of increased or decreased status rigidity, as the rate in the past is not available, and may have been

[25] "The Nine Hundred," *Fortune*, Vol. 21 (November 1952), p. 236.
[26] C. Wright Mills, "The Middle Classes in Middle-Sized Cities," *American Sociological Review*, Vol. 11 (October 1946), p. 258.

50 per cent or 90 per cent. In the absence of data for another generation, a conclusion as to time trends is not warranted.

In the study to which this research owes its comparison data and much of its methodology, Taussig and Joslyn also concluded after analysis of their data that the trend in the business elite at least has been to increased occupational rigidity. In 1932 they concluded: "It is entirely possible that by the middle of the century more than two-thirds of the successful businessmen in the United States will be recruited from the sons of business owners (large or small) and business executives (major or minor)." [27] This conclusion was reached after careful adjustment of the data of the study to correct for differences in career advantages between younger and older men. Despite this, it seems unlikely that generalizations may be made, regarding time trends in mobility, from data on a single generation. To examine the problem accurately, comparisons between two generations must be conducted.

The single substantial study comparing two generations of population with respect to occupational mobility is that recently published by Natalie Rogoff. Comparing 1910 and 1940, with populations drawn from Indianapolis, she concludes that little change in the direction or extent of occupational mobility has taken place.

For the population as a whole, the average mobility rate did not change over the thirty year time span. During both time periods occupational moves were made, on the average, by about four-fifths as many men as expected . . . If we use these mean mobility rates as a single measure of the openness or rigidity of the occupational structure, they indicate that no change took place during the past three decades.[28]

This study provides one of the few substantial indications of relatively constant mobility rates through time in American society. The work of Stuart Adams should also be cited in this connection, for, while not dealing directly with time trends as such, his study of lawyers [29] in particular raises important and substantial questions concerning the assumption of increasing occupational rigidity.

A number of factors have been held to be closely related to mobility,

[27] Taussig and Joslyn, op. cit., p. 235.
[28] Rogoff, op. cit., p. 46.
[29] Stuart Adams, "Regional Differences in Vertical Mobility in a High Status Occupation," American Sociological Review, Vol. 15 (April 1950), pp. 228–35.

occupational and social, and these have been examined both as they affect present mobility rates and patterns, and as they might affect mobility trends.

1. Differential fertility rates have been observed between occupational and class groups. In general, an inverse relationship between socioeconomic level and birth rate has been observed, which suggests the possibility that the net rate of reproduction at the higher status levels is such as to require some mobility from lower (higher reproduction) levels to maintain the population balance. Decreasing differences in birth rate by socioeconomic levels have provided a basis for postulating decreased mobility in the future.

2. Immigration has long been held to have made for increased mobility in American business, by providing a source of population for lower status positions and facilitating mobility by the rest of the population. The probable future effects of this factor were summarized by one author as follows: "Now the thin stream of newcomers is mostly composed of persons from higher social and economic levels; laborers in general can no longer afford to immigrate, even if they could escape their national masters. Thus instead of a strong upward current, immigration now produces a slight downward movement in our society."[30]

3. The "frontier" theory is closely related to the above in suggesting that in the American past new territories and communities to the west provided a social *tabula rasa* for ambitious young men. From this it has been argued that the end of the frontier brought with it decreased mobility. The point is not well supported by evidence, and an ingenious though hardly conclusive study by Adams[31] challenges it.

4. The well-documented role of education in defining future social position has focused much attention on the role of the school in accelerating and retarding mobility. Values and beliefs relating to "equal opportunity" are most sharply focused in this area, and as a result much attention has been paid to the fact that the schools function to the primary advantage of the higher social and economic status levels, and that the lower status students at all levels of our educational system are considerably disadvantaged. Given the importance to mobility of both technical and social training, emphasis has been placed

[30] Sibley, *op. cit.*, pp. 324–25.
[31] Adams, *op. cit.*

on the fashion in which schools tend to depress the mobility rate. Less attention has been drawn to the concomitant fact that they serve as training grounds, in a limited number of cases, for mobility. Few, if any, data are available which would support any conclusion on time trends in mobility as regards the educational system.

5. Differences in inherent abilities, particularly intellectual, have been postulated for the several social classes in America. Taussig and Joslyn in particular argued, not entirely successfully, for the importance of genetic differences among the several occupational strata in determining occupational inheritance and mobility rates. This view has not been well supported, and more recent work has provided evidence that abilities are distributed normally throughout the population.[32] The question is difficult to resolve, but from a sociological point of view the most tenable hypothesis, in lieu of more precise evidence, is clearly that such genetic differences on a class basis do not exist.

6. Marriage as a factor in occupational mobility is commonly recognized and little studied. In his sample, Centers found the differences between the occupations of the wife's father and the husband's father to be of about the same order as the differences between the occupations of father and son.[33] Studies of time trends in the relation between marriage and mobility have not been conducted, and, in general, it seems likely that this factor would more profitably be studied in the context of female mobility.

7. This brief review cannot deal with all factors shown or believed to influence occupational mobility rates, past and present. Mobility is a complex phenomenon, interrelated with the broadest range of social variables. An additional variable relevant to the question of time trends in mobility should be cited, however. This is the problem of the extent and intensity of the motivation or drive to a different, and especially higher, social position. The existence of strong belief in the possibility of economic and social advancement rather generally in the American population has been demonstrated for various time periods and populations. That the nature and extent of this belief varies with social circumstance would be expected and has been demonstrated.

[32] Kenneth W. Eells, et al., Intelligence and Cultural Differences (Chicago: University of Chicago Press, 1951).

[33] Richard Centers, "Marital Selection and Occupational Strata," American Journal of Sociology, Vol. 54 (May 1949), pp. 530–35.

Occupational Mobility

This factor of belief is important both in terms of the acquisition of formal training and in terms of job behavior.

Motivation as reflected in expressed attitudes has been examined over a period of time. As an indication of the somewhat contradictory evidence available, one author recently concluded that "there is reduced striving for success among the lower classes, and awareness of lack of opportunity, and a lack of valuation of education, normally the major avenue to achievement of high status." [34] But another review of the evidence available reached a different, if not totally contradictory conclusion: "The war, however, has not shaken the average man's belief in America as the land of opportunity. Today, he is even more convinced than before the war that his own prospects are better than those that his father had." [35] However, "two related groups, factory workers and union members, are noticeably less enthusiastic regarding both job satisfaction and opportunities for advancement than the rest of the population." [36]

In balance it would appear that there is little evidence in the literature that would substantially support generalizations regarding the direction American society has moved and is moving in terms of occupational mobility. The general view that mobility is diminishing is not verified, and much of the basis for the view rests on *post hoc* arguments deriving from a consideration of a variety of social variables which may or may not influence mobility.

A further aspect of mobility is relevant to this discussion. The question of time trends in mobility as examined here involves the change in the occupation of the son as compared with the occupation of his father. This change may result from two kinds of social change, only one of which is relevant to the question of the open or closed nature of the society. Changes in the occupational distribution of the total population from one generation to the next will account for some proportion of changes in occupation from father to son. The question concerning trends in mobility rates is whether the amount of occupational mobility taking place is greater or less than would be expected as a result of changes in the occupational distribution of the population.

[34] Herbert H. Hyman, "The Value Systems of Different Classes," in *Class, Status and Power*, edited by Reinhard Bendix and Seymour Lipset (Glencoe, Ill.: The Free Press, 1953), p. 438.

[35] "Jobs and Occupations: A Popular Evaluation," *op. cit.*, p. 13.

[36] *Ibid.*

The American Business Elite

Over the past several decades there have been important shifts in the occupational structure. The categories of unskilled laborer and farmer have declined in relative size most sharply, while the professional and clerical occupations have considerably increased. These broad changes, and their implications, were recently summarized as follows:

Occupational change and movement in the United States have raised the prestige level of the average occupational position in the labor force. Or, perhaps better the other way around, net occupational movement has been toward the jobs of higher prestige. When the results of studies of occupational shifts are considered in the light of studies of occupational prestige, there can be no doubt that expanding occupations on the whole are those of higher prestige levels, whereas the contracting occupations are on the whole found at lower prestige levels.[37]

These results may be encouraging in terms of the "American Creed," but an important question remains to be answered. Granted that the change in occupational structure has required widespread inter-generational mobility, it still must be asked whether the possibility of free upward movement — apart from increase in the number of places available — has increased or decreased.[38]

Selective Summary of Findings

A brief summary of some of the more important findings for the basic research questions we asked about occupational succession, vertical mobility, and the characteristics of the American business elite is presented here rather than in a later chapter of conclusions in order to equip the reader with an over-all view of the results and to enable him to examine the particulars presented in each chapter within the larger context of our conclusions.

The text of each chapter, beginning with the following one on the occupational origins and continuing through those on territorial origins and mobility, education, the business system and business careers, family background and marriage, is largely composed of interrelated generalizations summarizing our findings. The nature of the contemporary business elite and the factors operating in the lives of those who have achieved this position are considered in relation to occupational

[37] Nelson N. Foote and Paul K. Hatt, "Social Mobility and Economic Advancement," *American Economic Review*, Vol. 43 (May 1953), pp. 370–71.
[38] *Ibid.*, pp. 374–75.

succession and vertical mobility. The effort will be made here to select those findings most likely to give the reader an immediate introduction to what was learned about the entire problem.

It must be emphasized that the purpose of this volume is to present the operations and findings of the research and only briefly to interpret the larger significances of our findings.[39]

The data on which the results of this study are based deal with the backgrounds and careers of men holding chief executive positions in the largest firms in each type of business and industry in America. Some 8300 questionnaire responses were obtained from these men, representing the total population of business leaders; their accuracy was examined; and the responses were analyzed. The questionnaire was devised to provide critical information on present-day business leaders in light of the study's objectives, as well as to ensure a maximum of accurate comparison with the 1928 results as set forth by Taussig and Joslyn. A detailed comparison of the two questionnaires is provided in Chapter VIII, along with a complete statement of the techniques used in the study, the basis for selecting and verifying the sample employed, the methods used to examine the reliability and validity of the response, and the basis for ensuring comparability between the 1928 and 1952 data.

The first important substantive questions asked were these: Who are the business leaders of contemporary America? What are their occupational origins? Who were their fathers and their paternal grandfathers? By comparing the proportions of business leaders of the different occupational backgrounds [40] with the proportions of such occupations in the total American society, we were able to determine which occupations were overrepresented and underrepresented among the leaders studied. Business executives or owners of large businesses produced about eight times (7.75) more than the proportions of these occupations in the general population would lead one to expect. Three other categories were also overrepresented in terms of their proportions in the general population: the sons of owners of small businesses ranked

---

[39] *Big Business Leaders in America*, by W. Lloyd Warner and James Abegglen (New York: Harper and Brothers, 1955) presents the results of the study to a nonprofessional audience and attempts to relate the personalities of the elite to the mobility process. Accordingly, many of the data and results are confined to this present volume for the professional audience.

[40] See Table 3, page 41.

second with 3.60, the sons of professional men third (3.50), and the sons of foremen (1.33) ranked slightly above expectancy.

Four of the eight general occupational categories were underrepresented. The sons of white-collar men (clerks and salesmen) were slightly underrepresented (0.80). These were followed by the sons of skilled laborers (0.63). The ratio of mobility into the business elite for the sons of farm tenants and owners is 0.45, which is superior in ranking only to two other categories, the semiskilled and unskilled laborers (0.16) and farm laborers (0.00).

Perhaps an easier way to report these results is to say that for every 10 men who might have been expected to be business leaders on the basis of their occupational backgrounds and the proportion of such men in the general occupational population, there were approximately 80 sons of business leaders, 40 sons of small business men, about 40 sons of professional men, and slightly over 10 sons of foremen. For every 10 that might have been expected from the category clerks and salesmen, there were only 8, for skilled laborers only 6, for farm tenants and owners between 4 and 5. Fewer than 2 out of the expected 10 turn up for the semiskilled or unskilled and almost none for farm laborers.

Although these great disparities among the several categories of occupational origins of the 1952 business leaders show clearly that many factors were operative to determine similarities and differences, a comparison of the findings of 1928 (Taussig and Joslyn) and today yields differences which not only speak in a limited way for themselves but indicate that more general interpretation would be significant. In 1928, the ratio for laborer backgrounds was 0.24 compared with 0.32 for 1952; the ratio of white-collar men improved from 0.71 in 1928 to 0.80 in 1952. The farmers changed little in these years (0.32 to 0.33). On the other hand, both the professional and business categories dropped, the former from 4.33 to 3.50 and the latter from 9.67 to 4.73. (See Table 8, page 48.) Clearly, there has been not only an increase in the proportion of the men who come from the lower ranks, but an accompanying decrease in the proportion of sons of highly placed men, particularly of businessmen. Certainly occupational succession (within the limits of this study) is more fluid, and more vertical mobility has been taking place. Because of space limitations, results having to do with other important aspects of mobility and occupational origin, including the relation of three generations to occupational succession and of rural and urban backgrounds, will be deferred until Chapter II.

The several geographical regions of the United States contributed disproportionately to the number of business leaders (see Chapter III). The following results are corrected for the size of the population in each of the regions involved. The Middle Atlantic states rank first (a ratio of 1.47), the New England states second (1.43), and the Pacific Coast states third (1.33). (See Table 20, page 70.) The southern states, including the East South Central, West South Central, and South Atlantic regions, produced a disproportionately smaller share. These regional differences seem to be related to differences in emphasis on industry and agriculture, as well as differences in standards of living and education. The present distribution of business leaders, compared with their places of birth, shows that a sizable number left New England and the West North Central states, and that a considerable proportion moved into the Middle Atlantic and Pacific regions. The movement to and from regions is not random but likely to take place in a fairly definite pattern.

The size of a man's birthplace, like the region in which he is born, plays a part in occupational mobility. Most of the men of the business elite were born in the big cities. When the proportions of the business leaders born in the several sizes of community are compared with the proportions for the total population, it is found that relatively few are from small-town or rural backgrounds.[41] When the occupation of father, the region of birth, and the size of birthplace are considered jointly, the very small part played by the small-town and rural South in business leadership is sharply revealed.

More important to the patterns of occupational mobility than the territorial origins of business leaders is their territorial circulation. Most of these men have been spatially mobile during their careers.[42] This movement is closely related to a general movement to large cities, but it is apparent that territorial mobility and vertical occupational mobility are closely related.

When the findings of this research are reviewed in terms of general

[41] See Table 30, page 87.
[42] See Table 27, page 82.

26

thinking regarding occupational mobility, it appears that the role of immigration in mobility has been misinterpreted. While it is quite true that immigrants do not often achieve the highest status positions in American business, their disadvantage is less than might be assumed, for 5 per cent of the business elite were foreign-born, while about 10 per cent of the U.S. population were born abroad. Further, and more significant, the sons of foreign-born men of lower status are successfully mobile in a higher proportion than the sons of native-born men of lower status.[43]

This general finding is consistent with the role territorial mobility has been found to play in occupational mobility. The relationship between these two forms of social movement is an intimate one: those men who are mobile through social space are also mobile through geographic space. It may be concluded from this that the act of movement, spatially, establishes many of the preconditions for social and occupational mobility. The territorially mobile man is disengaged from the web of relations that determines his social position, and the son of an immigrant is that man least engaged with his cultural past. The physical mobility of Americans is a precondition to the changes in social position that have been found to take place increasingly in American business.

The previous questions and answers have dealt with the kinds of persons who have high-status business positions, the proportions of individuals who are mobile or are the sons of those in the elite, and their geographic origins. It is essential for an understanding of these social facts to examine some of the factors that influence them. In the formulation of this research the following questions were asked with respect to education and mobility:

How important is education, both the amount and kind, in successful mobility? It is clear that in America education is believed to be an important factor in social movement. Both the amount and kind of education received by these leaders should be determined to establish the relative influence of this factor in reaching higher social status.

When the general educational level of business leadership is established, relative to the nation as a whole, the problem arises whether a relatively higher education is necessary to upward movement, and if it is of special importance for any particular group (e.g., the laborer's son). Is college education necessary? Is business or trade training of

[43] See Table 38, page 94.

particular advantage in "getting ahead," as opposed to a more general liberal arts background?

Most of the business leaders were college men, well over half being college graduates. Seventy-six per cent of the men studied had gone to college, 57 per cent had graduated, 19 per cent had not. However, one fifth of the whole group (19 per cent) had not only graduated but had gone on to advanced graduate study. Comparatively, the American businessman tends to be a highly educated man: whereas 76 out of every 100 of the business elite had gone to college, only 13 of every 100 adult males (30 years and over) in the general population had some college training; 57 of every 100 business leaders had graduated, as compared with 7 out of every 100 in the general population.[44]

More than half of the adult males in the general population had not attended high school, compared with only 4 out of 100 leaders. Nine per cent of the leaders had some high school but did not graduate and 11 per cent graduated but did not go on to college, compared with 16 per cent in each of these two categories in the general population.[45]

But what kinds of men received a higher education? Were they sons of the elite or men from the wrong side of the tracks? Who were the men who did not go on to college? Nine out of every 10 sons of professional men and business leaders had been to college and 7 of the 10 had graduated.

Over half of the sons of semiskilled or unskilled laborers had been to college (52 per cent) and 36 per cent had graduated. Seven out of every 10 sons of fathers of the white-collar level had been to college and 5 out of 10 had graduated.[46] In general, men originating from all levels went to college, but those from higher levels attended and graduated from college in higher proportions. Another moderately accurate measurement of the effect of occupational rank on education is obtained from a comparison of the percentages of men of diverse origins who did not graduate from high school. Whereas only 3 per cent of the sons of professional men and 3 per cent of those of business leaders quit school before graduating from high school, one third of the sons of unskilled and semiskilled laborers and one fourth of the sons of skilled laborers failed to go on. The other levels fell between the two extremes.

Despite the fact that men from higher levels receive more education

[44] See Table 39, page 96.   [45] Ibid.   [46] See Table 40, page 98.

than those from lower levels, at all levels of occupational background college graduates make up the largest single educational group.

In general, the business leaders as a group were better educated than their fathers. Only 13 per cent fell below the level of high school graduation, compared with 54 per cent of their fathers; on the other hand, only 28 per cent of the fathers had graduated or had some college experience, while 76 per cent of the contemporary business leaders were graduates or had spent some time in college.[47]

Business leaders of 1952 are better educated than the leaders of 1928.[48] For example, whereas in 1952 only 4 out of every 100 leaders had less than a high school education, 27 did in the earlier group; and only 32 per cent were college graduates in 1928, compared with 57 per cent in 1952. In 1952, the proportion of college graduates from each occupational category, including skilled and unskilled laborers, was greater than the proportion of college graduates in the entire sample for 1928.[49] Furthermore, a large number of these men, both those with and those without college training, prepare themselves for careers by taking commercial training — in colleges or universities, by correspondence courses, or in business colleges. One fourth of the leaders had taken correspondence courses or gone to business college and one third had some kind of commercial training in a college or university.[50]

Education is now one of the principal avenues to business leadership. The mobile men use it in greatly increased numbers in their drive to places of leadership and power. Clearly education helps many from all levels to reach the top, yet financial and other restrictions on access to higher education is also an important factor in the maintenance of occupational inheritance by the elite.

In terms of the effect on the individual's hopes and beliefs, the factors in getting to the top include also the amount of time he must work to achieve this goal. This study asked a number of questions related to this problem. Some of them were as follows:

How long did it take for top executives to reach their present positions from the time of their entry into the business world?

What were the differences in length of time required for the sons of business leaders and for those whose fathers occupied lower economic ranks?

[47] See Table 41, page 100.
[48] See Table 49, page 109.
[49] See Chapter IV for a full discussion.
[50] See Table 51, page 112.

Occupational Mobility

What is the relation between achievement time and the separate factors of education, financial aid, and influential connections? For example, to what extent, if any, does a man improve his chances of *early* success by obtaining a college degree?

The average business leader in our study has almost reached his fifty-fourth birthday (53.7 years). He entered business a few months after reaching his majority (21.4 years). It took him almost twenty-four years to reach his present business position. Occupational origin has an effect on the age of entering business: sons of laborers become self-supporting earlier (before reaching nineteen) than those of any other occupational category. The sons of professional men and businessmen do not enter business until they are nearly twenty-two.

The length of time before reaching a top business position was shortest for the sons of major executives (20.6 years) and longest for the sons of laborers (26 years). The sons of farmers took about a year less than those of laborers (25.1 years). On the whole, territorial mobility, while an integral part of the mobility process, seems to be related to retardation of the career, although some men would probably not have advanced so far if they had not been territorially mobile in their careers. Men who have moved about a lot tend to achieve business leadership later than those who stay closer to home.[51]

These successful men tended to move from one firm to another; only a fourth of those we studied remained with a single firm. These changes occurred before as well as after they had attained high position. Usually, the men from lower levels who were mobile moved from firm to firm more often than those from higher ranks. Furthermore, men of college education moved less often.

The careers of most men in the business elite begin with white-collar and professional jobs. Few of the business elite began in laboring occupations during their careers and of those who did, few remained long.[52] The occupation of the father is an important factor, however, in determining the point at which the career begins, for 24 per cent of the sons of laborers began their careers in laboring jobs in the shop, while only 12 per cent of the sons of big business men began at this level. The professions were the point of departure in the careers of nearly a quarter of the men, with engineering and law predominating.

Education plays a considerable role in determining the career line

---

[51] See Chapter V, pages 128–37, especially Table 66, page 129.
[52] See Table 53, page 118.

and the kind of experience obtained. The lesser the education, the lower the level at which the career was launched; the higher the education, the greater the proportion of men who began their careers at a higher rank. About a third of the men with less than high school education started as laborers; only 11 per cent of the college graduates began at the bottom. On the other hand, 36 per cent of the college graduates began in the professions. Whereas over half of those with less than college education began their careers in clerical roles, only 22 per cent of college graduates were so employed when they started.[53]

It is sometimes assumed that the rapidly expanding businesses are more likely places for the college graduate than for those with lower educational achievement. This does not appear to be true. The majority of the business elite in slowly expanding businesses, no matter what their occupational origins, are college graduates, whereas the men with less formal education are more frequent in businesses that are growing more rapidly. Further, the gigantic business organizations place considerable emphasis on college education. Sixty-two per cent of the chief executives of the largest firms are college graduates. The giant firms also tend to be places for occupational advancement for those from lower ranks with college education. The smaller firms are the organizations where mobility from lower levels is most difficult. Men with college education from the lower ranks seek and find advancement in the largest corporations. It is these organizations rather than the smaller ones which are more likely to welcome talent and training no matter what their origins; here the mobile elite prosper.

American business and industry is a system of widely differing institutions and activities, and these differences also influence the extent and nature of occupational mobility. Among the several types of business and industry, certain categories of business include in their leadership higher proportions of sons of laborers and farmers, men with less formal education, and men from underrepresented geographic regions than others do. For example, 58 per cent of the leaders of brokerage and investment firms are sons of major executives, owners of large businesses, or professional men;[54] 71 per cent are college graduates; most are born in the North (60 per cent). This type of business represents the extreme of social exclusion in American business.[55]

[53] See Table 57, page 122.
[54] See Table 79, page 146.
[55] See Tables 80 and 81, pages 148 and 149.

Occupational Mobility

The influence of a father's occupational position may be felt directly as an economic or less directly as a social fact. In America many directly inherit their positions in the birth elite or influence may be exerted through the family's general socioeconomic status. Relatives and friends may help directly through financial aid or intercession, or indirectly through less easily identified influences on what a man is as a person or how he may be evaluated. What effect do these varying degrees and kinds of influence have on the men from diverse backgrounds? [56]

A good test of the effect of influence is to compare the amount of time it takes for men with and men without influence to achieve top positions. There is little or no effect on the length of time when only friends are involved.[57] However, men with relatives in the firm took less time — 19 to 20 years, compared with approximately 24 years for all types. Only two categories of occupations reported influential relatives in the firm: the sons of executives and the sons of owners of large businesses. Fifty-six per cent of the first and 36 per cent of the latter had relatives in the same firm. Only 9 per cent of the sons of professional men and the same percentage of the sons of small owners had relatives in the firm. All the remaining occupations had less than 6 per cent reporting relatives in the firm.

The percentage of sons in the same enterprises as their fathers varies with both the size and type of enterprise — the larger the firm the smaller the proportion of men with fathers in the same firm.[58] The principal industries in which fathers and sons are found in the same enterprises are real estate, wood and coal products, personal services, and security and commodity brokers. Throughout the larger enterprises there has been a decided decrease in the proportion of men in the same firm as the father. The stronghold of inherited position today in America is in the smaller enterprises; the larger enterprises are more open to competition for men rising from lower occupational levels.[59]

Only a very small percentage of the business leaders received financial aid — some 6 per cent.[60] Of those who did, the sons of big business

[56] See Chapter VI, pages 158–64.
[57] See Table 89, page 161.
[58] See Chapter VI, pages 164–71.
[59] See Table 95, page 167.
[60] See Table 99, page 171.

men far outranked all others: 17 per cent compared with 6 per cent of the sons of professional men, 3 per cent of small business men,[61] and less than 1 per cent (0.6) of the sons of laborers. There has been a decided decrease in such help since 1928. At that time, 13 per cent of the leaders had been assisted financially, as compared with 6 per cent in 1952.

The research questions and answers until now have been directed to the relations of fathers and sons and the family of birth, emphasizing the effect of social and economic place on the careers of American business leaders. We turn now to another social factor. The marriages of Americans influence, and are influenced by, the patterns of their careers. Do such men marry above or below their levels of origin? Do men of lower rank marry women of similar status or do they marry above themselves? Do the sons of big business men marry the daughters of men of the same high position or do they often marry the ambitious daughters of fathers from the lower occupational ranks? The answers to these questions are important in their own right, but their social implications for rank and social mobility are still more important, for if men born to high rank marry women of similar origin the effect is to decrease the fluidity of the society and to increase closure; on the other hand, frequent marriage above or below the level of origin reduces the effect of status and emphasizes the values of freedom of choice, individuality, and flexibility of status. These statements become even more significant when two or more generations, which do or do not emphasize hereditary status at marriage, are involved.

Approximately half of the wives of the business leaders studied (51 per cent) were the daughters of business or professional men, and about a sixth were from the laboring class. Men born to high station married women from similar backgrounds in greater proportion than did any other class; but in general the men studied married women from their own occupational level more than any other group of women. The men whose fathers were white-collar workers married out of their occupational origins more than any others did; men with laboring, farmer, and big business backgrounds were more likely than others to marry within their occupational origins. In general, both endogamic and exogamic factors seem to be operating in the choice of mates. Flexibility, individual choice, freedom to go beyond the confines of

[61] See Table 99, page 171, and Chapter VIII for definition of terms.

the occupational level — all are exhibited in the kinds of marriages made by the business leaders.[62]

When the effect of the paternal grandfather's generation on the marriages of the elite is examined there appears to be a definite relation between choice of mate and status of the grandfather. If he was of high status it is more likely that his grandson (the business leader) will marry a highly placed woman than if he was of lower status, this being true even if the father of the leader was a big business man. Furthermore, the lower the status of the grandfather the greater the likelihood the grandson will not marry a highborn woman.[63]

The effect of a college education is to increase the likelihood of marriage at higher levels. Both inherited status and education influence the selection of the mates of business leaders.[64]

The question arises, what effect did in- and out-marriage have on the careers of these men? The sons of the elite who married the daughters of laborers took 23 years to achieve their positions at the executive level; those who married at their own level took two years longer (25 years). The laborer who "marries the boss's daughter" takes almost exactly the same amount of time for achievement as the one who marries someone from his own level of origin (25.9 years for the first, 26.1 for the latter). The general effect of marriage on the career is quite similar for all categories; there is only a limited range of difference in time for the careers of men who marry above or below their occupational origins.[65] The status of the wife generally does not have a direct effect on accelerating the career of the business leader.

The results of this investigation must be evaluated in terms of the limitations imposed by the study's design. Occupational mobility into business leadership is examined here in some detail. The results do not bear directly on questions of mobility and occupational rigidity in government and political hierarchies, military or professional positions, or on any other of the several categories of social power. Only to the extent that mobility into the business elite and business-career patterns are a function of more general variables in our social system may the results of this study be related to occupational mobility in other hierarchies.

[62] See Chapter VII, pages 178–83 for the marriages of the elite.
[63] See Chapter VII, pages 183–89.
[64] See Chapter VII, pages 189–98.
[65] See Chapter VII, pages 201–4.

The American Business Elite

Further, occupational mobility for only one of the many groups that make up the American business world has been reported. In particular, two important categories of business positions have not been examined. The first is composed of those positions at the level immediately below the management positions studied. These involve a wide range of functions, and mobility at this level of American business and industrial firms may only be inferred from this data. It appears, from the analysis in Chapter V, that more of these positions than of the top positions are held by men from lower status backgrounds, as would be expected. Whether mobility at this second level is increasing is not known, but the most reasonable assumption would appear to be that it follows the same general pattern of mobility into top-level positions.

The other category not studied in this research is that of executive positions in firms smaller in size than those studied, though important in the economy. In general, it appears from the analysis of the business elite that mobility is more limited in smaller firms, and a higher rate of occupational inheritance obtains. Whether this more limited mobility takes place at all levels of lesser size is not known, and it is quite possible that it is in firms of intermediate size (the smallest in our sample of companies) that mobility is most restricted.

It is also important to note that this study deals only with occupational mobility; the questionnaire does not provide data on the more general problem of social class mobility. That occupational rank and social class are closely related is well established. Nevertheless, social class position and occupational position are not identical, and the important variations between the two are not touched on here. It is probable that the social class positions, as measured by status and prestige in their communities, of the men in business leadership from lower level occupational backgrounds are not generally so high as those of the leaders whose fathers were of the business elite. The extent and nature of these differences, and time trends in these respects, are not dealt with in this research.

In the broadest sense, this research indicates that at the levels studied here American society is not becoming more castelike; the recruitment of business leaders from the bottom is taking place now and seems to be increasing. Mobility to the top is not decreasing; in fact, for the last quarter century it has been slowly increasing. In spite of the pessimistic predictions about an immobilized society, this evidence shows that our society, although much like what it has been in past generations, is more flexible than it was; more men and their families are in social motion; pessimism about decreased flexibility and mobility is not warranted.

Despite these facts, the operation of rank and the effects of high birth are strongly evidenced in the selection of the American business elite. Men born to the top are more likely to succeed and have more advantages than those born further down. There is not full freedom of competition; the system is still sufficiently status-bound to work to the considerable advantage of men born to higher position. Fathers at the elite levels still find it possible to endow their sons with greater opportunity than those further down enjoy. Nevertheless, they do so now in decreased numbers. The sons of men from the wrong side of the tracks are finding their way increasingly to the places of power and prestige. The values of competitive and open status are felt more today than yesterday and those of inherited position and fixed position, while still powerful, are less potent now than they were a generation ago.

CHAPTER II

Occupational Origins of the Business Elite

The Occupations of the Fathers

THE problem of occupational succession will be examined in this chapter, with particular attention to two questions: Do the sons of the elite retain the positions of their fathers? Do the sons of men in other occupations move into the business elite? After viewing the occupations of the fathers of business leaders, we will extend our limits to include the paternal grandfathers' occupations, in order to learn about mobility that takes two generations rather than one. This analysis will be followed by a comparison of the results of 1952 with those of 1928 to discover whether mobility into business leadership is increasing or decreasing.

The occupational background of present-day American business leadership is shown in Table 1. The distribution is for the occupation of the father at the time the business leader became self-supporting. The distribution for all 22 occupational categories used in the 1952 questionnaire is given on the right of Table 1, showing the percentage of fathers in each occupational group. These occupations are combined into eight broader categories in the column on the left.

Fifteen per cent of the 1952 business leaders are the sons of laborers: only 4.5 per cent are the sons of unskilled or semiskilled laborers, and 10.3 per cent the sons of skilled laborers. Nine per cent of the 1952 business leaders are the sons of farmers, unequally distributed through the farmer categories: almost half are the sons of those of the upper category, farm owners or managers with paid help; less than 1 per cent are the sons of small tenants or farm laborers.

Eight per cent of the business elite are the sons of white-collar workers, clerks or salesmen — the last in the majority. It would ap-

37

Occupational Mobility

Table 1. Occupations of the Fathers of 1952 Business Leaders

Occupation of Father (7 Groups)	Percentage	Occupation of Father (22 Groups)	Percentage
Laborer	15	Unskilled or semiskilled worker	4.5
		Skilled worker or mechanic	10.3
White-collar worker	8	Clerk or retail salesman	2.5
		Salesman	5.9
Business executive	26	Foreman	3.1
		Minor executive	7.4
		Major executive	14.6
Business owner	26	Owner of small business	17.7
		Owner of medium business	6.4
		Owner of large business	2.4
Professional man	14	Doctor	2.2
		Engineer	2.2
		Lawyer	3.2
		Minister	2.3
		Other	4.2
Farmer	9	Farm tenant or farm worker	0.3
		Tenant with paid help	0.4
		Farm owner without paid help	3.7
		Owner or manager with paid help	4.2
Other occupations	2	Military career	0.3
		Government service	1.8
		Other occupations	0.4
Total	100	Total	100.0

pear that the larger proportion of sons of white-collar workers who move to top business positions are sons of salesmen, the upper level of this category.

When foremen are included in the category, 26 per cent of the 1952 business leaders are the sons of business executives. Almost 15 per cent are the sons of major executives (owner through general manager, as listed on the questionnaire). The major executive group produces as many business leaders as does the entire laborer population, despite its very much smaller proportion in the general population.

Of the 1952 business leaders, 26 per cent are the sons of men who owned their own businesses, the majority small businesses. Despite their rapidly diminishing numbers, the owners of large businesses as designated here (annual volume in sales or income of $100,000 or more) are as important a source of future business leaders as the entire lower level white-collar group.

The professions are a major source of the business elite: 14 per cent of the 1952 business leaders are sons of professional men, most of whom are in the four major professions of law, medicine, engineering, and the ministry. More than 3 per cent of the 1952 business elite is made up of sons of lawyers.

The remaining 2 per cent of the business leaders studied are sons of men from the other occupations — military service or government service. A small number — less than 1 per cent — of the business elite have military backgrounds. A larger number of the fathers of business leaders had careers in government service. Examination of the questionnaires (on which the respondents very often in these cases wrote a more complete description of the father's occupation) indicates that those in the government service group are spread through the entire range of federal and state governmental positions, from clerical through judicial, both appointive and elective.[1]

It is clear that all occupational groups are not equally represented in top-level business positions. Certain occupational groups supply a greater share of business leaders than their proportion in the general population: we have seen that the sons of business owners and executives are present in positions of business leadership in 1952 in a greater proportion than would be expected; conversely, proportionately fewer sons of laborers or farmers are in the business elite. If there were uninfluenced mobility to all occupational positions in U.S. business and industry, the occupational origins of business leaders would be approximately the same as the occupational origins of the male adult U.S. population. The first question in the study of occupational mobility is the degree to which the several occupational groups are overrepresented or underrepresented in the background of the business elite.

As noted, the information on the occupational origins of business leaders provides the occupation of the fathers at the time the sons, the

[1] The remaining 34 questionnaires analyzed indicated the father's occupation in a way that made reclassification hazardous. Responses included listing of the father's occupation as "merchant," "broker," or "importer." We may assume that these, like the government service group, would distribute throughout the range of more specific occupational categories.

Occupational Mobility

1952 business leaders, became self-supporting. The average age of the businessmen studied is about 53. Since the average age for becoming self-supporting is about 20, the occupations of the fathers are given, on the average, for the time period near the 1920 census of population. Therefore, the comparison will be between the fathers of the business leaders and the occupations of the male adult U.S. population in 1920.[2]

Table 2. Occupational Distribution of the Fathers of Business Leaders and of the U.S. Male Adult Population for 1920

Occupation	Percentage of Fathers of 1952 Business Leaders	Percentage of Total U.S. Male Adult Population in 1920
Unskilled or semiskilled laborer	5	31
Skilled laborer	10	16
Owner of small business	18	5
Clerk or salesman	8	10
Foreman	3	2
Minor or major executive; owner of large business..	31	4
Professional man	14	4
Farm laborer	0	7
Farm tenant or owner	9	20
Other occupations	2	1
Total	100	100

Table 2 presents the data necessary for answering the question of the relative degree of overrepresentation or underrepresentation of the occupational groups in the business elite. The ten occupational categories are those for which a comparison is possible; the nature of the U.S. census data for 1920 does not permit comparison for some of the occupations listed on the questionnaire.

Comparison of the columns shows that, while 31 per cent of the 1920 adult male population were unskilled or semiskilled laborers, only 5 per cent of the 1952 business leaders are the sons of unskilled or

[2] It should be noted that this comparison will provide a conservative estimate of the amount of occupational rigidity in American society, owing to the effects of differential fertility. The assumption in the comparison described is that fathers of all occupational groups provide an equal number of sons in the succeeding generation. As is well known, fertility rates in the United States for this time period are such that the lower occupational groups will in fact have proportionately more offspring. Because of the difficulty of making an adjustment for differential fertility, this factor is not accounted for. The effect is to underestimate somewhat the proportion of sons from farm and laboring backgrounds especially, and to overestimate the proportion of sons of business and professional men.

Occupational Origins of the Business Elite

semiskilled laborers. On the other hand, while only 4 per cent of the 1920 adult males were business executives or owners of large businesses, 31 per cent of the 1952 business leaders are sons of business executives or owners of larger businesses. This very large difference between the proportions in the population and in the background of business leaders is the measure of the underrepresentation of the sons of laborers of the unskilled or semiskilled categories, and the overrepresentation of the sons of upper level businessmen.

Thus the two sets of proportions in Table 2 provide the basis for a systematic answer to the question of the rigidity or fluidity of the U.S. occupational structure with respect to the American business system. To obtain a single measure of the difference shown in Table 2, the ratio of one proportion to the other may be taken. If the movement of the sons of the last generation into their careers and occupational positions had been uninfluenced by the occupational position of their fathers, the proportions shown in Table 2 would be the same for both columns, and the ratio between 1920 census data proportions and fathers of 1952 business leaders would be 1.00. If fewer sons became business leaders than the proportions of fathers would indicate, the ratio would be less than 1.00.

The ratio of the proportion of each occupational group in the 1920 population to the proportion of fathers of 1952 business leaders in each occupational group is presented in Table 3. Thus, in 1920, 31 per cent of the adult male population were unskilled or semiskilled laborers. If the sons of laborers had achieved top business positions in pro-

Table 3. Sources of 1952 Business Leaders: Ratio of Proportion of Fathers in Occupational Group to Proportion of Occupational Group in Adult Male Population in 1920

Occupation	Ratio *	Rank Order (1–9)
Unskilled or semiskilled laborer	0.16	8
Skilled laborer	0.63	6
Owner of small business	3.60	2
Clerk or salesman	0.80	5
Foreman	1.33	4
Executive or owner of large business	7.75	1
Professional man	3.50	3
Farm laborer	0.00	9
Farm tenant or owner	0.45	7

* Proportional representation = 1.00.

41

portion to their representation in the population, about 31 per cent
of the fathers of 1952 business leaders would have been unskilled or
semiskilled laborers. The ratio in that case would be 31:31. However,
the observed ratio is 31:5, or 0.16, as shown in Table 3.

When this measure of occupational mobility is used, it is possible
to rank the occupational groups in terms of their representation in
the 1952 business elite. For the sons of farm laborers, such mobility
is almost impossible; this is the most disadvantaged group in the
population in this as in other respects. The ratio of mobility in this
case is actually 0.00, as almost no sons of farm laborers appeared in
the study. The sons of semiskilled or unskilled laborers are the next
most disadvantaged group with a ratio of 0.16. A measure of the very
limited mobility into the top level of American business on the part
of the nonurban population is provided by the fact that the sons of
all farm tenants and owners are next to the lower labor category, with
a ratio of 0.45.

Following these three lowest groups in order of increasing proportion of sons in top business positions are skilled laborers, 0.63; white-
collar workers (clerk or salesman), 0.80; foremen, 1.33; professional
men, 3.50; owners of small businesses, 3.60; business executives or
owners of large businesses, 7.75. The number of business leaders supplied by this last group is eight times its proportion of the general
population.

Table 3 clearly shows the differences between occupational groups
in providing the business leaders of 1952. The 1952 business elite is
made up in greatest part of the sons of men of relatively high occupational status, the sons of business and professional men. It is clear,
when these proportions are compared with the proportions in the
population, that a man's birth into the business and professional
echelons enormously increased the probabilities of his subsequently
holding similar positions.

This description is still incomplete. The occupational groupings
shown in Tables 2 and 3 are, of course, very broad. Each category of
occupation includes a wide variety and range of more specific occupations. As indicated in the discussion of the total questionnaire return,
there is a general tendency for the elite to come not only from the
upper occupational groups, when these groups are broadly defined,
but also from the upper level within each group. Thus, for example,

most of the men studied are sons of businessmen; few are sons of farmers. Further, of the sons of farmers, most are sons of higher status farmers. While these occupations may be meaningfully combined, as they have been for the preceding analysis, this broad grouping tends to obscure the full picture of occupational mobility.

Given the questionnaire and the census data available, it is possible to examine in more detail one of the occupational groupings shown in Tables 2 and 3, that of the professions. In the questionnaire, provision was made for checking separately the professions of doctor, engineer, lawyer, and minister as the occupation of the father. The remaining professions of teacher, writer, architect, and the like, were combined into an "other" category.

Table 4. The Professions as Sources of 1952 Business Leaders

Profession	Percentage of 1920 Male Adult Population	Percentage of Fathers of 1952 Business Leaders	Ratio
Lawyer	0.46	3.2	8.00
Minister	0.41	2.3	5.48
Engineer	0.52	2.2	4.80
Doctor	0.51	2.2	4.78
Other professions ...	2.47	4.2	1.89

Table 4 presents the results of this more detailed examination of the professions as sources of 1952 business leaders. It should first be noted that the specific professions asked for in every instance produce more business leaders, in proportion to their figures in the population, than the other professions combined (see the last column). The four well-defined and relatively highly evaluated professions all appear as major sources of business leaders. Further, in terms of relative size in the population, the single profession of law ranks higher — with a ratio of 8.00 — as a source of the business elite than any other occupation examined in the study. This is not to say that the sons of lawyers are more likely to become business leaders than are the sons of any other group in the population. Clearly, if it were possible to further refine the "owner of large business" or "major executive" categories and compare them with fairly precise census data, the higher groups within each category would also be seen to be relatively very much more important than the category taken as a whole. It may be assumed that if it were possible, from the questionnaire and from the census data, to separate out more specific categories within the remaining occupational groups, the same relationship would hold. Certain of the occupations would be very highly represented in business leadership, even within the more advantaged broad groupings.

This research has been designed to answer the question of whether, in the hierarchy under study, the American social system is one of increasingly fixed occupational position, or of continued or increasing fluidity. The general outline of the facts concerning occupational mobility into the present American business elite has been presented. It is now possible to turn to the following question: Is occupational mobility increasing or decreasing in the United States?

The information gathered and the men studied in the 1952 research are comparable to those studied in 1928.[3] Comparing the results of the two researches makes it possible to discover the general trends in U.S. society over the past two and one-half decades.

Occupational Mobility in 1928 and 1952

Table 5 presents the distribution of respondents by father's occupation, for 1928 and 1952. The occupational categories employed in Table 5 are those used in the 1928 research. The 1952 category "foreman" has been combined with that of "minor executive" for this analysis. The numbers on which the 1952 analysis is based are the same as those of the 1928 study. A detailed comparison of the men studied in 1928 with those studied in 1952 is provided in Chapter VIII.

A comparison of the distributions for the two time periods, as given in Table 5, indicates first that a larger percentage of men whose fathers were laborers move into business leadership at the present time than in 1928: 15 per cent in 1952 as against 11 per cent in 1928. The proportion of sons of farmers declined from 12 per cent in 1928 to 9 per cent in 1952, while the proportion from white-collar backgrounds and from the professions increased. The minor executive category supplies a larger percentage of sons, while the remaining business categories — major executives or owners of businesses, both large and small — supply a lower percentage of the 1952 business elite.

A simple comparison of the proportions given in Table 5 is not sufficient to define the trends in occupational mobility to which the study is addressed. There has been a general trend since the turn of the cen-

[3] A detailed comparison of the two studies is provided in Chapter VIII.

Occupational Origins of the Business Elite

tury to a decline in the over-all U.S. farm population and an increase in the white-collar and professional groups. Before we draw conclusions as to occupational mobility, the over-all population trends must be examined as well as trends in mobility to business leadership. The joint consideration of both factors provides the needed data.

Just as the comparable figures on which mobility estimates for the 1952 business elite may be based are those of the adult male population in 1920, so the 1928 business elite must be studied in terms of the occupational distribution of the adult male population in 1900. Table 6 is a comparison of the two distributions: the occupational backgrounds of 1928 business leaders, and the occupational distribution of the total adult male population in 1900.

The 1900 census data present many difficulties in this kind of study,

Table 5. The Occupations of the Fathers of 1928 and 1952 Business Leaders

Occupation of Father	Percentage in 1928	Percentage in 1952
Unskilled or semiskilled laborer	2	5
Skilled laborer	9	10
Farmer	12	9
Clerk or salesman	5	8
Minor executive *	7	11
Owner of small business	20	17
Major executive	17	15
Owner of large business	14	9
Professional man	13	14
Other	1	2
Total	100	100

* The figure for 1952 includes "foremen."

Table 6. Occupational Distribution of Fathers of 1928 Business Leaders and Total Male Adult U.S. Population in 1900

Occupation	Percentage of Fathers of 1928 Business Leaders	Percentage of Total Male Adults in 1900
Skilled or unskilled laborer	11	45
Clerk or salesman	5	7
Business owner or executive	58	6
Professional man	13	3
Farmer	12	38
Other	1	1
Total	100	100

45

and a further combination of the questionnaire categories was required to obtain an accurate comparison of the two sets of proportions. The maximum number of occupational categories on which reliable estimates may be based is six. Table 6 shows the major differences between the two distributions among these categories. For the 1928 business elite, as with that of 1952, national occupational origins and business leader origins differ markedly; there is wide variation between the occupations of the 1900 male population and the occupational background of the 1928 business leaders.

Table 7. Occupational Mobility Rates: 1928 and 1952 Business Leaders' Fathers
Compared with Adult Males of 1900 and 1920

Occupation	Comparison for 1928 Group		Comparison for 1952 Group	
	Fathers of Business Leaders	U.S. Adult Males of 1900	Fathers of Business Leaders	U.S. Adult Males of 1920
Laborer	11%	45%	15%	47%
Clerk or salesman	5	7	8	10
Business owner or executive	58	6	52	11
Professional man	13	3	14	4
Farmer	12	38	9	27
Other	1	1	2	1
Total	100	100	100	100

The question of changes in occupational mobility in American business and industry is studied in Table 7. In 1928, 11 per cent of the business leaders studied were sons of laborers, as compared with 15 per cent in 1952 — an increase of 4 per cent. At the same time, the total proportion of laborers in the population increased from 45 per cent in 1900 to 47 per cent in 1920. The increase in the sons of laborers in positions of business leadership is greater than the increase in the proportion of laborers in the population.

While the number of business leaders who are sons of white-collar workers increased from 5 to 8 per cent from 1928 to 1952, a partly compensating increase from 7 to 10 per cent took place in the proportion of white-collar workers in the population.

In the case of business executives and the owners of businesses, while the proportion of sons of these men who become business leaders declined from 58 per cent in 1928 to 52 per cent in 1952, the proportion in the population increased from 6 per cent in 1900 to 11 per cent in 1920. The proportion of men in business leadership from professional backgrounds increased from 13 to 14 per cent, while the increase in the population was from 3 to 4 per cent. The proportion of farmers in the male adult population declined more than that of any other group in the period 1900 to 1920 — from 38 to 27 per cent. This decline parallels a decline in sons of farmers who became business leaders, from 12 per cent in 1928 to 9 per cent in 1952.

Thus it is necessary, in studying the meaning of these changes in mobility, to account at once for two changes: first, the general population shifts which would be expected to change the distribution by occupational background in the next generation; and second, changes in the occupational background of business leaders. By relating occupational background data to population shifts, a direct comparison of the two time periods of 1928 and 1952 in terms of occupational mobility is possible. This will indicate the nature of the changes in our social system with respect to occupational mobility into the business hierarchy.

Let us review briefly the method employed — that of deriving the ratio between the percentage of the population in each occupation and the percentage of business leaders from each occupational background. Given chance movement, that is, if the sons from all occupational categories moved into business leadership in equal proportions, the same proportion would be found in each business leader group as in each population group. For example, 45 per cent of the U.S. adult male population of 1900 belonged to the laborer group. In 1928, 11 per cent of the business leaders had fathers who were laborers. If the sons of laborers had been represented fully in business leadership, about 45 per cent of the business leaders would have been sons of laborers. In this case the ratio would be 45:45; that is, there would have been full representation of the laboring group in the business leadership of 1928. The actual observed ratio is 45:11 or 0.24, as indicated in Table 8.

In 1920, 47 per cent of the U.S. adult male population belonged to the laboring group. In 1952, 15 per cent of the business leaders were sons of laborers. If the sons of laborers had been represented fully in the business elite, about 47 per cent of the 1952 business leaders would have had fathers who were laborers. Instead of this ratio of 47:47 (1.00), we find a ratio of 47:15, or 0.32.

This ratio of 0.32 for 1952 compares with the ratio of 0.24 for the

Occupational Mobility

1928 business elite, which indicates two things. In both periods the sons of laborers were substantially underrepresented in the business leadership of the United States. But their representation has increased from 1928 to 1952 beyond their proportionate increase in the general population.

Table 8. Changes in Occupational Mobility in American Business from 1928 to 1952

Occupation	1928 Ratio *	1952 Ratio *
Laborer	0.24	0.32
White-collar worker	0.71	0.80
Professional man	4.33	3.50
Businessman	9.67	4.73
Farmer	0.32	0.33

* Proportional representation = 1.00.

It will be remembered that the white-collar force increased noticeably between 1928 and 1952, both in percentage of the total working force and in representation of sons in the business elite. The measurement of the actual differences, in terms of the 1928 and 1952 ratios, shows that the sons of white-collar workers made a gain from 0.71 to 0.80. While the sons of white-collar workers are underrepresented in the business elite in both time periods, their proportionate share is much greater than that of sons of laborers. As with the latter, an increasing proportion of sons of white-collar workers make their way to the top of the U.S. business hierarchy.

As in the case of the white-collar group, there are more professional men in the population and more of their sons in the business elite in 1952 than in 1928. In contrast to the white-collar group, the ratio of professional men in 1928 shows they are overrepresented in business leadership. Instead of an expected ratio of 1.00, they actually show a ratio of 4.33, which indicates that over four times more sons of professional men were in business leadership in 1928 than would have been expected from their incidence in the population. The 1952 ratio is 3.50. Thus sons of professional men continue to have a substantial advantage in terms of mobility in business. However, although the number of sons of professional men in the business elite has increased as of 1952, their ratio to their proportion in the population has decreased from 4.33 to 3.50.

Occupational Origins of the Business Elite

The most marked change from 1928 to 1952 is the decline in representation in business leadership of the sons of businessmen. In 1928, the 6 per cent of the population whose fathers were businessmen were represented by 58 per cent of the business elite. In 1952, although the proportion of businessmen in the population had increased perceptibly, from 6 per cent to 11 per cent, their representation among business leaders had declined from 58 to 52 per cent. As shown in Table 8, the change in ratio is from 9.67 in 1928 to 4.73 in 1952.

The data on the farmer require special attention. In the 1928 study Taussig and Joslyn remark on

the surprisingly poor showing of the farmer class in respect to productivity in business leaders. Its position in this respect is lower than that of any other class, save only that of unskilled and semi-skilled labor. This situation is to be explained in part at least by the differing geographic and demographic distribution of farmers, as compared with men in other occupations, during the period 1870 to 1880. The effect of this differing distribution was, in essence, to require of farmers' sons a considerable degree of territorial mobility, in addition to the vertical occupational mobility required of them in common with laborers' sons, in order to put themselves in a position to become business leaders.

Consideration of the farmers' situation of the past few decades indicated some basis for predicting that the findings of 1928 would be changed in the 1952 results and for expecting a greater proportion of farmers' sons in positions of business leadership. For a considerable time, and most notably since the turn of the century, the number of farmers in the working population has declined relative to other occupational groups, and more recently there has also been an absolute decline in the number of farmers in the United States. For this study it is important to note that during the period from 1910 to 1934 the farmer group underwent a net loss of 276,000 persons.[4] The sons of farmers were forced by circumstance, if not by choice, to turn to the cities for places in the job market during much of this period. "A cityward trend of the population is distinctly favored by the much higher reproduction rate in agricultural areas, involving the continual accumulation of surplus population in these areas. Figures indicate a sur-

[4] H. Dewey Anderson and Percy E. Davidson, *Occupational Trends in the United States* (Stanford University, Calif.: Stanford University Press, 1940). For the agricultural data, see Chapter II, pp. 71–99.

plus of some 1,200,000 children accumulated in the rural-farm population above replacement needs during the five-year period 1925–1929." [5]

Thus it might be expected that, with an increasing number of sons of farmers entering the urban job market during the period under study, the demographic disadvantage referred to in the 1928 research would be partially overcome. Further, with the enormous expansion in the transportation and communication network in the nation during the period under study, the relative isolation of most farmers from the larger U.S. society appears substantially reduced. There are fewer social differences between rural and urban populations as a result of this much greater social interaction. It was therefore to be expected that these forces would have worked to increase the participation of the sons of farmers in vertical social mobility in American business and industry.

This is not the case. The low level of representation of farmers' sons in 1928 business leadership continues in 1952. This is true despite the fact that, in general, vertical occupational mobility in U.S. business and industry has increased. Whereas in 1928 the ratio was 0.32, the ratio for the farmer in 1952 is 0.33. Technological and demographic revolutions have not changed the fact that the farmer's son has very limited access to mobility into the business elite.

A summary of the general trends in occupational mobility between 1928 and 1952 is presented in Table 9. Excluding "other" occupations, we contrast the three underrepresented occupational groups of laborer, farmer, and white-collar worker with the categories of businessman and professional man. Twenty-nine per cent of the 1928 business leaders came from the three underrepresented occupational groups, who made up 91 per cent of the population; 71 per cent of the 1928 busi-

Table 9. Equality and Inequality, 1928 and 1952: Comparison of Business Leaders' Fathers and Adult Male Population in Terms of Two Occupational Groupings

Occupational Group	Comparison for 1928		Comparison for 1952	
	Male Adults in 1900	Fathers of 1928 Leaders	Male Adults in 1920	Fathers of 1952 Leaders
Laborer, farmer, white-collar worker	91%	29%	84%	34%
Business, professional man	9	71	16	66
Total	100	100	100	100

[5] *Ibid.*, p. 71.

ness elite were sons of 9 per cent of the population. In 1952, 34 per cent of the business leaders were sons of farmers, laborers, or white-collar workers, while their fathers comprised 84 per cent of the population. The proportion of the higher status occupational groups in the population increased from 9 to 16 per cent, but their representation in the business elite decreased from 71 to 66 per cent. While more men in the population were sons of business and professional men, proportionately fewer business leaders were drawn from this group.

Three Generations of Mobility

The study, up to this point, has considered occupational mobility in the minimum time range of two generations — the relationship between the occupation of the father and the occupation of the son. Occupational mobility may, however, be examined more accurately and meaningfully over a longer span of social time. Therefore, this study was designed to examine occupational status through the male line over three generations, and present-day business leaders were asked for their own position, the occupation of their father, and, in addition, the occupation of their paternal grandfather. Within the limits of the male line, it is possible to analyze occupational mobility over the broad range of nearly a century. The grandfathers of the men studied shaped their careers in America's industrial revolution following the Civil War; the present business elite have seen the opening of the atomic era. It is against this sweep of events and time that the history of occupations from father to son and, again in the next generation, from father to son will be traced out.

The occupational distributions for the three generations are given in Table 10. The first and second columns present the distribution, by percentages, of the grandfathers of the 1952 business elite among the 22 occupational groups of the 1952 questionnaire and among the eight broader groups. The next columns present the distribution of fathers of the 1952 business elite, as given in Table 1. As indicated in the columns on the right, the present business elite are executives, with a few owners of large businesses included.

A comparison of the distributions for grandfather and father indicates the changes in over-all distribution by occupation for these two preceding generations. While 19 per cent of the grandfathers were laborers, this proportion is reduced to 15 per cent in the next genera-

Table 10. Occupational Mobility in Three Generations: Occupations of the Fathers and Paternal Grandfathers of the 1952 Business Leaders

Occupation	Paternal Grandfather		Father		Business Leader	
	22 Occupational Groups	8 Occupational Groups	22 Occupational Groups	8 Occupational Groups	22 Occupational Groups	8 Occupational Groups
Skilled or semiskilled laborer	7.2%	19%	4.5%	15%	0.0%	
Skilled laborer	11.8		10.3		0.0	
Farm tenant or farm worker	2.4	35	0.3	9	0.0	
Tenant with paid help	0.9		0.4		0.0	
Farm owner without paid help	19.4		3.7		0.0	
Owner or manager with paid help	11.9		4.2		0.0	
Clerk or retail salesman	1.1	2	2.5	8	0.0	
Salesman	1.2		5.9		0.0	
Foreman	0.8	3	3.1	11	0.0	
Minor executive	2.2		7.4		0.0	
Major executive	4.7	5	14.6	15	99.0	99%
Owner of small business	17.6	24	17.7	26	0.0	1
Owner of medium business	5.5		6.4		0.0	
Owner of large business	1.4		2.4		1.0	
Doctor	1.9	10	2.2	14	0.0	
Engineer	0.9		2.2		0.0	
Lawyer	2.1		3.2		0.0	
Minister	2.6		2.3		0.0	
Other	2.3		4.2		0.0	
Military career	0.6	2	0.3	2	0.0	
Government service	1.0		1.8		0.0	
Other	0.5		0.4		0.0	
Total	100.0	100	100.0	100	100.0	100

tion. The most striking difference is the movement out of the farm population between these two generations; the relatively minor position of the farmer in supplying business leadership in 1952 was examined earlier, but when seen over a period of three generations the role of farm backgrounds in business mobility assumes greater importance. The movement off the farm into urban occupations takes place in the preceding generation; it is the grandfather who was a farmer, while the father moves into an urban occupation, and the son is mobile, in the vertical dimension, into business leadership. Thirty-five per cent of the paternal grandfathers of the business elite were farmers, and only 9 per cent of the fathers were farmers.

The remaining categories show increases from the grandfather's generation to that of the father in the percentages engaged in the occupation. Substantially greater proportions of the fathers are white-collar workers (an increase from 2 to 8 per cent), and the categories of minor and major business executive show large increases from paternal grandfather to father. An increased number of fathers are in the professions as well.

Two general trends may be noted. First, Table 10 makes it clear that there was in this preceding transition from one generation to another a good deal of mobility into higher occupational groups. At the same time, there is a major movement from the farm into urban occupations.

This table indicates only the over-all, general shifts in occupation. As families are mobile through the occupational structure over several generations, what are the occupational routes they follow? Especially in the case of farm families, how does the move from farm to city take place? What are the transition occupations from which the grandson of the farmer is able to move into the business elite?

To examine the data on intergenerational mobility, it is necessary to follow the sequence of movement in each of the occupational groups as the family unit shifts its position in the occupational structure. Table 11 presents the distribution of the fathers of 1952 business leaders, for each of ten occupational groups, by the occupations of the fathers' fathers of each group. Thus, the first column of Table 11 indicates that 51 per cent of the fathers who were unskilled or semiskilled laborers were the sons of unskilled or semiskilled laborers. Ten per cent were the sons of skilled laborers. Few of the fathers of 1952 busi-

Table 11. Movement of 1952 Business Leaders' Fathers out of Occupations of Paternal Grandfathers: Distribution of Fathers in Each of Ten Occupational Groups According to Occupation of Father's Father

Occupation of Father's Father	Occupation of Father										Distribution of Fathers' Fathers in Occupational Groups
	Semiskilled or Unskilled Laborer	Skilled Laborer	Owner of Small Business	Clerk	Minor Executive	Major Executive	Owner of Large Business	Professional Man	Farmer	Other	
Unskilled or semiskilled laborer	51%	14%	6%	6%	8%	2%	3%	2%	2%	8%	7%
Skilled laborer	10	34	11	12	16	9	7	7	4	10	12
Owner of small business	3	9	30	21	16	22	25	8	5	14	17
Clerk	0	1	1	7	4	3	3	1	0	2	2
Minor executive	1	1	2	3	8	4	2	3	0	2	3
Major executive	0	1	2	3	3	18	4	4	0	6	5
Owner of large business	2	1	3	7	6	11	24	12	1	5	7
Professional man	3	5	5	9	8	11	7	26	5	8	10
Farmer	29	33	38	29	29	18	24	33	82	37	35
Other	1	1	2	3	2	2	1	4	1	8	2
Total	100	100	100	100	100	100	100	100	100	100	100

Table 12. Ratios of Movement out of Occupations of 1952 Business Leaders' Paternal Grandfathers into Occupations of Fathers*

Occupation of Father's Father	Occupation of Father										Mean Mobility Ratio out of Occupation
	Semiskilled or Unskilled Laborer	Skilled Laborer	Owner of Small Business	Clerk	Minor Executive	Major Executive	Owner of Large Business	Professional Man	Farmer	Other	
Semiskilled or unskilled laborer	6.86	2.00	0.71	0.86	1.14	0.29	0.43	0.28	0.29	1.29	0.81
Skilled laborer	0.67	2.92	0.92	1.00	1.33	0.67	0.58	0.58	0.33	0.75	0.76
Owner of small business	0.18	0.47	1.76	1.23	0.94	1.24	1.35	0.65	0.24	0.82	0.79
Clerk	0.00	0.50	0.50	3.50	2.00	1.50	1.50	1.00	0.00	1.00	0.89
Minor executive	0.33	0.67	1.00	1.00	2.67	1.33	0.67	1.00	0.00	0.67	0.74
Major executive	0.00	0.20	0.40	0.60	0.60	3.60	0.60	0.80	0.00	1.60	0.53
Owner of large business	0.43	0.14	0.43	1.00	0.86	1.57	3.71	1.14	0.14	0.57	0.70
Professional man	0.40	0.40	0.50	0.70	0.80	1.20	0.80	2.70	0.50	0.80	0.68
Farmer	0.89	0.94	1.09	0.89	0.80	0.54	0.69	0.94	2.37	1.00	0.86

* Mean = 0.75; diagonal mean = 3.34.

ness leaders who were unskilled or semiskilled laborers were the sons of small business owners, clerks, business executives, or professional men. However, 29 per cent were the sons of farmers, which indicates a substantial movement from the farm in the grandparent's generation, to laboring jobs in the father's generation, to business leadership in the son's generation.

Succeeding columns in Table 11 present, in percentages, the occupational distribution of the fathers, in terms of the occupations of the paternal grandfathers. In contrast with the laborer group, 22 per cent of the fathers who were major executives were sons of owners of small businesses, 4 per cent were sons of minor executives, 18 per cent were sons of major executives, and 11 per cent were sons of owners of large businesses. Thus, 55 per cent of the fathers of the business elite were in turn sons of businessmen; only 11 per cent were sons of laborers; while 18 per cent were sons of farmers.

The broad outlines of movement from father's father to father may be followed similarly for each occupational group. On the extreme right of Table 11 is the total distribution of paternal grandfathers of the 1952 business elite by occupation, a ten-category summary of the data in Table 10. By relating the distributions in each column to the over-all distribution by grandfather's occupation, we may see the data in Table 11 in concise form.

If occupational mobility from the paternal grandfather to the father takes place in a random fashion, and the paternal grandfather's occupation does not influence the choice (or necessity) of the father in entering an occupation, it would be expected that all the vertical columns in Table 11 would approximate that on the extreme right. In other words, since about 7 per cent of the grandfathers were unskilled or semiskilled laborers, about 7 per cent of all the fathers would be expected to be sons of unskilled or semiskilled laborers. To take another type of example, 10 per cent of the fathers' fathers are professional men. If this occupation had no effect on the father's choice of occupation, sons of professional men would appear in equal proportions in all occupations, and 10 per cent of the fathers, whether laborers, farmers, or executives, would be sons of professional men. Because 35 per cent of the grandfathers were farmers, it would be expected that about 35 per cent of the fathers who are unskilled or semiskilled laborers would be from farm families. On the other hand, if no occupational mobility took place and the son had no choice but to enter his father's occupation, then Table 11 would read 100 per cent on the diagonal and would have no other entries. All men in an occupation would be sons of men from that occupation.

The ratio method employed in Tables 3, 4, and 8 may again be used to measure in summary form the degree of rigidity or fluidity in occupational mobility. Table 12 presents the ratios of the occupational background of fathers in a given occupation against the total distribution, by occupation, of all grandfathers. It shows the extent and direction of occupational continuity and mobility from the grandfather's to the father's occupation. In the first column on the left, the fathers who were unskilled or semiskilled laborers are drawn in greatest numbers from paternal grandfathers who were in the same occupational group (ratio of 6.86). The diagonal ratios of Table 12 are then a measure of occupational continuity, the tendency of father to follow grandfather in each of the occupational groups.

The farm population supplied the next greatest number, proportionately, of unskilled or semiskilled laborers in the father's generation (a ratio of 0.89). There was some downward mobility into the laboring group from large owner and professional backgrounds. On the whole, however, there was little movement into laboring occupations from higher status groups. In general, men from farm backgrounds became laborers in considerable numbers as sons of laborers were mobile into white-collar occupations.

To further explore Table 12, two contrasting occupational groups may be examined — the backgrounds of fathers who were major executives, and of fathers who were farmers. All occupational groups studied, except the laboring group and the farmer, exceed the "expected" ratio of 1.00 of mobility into the major executive group. That is, considerable movement out of all occupational groups into the level of major executive in business and industry took place in the generation of the fathers of the 1952 business leaders. At the same time, a large proportion of the fathers who were business leaders were the sons of big business men (a ratio of 3.60). There was, then, a general tendency for the fathers to move into business leadership, as well as a considerable tendency for the sons whose fathers already had such positions to retain them.

In contrast, there was almost no mobility onto the farm. None of the occupational groups of grandfathers supplied a large share of sons to farming. Almost all the fathers of 1952 business leaders who were farmers were the sons of farmers. At the same time, it should be noted, the farm population supplied a considerable proportion of all those in the lower occupational groups, as well as those in the professions. (It is probable that the proportion of sons of farmers entering the professions is a reflection of the rise of the great state universities and the use of education by some farmers' sons as a means of mobility. The point will be further examined.) It would appear that at least in this generational sequence, which terminates in the business elite, there was a great deal of movement off the farm between the generation of the paternal grandfather and that of the father, especially into labor, small business, and the professions. A transition generation passes before the mobile farm offspring (the grandson) attains the heights of the business hierarchy. Movement back onto the farm from other occupational groups is nearly a dead end in terms of potential business mobility.

The column on the extreme right of Table 12, the average mobility ratio out of a given occupation, provides a measure of over-all movement. There is a very large amount of mobility on the part of all occupational groups. Indeed, three fourths of the maximum possible mobility actually takes place (ratio of 0.75, when 1.00 is the maximum). In this system of movement, it is the lower occupational groups — white-collar worker, farmer, and laborer — that are occupationally mobile in the greatest proportions.

All this movement converges by definition on a single specific locus, the business elite of America. A glance back through time, down the male line, shows that an enormous amount of social movement has taken place. This movement is not purposeless. There are definite patterns, or definite channels, by which families are seen to shift occupational position as the process of vertical mobility takes place over the generations. It is the exceptional family whose position remains stable until the grandson assumes business leadership.

The comparison of occupational groups in respect to the amount of occupational stability, or occupational inheritance, from paternal grandfather to father is given in Table 13. The distribution shows the percentage of business leaders' fathers who were sons of men in the same occupation as their own. The column of ratios presents a more

Occupational Mobility

accurate measure of stability, since it is adjusted for the total proportion of fathers' fathers in the occupational group. The occupations are listed in rank order, from the highest ratio of stability to highest mobility, from unskilled laborer to owner of small business.

Occupational stability is greatest at the two extremes of the occupational ranking, with stability in the unskilled and semiskilled laborer group much higher than in any other occupation. The occupation of

Table 13. Occupational Stability from Paternal Grandfathers to Fathers of 1952 Business Leaders

Occupation	Percentage of Fathers in Same Occupations as Fathers' Fathers	Ratio
Unskilled or semiskilled laborer	51	6.86
Owner of large business	24	3.71
Major executive	18	3.60
Clerk or salesman	7	3.50
Skilled laborer	34	2.92
Professional man	26	2.70
Minor executive	8	2.67
Farmer	82	2.37
Owner of small business	30	1.76

owner of a small business seems to be pivotal, with a high degree of circulation and low inheritance. This is consistent with other studies that have established the high mortality rate of this kind of business and movement into and out of ownership of small business (by laborers especially).

The ten occupational groups can be further combined to determine, when the intergenerational movement is viewed most broadly, the routes of mobility employed over these generations. We are studying three generations: the occupational sequence from grandfather, to father, to son — the last being the business elite of the present sample. To establish in broad outline the source of the fathers recruited into each occupational level, the pattern and sequence is presented by the horizontal distribution of Table 14.

As has been noted, the farmer leads all occupational groups in the amount of movement out of the paternal grandfather's occupation. Sons of farmers moved, in substantial numbers, into all occupational groups except the major executive group. Movement from the farm,

Table 14. Patterns of Occupational Mobility for 1952 Business Leaders: Mobility Ratios of Six Occupational Groups *

Occupation of Father's Father	Percentage of Fathers' Fathers in Occupation	Occupation of Father						Mean Mobility out of Occupation
		Major Exec-utive	Profes-sional Man	White-Collar Worker	Business Owner	Laborer	Farmer	
Major executive	5	3.60	0.80	0.60	0.60	0.20	0.00	0.44
Professional man	10	1.20	2.70	0.80	0.60	0.40	0.50	0.70
White-collar worker	5	1.40	1.00	2.20	0.80	0.40	0.00	0.72
Business owner	25	1.32	0.80	1.04	1.56	0.32	0.24	0.74
Laborer	20	0.55	0.45	1.10	0.70	2.65	0.30	0.62
Farmer	35	0.54	1.00	0.86	0.97	0.71	2.37	0.86

* Mean = 0.68; diagonal mean = 2.51.

59

in the father's generation, into all other occupations exceeds the mean interoccupational movement of 0.68 except that proportionately fewer major executives in the father's generation were supplied by the farm than by any other background. At the same time, there was little occupational mobility into farming. There was a general dispersal of farm offspring throughout the lower occupational structure and into the professions.

The movement from the farm to business leadership is clearly a three-generation process. The son of the farmer supplies, in substantial measure, all occupational groups except the major executive group. His son in turn achieves business leadership. The most common route for the farm son was from the farm through the professions (1.00) or business ownership (0.97), to business leadership in the third generation.

For the son of a laboring father, the route was more circumscribed. Movement by the father out of the laboring group was not so frequent (0.62); it was most often into the white-collar group (1.10) and subsequently to business leadership.

The business-owner group and the white-collar group are the intermediate stages in these intergenerational mobility sequences. Movement between them is substantial, and both are important sources of future business leaders. It is through these occupations that the laboring and farming families move to business leadership.

Professional men in the father's generation are drawn from all of the occupational groups studied, with the laboring group least represented. There is, besides, some downward mobility from the professions into the occupations of laborer and farmer. The major executive group, when viewed in this fashion, is the most stable of the occupational groups. The mean mobility rate out of the major executive group is much lower (0.44) than for any of the other occupations studied, with little or no mobility out of this occupation into laboring or farming groups. Sons of major executives enter only one non-business occupational group, the professions, in substantial proportions (0.80). Movement into the major executive group occurs, as noted, from all occupational backgrounds, with the white-collar and business groups most important.

The sequences of vertical mobility over the three generations, for the urban occupational groups, may be summarized as follows:

Occupational Origins of the Business Elite

Paternal Grandfather	Father	Son
Laborer	White-collar worker or business owner	Major executive
Business owner	Major executive	Major executive
Business owner	White-collar worker or professional man	Major executive
White-collar worker	Major executive	Major executive
White-collar worker	Professional man or business owner	Major executive
Professional man	Major executive	Major executive
Professional man	White-collar worker	Major executive

It would seem likely that, if these categories were further refined, the groups would divide into higher and lower status levels with alternative sequences for each. Thus, for example, the movement directly into the major executive group from the professions obtains primarily for the grandfathers in the higher status professional positions, while the alternative route over three generations, through white-collar positions, obtains primarily for lower status professional positions. There may be a similar differentiation in the business-owner and white-collar sequences.

Against this outline of occupational mobility, over three generations, of the 1952 business elite, the examination of changes in these sequences may be made by comparing 1928 with 1952. The occupations of the paternal grandfathers and fathers of the 1928 business leaders, and of the 1952 comparison group are given in Table 15.

As would be expected from the higher vertical mobility rates at the present time than in 1928, more of the paternal grandfathers of the 1952 business leaders occupied lower occupational positions than did the paternal grandfathers of the 1928 business leaders. Three per cent of the 1928 paternal grandfathers were unskilled or semiskilled laborers, compared with 7 per cent of the grandfathers of the 1952 elite. For both groups, there is the same upward trend occupationally between the two antecedent generations, and in somewhat the same proportions. Thus, for example, the proportions of unskilled or semiskilled laborers shifted from 7 to 5 per cent from grandfather to father of the

Occupational Mobility

1952 group, and the proportions changed from 3 to 2 per cent for the 1928 group. Five per cent of the paternal grandfathers of the 1952 group were major executives while 15 per cent of the fathers were major executives. For the 1928 group 6 per cent of the grandfathers and 17 per cent of the fathers were major executives.

Table 15. Occupations of Paternal Grandfathers and of Fathers of 1928 and 1952 Business Leaders

	1928 Leaders		1952 Leaders	
Occupational Group	Paternal Grandfather	Father	Paternal Grandfather	Father
Unskilled or semiskilled laborer	3%	2%	7%	5%
Skilled laborer	9	9	12	10
Owner of small business	17	19	17	18
Clerk or salesman	2	5	2	8
Minor executive	4	7	3	11
Major executive	6	17	5	15
Owner of large business	8	14	7	8
Professional man	12	13	10	14
Farmer	37	13	35	9
Other	2	1	2	2
Total	100	100	100	100

In summary, the general trends are clear. It will be noted that in both 1928 and 1952 a good deal of occupational mobility took place from the paternal grandfather's to the father's occupation. This mobility was generally off the farm, and from the laboring and white-collar categories into higher business positions.

Further, just as the 1952 business leaders are drawn from somewhat lower occupational groups than the 1928 business leaders, so on the whole their grandfathers occupied the lower occupational brackets in greater numbers than did the grandfathers of the 1928 business leaders. The conclusion of a trend to increased occupational mobility, drawn from the earlier analysis, is given further support by the data for the longer time period. Comparisons between the grandfathers, and the fathers, of the 1928 and 1952 business elites show that, in general, there is little difference in the kind and direction of occupational sequences. However, there have been noticeable increases in recruitment from lower occupational categories over three generations during the last decades.

Given the general increase in mobility noted for 1952 as compared

Occupational Origins of the Business Elite

with 1928, it is important to compare the occupational origins of the business elite for the two time periods in terms of changes and similarities in the patterns and sequences of occupational mobility. The great increases in the relative sizes of the white-collar and professional groups in the population and the relative decline of the farm population raise questions as to changes in the channels by which occupational mobility leads to positions of business leadership in the third generation. It has, for example, been held that the white-collar occupations have tended to become blind alleys, that they are occupations from which further occupational mobility is difficult although mobility from laboring backgrounds into white-collar occupations is frequent. Is there any evidence from this study that America's basic occupational structure has changed qualitatively?

Table 16 presents, for six occupational groups, the direction and extent of mobility by the fathers of 1928 business leaders out of the occupations of the paternal grandfather. The table has been constructed on the same basis as Table 14 above, with the preliminary tables omitted. Table 17 presents the direction and extent of mobility of the fathers of the 1952 comparison group.

A comparison of Tables 16 and 17 indicates that, on the whole, assumptions as to changes between the two samples in the sequence of occupational mobility in the antecedent generations are not supported. Those occupations of the fathers' fathers from which the fathers of 1928 business leaders moved into their own occupations are generally the same as those from which the fathers of the 1952 leaders moved. As with the fathers of the 1952 business leaders, farmers' sons who are fathers of 1928 business leaders moved into all other occupational groups, except the major executive group, in substantial proportions. There was for 1928 as for 1952 little movement from other occupations into the farm group. The 1928 business leaders' fathers who were major executives, like the fathers of the 1952 leaders, are drawn from professional, white-collar, and business-owner backgrounds, but only in small proportion from laboring or farming backgrounds.

The essential similarity in the patterns of occupational sequence over the three generations for both business elites seems clear. This similarity must be seen also in the light of a general difference between the two time periods, as shown in Table 18. When occupational sta-

63

Table 16. Mobility Ratios of Six Occupational Groups: Movement of 1928 Business Leaders' Fathers out of Occupations of Fathers' Fathers

Occupation of Father's Father	Occupation of Father						Mean Mobility out of Occupation *
	Major Executive	Professional Man	White-Collar Worker	Business Owner	Laborer	Farmer	
Major executive	4.17	0.50	0.83	0.33	0.00	0.17	0.37
Professional man	1.08	3.17	0.83	0.67	0.33	0.25	0.63
White-collar worker	1.40	0.60	3.20	0.80	0.40	0.20	0.68
Business owner	0.92	0.69	0.85	1.69	0.38	0.15	0.60
Laborer	0.54	0.38	1.08	0.77	4.08	0.23	0.60
Farmer	0.63	0.87	0.87	0.84	0.82	2.32	0.81

* Mean for all groups = 0.62; diagonal mean = 3.10.

Table 17. Mobility Ratios of Six Occupational Groups: Movement of 1952 Business Leaders' Fathers out of Occupations of Fathers' Fathers

Occupation of Father's Father	Occupation of Father						Mean Mobility out of Occupation *
	Major Executive	Professional Man	White-Collar Worker	Business Owner	Laborer	Farmer	
Major executive	3.60	0.80	0.60	0.40	0.20	0.00	0.40
Professional man	1.20	2.70	0.80	0.60	0.40	0.50	0.70
White-collar worker	1.17	0.83	2.00	0.83	0.33	0.17	0.67
Business owner	1.32	0.80	1.00	1.56	0.36	0.20	0.74
Laborer	0.57	0.47	1.16	0.73	2.74	0.32	0.65
Farmer	0.54	1.00	0.86	0.97	0.91	2.40	0.86

* Mean for all groups = 0.67; diagonal mean = 2.50.

Occupational Origins of the Business Elite

Table 18. Occupational Stability in 1928 and 1952

Occupation	Ratio of Fathers' Mobility out of Occupation		Ratio of Fathers' Occupational Stability	
	1928	1952	1928	1952
Major executive	0.37	0.40	4.17	3.60
Laborer	0.60	0.65	4.08	2.74
Professional man	0.63	0.70	3.17	2.70
White-collar worker	0.68	0.67	3.20	2.00
Business owner	0.60	0.74	1.69	1.56
Farmer	0.81	0.86	2.32	2.40
Mean	0.62	0.67	3.10	2.50

bility for the two time periods is examined, an important and consistent difference between the two periods is seen in the fact that there is generally more mobility and less occupational stability for the fathers of the 1952 business leaders than for the fathers of the 1928 business leaders.

The mean mobility out of the paternal grandfathers' occupations by the fathers of 1952 business leaders exceeds that of the 1928 group. That is, more of the fathers of the 1952 business leaders were occupationally mobile, and the trend to increased vertical mobility observed in the present-day business elite may be seen as extending back to the previous generation. A concomitant of this increased mobility by the fathers out of the grandfathers' occupations is the decreased occupational stability, as shown in Table 18 in the column to the right, with fewer men continuing in the occupation of their fathers. An exception is the farm population, where stability increases slightly. For the other occupations, the fathers of the 1952 business leaders remained in the same occupations as the paternal grandfathers less often than did the fathers of 1928 business leaders.

Thus it appears that the increased occupational mobility is a characteristic not only of the present-day business elite, but of their fathers as well. It would appear that the trend to increased mobility into different and higher occupational positions is a deep and long-lasting trend in American society. The sequences of occupational mobility over three generations have largely remained the same for the two time periods studied. However, there has been a general trend to greater occupational mobility that finds ultimate expression in greater vertical mobility from lower occupations into the business elite of the present time.

The data of this research allow a further examination of occupational mobility into business leadership, extending over a longer time period than that of 1928 to 1952. The fathers of the 1928 and 1952 business leaders who were themselves major executives or the owners of large businesses provide a sample of business leaders for two additional time periods. The fathers of the 1928 business leaders who were major executives or owners of large businesses may be defined as business leaders of about 1900. The 1952 business leaders' fathers who were major executives or owners of large businesses may be defined as business leaders of 1920. The questionnaire data on the occupations of paternal grandfathers provide the information as to the occupations of the fathers of these two additional groups.

Table 19. Long-Range Trends in Occupational Mobility into U.S. Business Leadership: Business Leaders of 1900, 1920, 1930, and 1950 from Specified Occupational Backgrounds

Occupation of Father	Business Leaders				Difference between 1900 and 1950
	1900	1920	1930	1950	
White-collar worker	5%	7%	12%	19%	+14%
Laborer	7	10	11	15	+8
Professional man	11	10	13	14	+3
Major executive	15	13	17	15	0
Owner of small business ..	19	23	20	18	−1
Owner of large business ..	17	16	14	8	−9
Farmer	24	21	12	9	−15
Other	2	0	1	2	
Total	100	100	100	100	0

Table 19 presents the four groups of business leaders for whom information as to occupation of the fathers is available. The samples are arranged chronologically, grouped according to the nearest convenient date — 1900, for the fathers of 1928 business leaders who were big business men; 1920, for the fathers of 1952 business leaders who were big business men; 1930, for the 1928 business elite; and 1950, for the 1952 business leaders studied.

The samples for the four time periods are not directly comparable. The "1930" and "1950" samples represent a careful selection from the very top of the business and industry hierarchy. The "1900" and

Occupational Origins of the Business Elite

"1920" samples presumably include a much wider range of business-men, including men of lesser position and men with smaller business firms. It would therefore be expected that the 1900 and 1920 samples represent an overestimation of the amount of occupational mobility during these two general time periods. They would be expected to indicate somewhat more mobility into business positions than actually took place during those periods in terms of the top of the business hierarchy.

Nevertheless, as Table 19 shows, despite this conservative estimate of occupational inheritance in the two periods, the analysis strongly supports the general conclusions already reached from the comparison of 1928 and 1952. Projecting the data to the turn of the century and including in it men born before the Civil War whose careers encompass our society's period of greatest commercial expansion, we find evidence of a long-term, continuing trend to a greater degree of vertical occupational mobility in American business.

As shown in Table 19, the farm population has been supplying an ever diminishing proportion of the nation's business leaders. This proportion seems to have been small but consistent, its diminution a function of the decline in relative size of the farm population in America. Over this half-century, the proportion of business leaders who come from white-collar backgrounds has steadily increased, from about 5 per cent of the business leaders of 1900 to about 19 per cent in 1950. This increase has paralleled and exceeded the increase in proportionate size of the white-collar population. The increase in the contribution of the white-collar group has nearly balanced the diminution of the proportion from farm backgrounds.

Sons of the owners of small businesses appear in a fairly constant proportion in positions of business leadership over the entire 50 years. There is some indication of a decline in their proportion. On the whole, this occupational category appears in the same intermediate role as in previous analyses, and is the source of about one fifth of America's top business leaders.

There has been a consistent decline in the proportion of the sons of owners of large businesses who assume positions of business leadership. While this is balanced by the movement away from business ownership in larger businesses in the American economy, taken together with the rather constant proportion of sons of major executives who move to top business positions, the proportions provide a measure of the degree to which occupational inheritance at the upper level has declined and vertical mobility has been increasing. The most graphic evidence for this increase in vertical mobility comes from the increase in the proportion of sons of laborers who move to the upper ranks of business over this period of time. In 1900 only 7 per cent of the men studied were sons of laborers. The proportion has increased until at present 15 per cent of the business elite are sons of laborers. This trend is in no way balanced by population changes, for the total proportion of skilled and unskilled nonfarm laborers has remained fairly constant for some time.

CHAPTER III

Circulation of the Elite

The Regions of the United States That Produce Leaders

OUR culture has established a series of contradictory images of the successful businessman and his geographic background. For example, the image of the hardfisted robber baron of some decades ago usually includes birth outside the United States, early immigration, and the hard road up. An eastern editor pointed his finger across the Hudson and adjured the young man to go West for fame and fortune. A midwestern editor customarily has his cartoonists portray the business leader as eastern-born, England-trained, and New York–domiciled.

All these elements of the businessman image are true, but none of them is wholly correct of course. All parts of this country, as well as other nations, have supplied members of the business elite. The productivity in business leadership of the various regions of the United States varies widely, however, and in systematic ways. It would appear that geographic origin, as well as occupational or status origin, plays a considerable part in the pattern of vertical mobility in American business.

The 1952 business leaders were asked in the questionnaire to indicate whether or not they were born in the United States and, if so, the state in which they were born. Information on the nativity of the father and the size of the community of birth was also obtained and will be considered later.

The proportions of business leaders born in the several census regions of the United States are given in the column on the left in Table 20.[1] The region in which the largest proportion of the 1952 business

[1] The problem of regional classification of the states has never been satisfactorily resolved. Because the census classification of states into regions gives a meaningful

69

Occupational Mobility

Table 20. Distribution of 1952 Business Leaders by Region of Birth and 1900 Adult Population by Region of Residence

Region	Percentage of Business Leaders Born in Region	Percentage of 1900 U.S. Population Living in Region	Productivity Ratio of Region
New England	10	7	1.43
Middle Atlantic	28	19	1.47
East North Central	26	22	1.18
West North Central	14	14	1.00
South Atlantic	8	14	0.57
East South Central	4	10	0.40
West South Central	4	9	0.44
Mountain	2	2	1.00
Pacific	4	3	1.33
Total	100	100	

leadership was born is the Middle Atlantic area (28 per cent of the total), closely followed by the East North Central states with 26 per cent, these two northeastern regions comprising over half (54 per cent) of the total. Fourteen per cent were born in the West North Central states, and 10 per cent in New England. Less than a quarter of the 1952 business elite were born in the remaining regions — the entire South, the Southwest, and the Far West.

If these proportions are to be evaluated fully, they must be adjusted to the distribution of the U.S. population. Ideally, the comparison should be between the business leaders born in a region and the male infants in each region in the United States at the time of the infancy of the men studied. Since these data are not available, the comparison made in Table 20 is with the distribution of the United States population by regions for 1900. The men studied were born at about the turn of the century, on the average. For accurate study of the regional productivity of business leaders, without allowing the relationships to be obscured by subsequent migrations of the population (especially the movement westward), the most appropriate available comparison is with the 1900 U.S. population.[2]

division of the states for the most part, and because much of the analysis of this study must be made in terms of census data, the census categories of regions are employed throughout. The map on page 71 presents the groupings of states employed in this analysis.

[2] An example of error resulting from the failure to correctly adjust data on geographic origins is to be found in the magazine article "The Nine Hundred," *Fortune,*

Regional Groupings of the States

The comparison of the proportion of business leaders born in each region with the "expected" proportion as given by the population of the region during a comparable time period is shown in Table 20 in the column on the right. Where the proportion of business leaders born in a region is the same as the proportion of U.S. population in the region, as in the Mountain states, the ratio in the column on the right is 1.00. New England ranks high with a ratio of 1.43; the Middle Atlantic states have a slightly higher proportion (ratio of 1.47); the Pacific states are the third most important, with a ratio of 1.33; and the East North Central states are also important (1.18). The West North Central states and the Mountain states are the birthplaces of their proportionate shares of business leaders. Only the northeastern states, in New England and the Middle Atlantic region, produce a proportionately greater share of business leaders than does the Far West.

It is quite clear from Table 20 that the only areas of the United States in which relatively few business leaders are born are the southern states — the East South Central, West South Central, and South Atlantic regions. We will not discuss this finding in detail at this point,

November 1952. The birthplace of the businessmen studied (average age about 60) was compared with 1950 census data. The appropriate comparison would have been with 1890 census data and owing to the increased population of the Far West, it is hardly surprising that it was found to be very low in production of business leaders. *Fortune* explained that the West was "too busy with its own growth, its emergent businesses, and its real estate . . ."

but the basis for this result is not hard to establish. In general, the regions' productivity in business leaders parallels closely their industrial development, and until recent years the South has lagged tremendously in this respect; moreover, its relatively meager industrial plant is often absentee-owned. Further, the low standard of living and level of education in the area are relevant to this outcome. (The proportions given in the middle column include persons of all races, as do all census data used in the study. This does not change the inferences to be drawn from the table, as discussed further in Chapter VIII.

With the mobile population under study, the data on place of birth provide only an outline of the geographic point of departure for these men. The distribution of the business leaders by the region in which they have their present business presents quite a different picture from that by region of birth. As would be expected, most of the 1952 business leaders are now located in the broad belt of highly industrialized territory extending from New York to Illinois and including New Jersey, Pennsylvania, Ohio, and Michigan. These states are included in the Middle Atlantic and East North Central regions in Table 21.

When the distribution of business leaders by the region in which their business is located is compared with the appropriate census data, three regions predominate. The comparison given is with the 1950 U.S. male adult population. The ratios exceed 1.00 in the case of the Middle Atlantic and East North Central regions, and New England. A comparison of the present distribution by regions with that at the time of birth, however, indicates that a definite pattern of movement has taken place. A large proportion of business leaders have moved, during their careers, out of New England and the West North Central states, while the proportion of business leaders has increased most in the Middle Atlantic and Pacific regions.

The extent to which each of the regions retains business leaders is examined in detail in Table 22. The Middle Atlantic states retain 75 per cent of the business leaders born there; the number of business leaders located in the region at the time of the study shows an increase of 73 per cent over the number born there. There is little movement out of, and a great deal of movement into, this region.

The Pacific states also retain a very high proportion of the men born there who become business leaders, and they gain a substantial number of leaders from other states. There is also low mobility out of

Circulation of the Elite

Table 21. Distribution by Region of Present Business of 1952 Business Leaders and 1950 Adult Male Population

Region	Percentage of 1952 Business Leaders	Percentage of 1950 Male Adult Population	Residence Ratio
New England	7	6	1.17
Middle Atlantic	38	21	1.81
East North Central	25	21	1.19
West North Central	9	10	0.90
South Atlantic	7	13	0.54
East South Central	2	7	0.29
West South Central	3	9	0.33
Mountain	1	3	0.33
Pacific	8	10	0.80
Total	100	100	

Table 22. Regional Retention of Potential Business Leadership

Region	Regional Stability (Percentage of Leaders Born in Region Who Are Now in Region)	Regional Gain or Loss (Percentage of Increase or Decrease over Number of Leaders Born in Region)	Average Ratio of Mobility out of Region
Middle Atlantic	75	+73	0.35
Pacific	69	+37	0.47
East North Central	61	−1	0.48
South Atlantic	47	−18	0.64
New England	43	−29	0.41
West South Central	42	−11	0.66
West North Central	36	−39	0.76
East South Central	29	−50	0.91
Mountain	18	−60	0.94

the region. It is clear that the rather low ratio (0.80) of leaders to population for the Pacific region at present, given in Table 21, is a function of a very rapid increase in total population, at a rate exceeding that of the increase in business leadership.

The regions are listed in Table 22 in the rank order of their retention of leaders, from the Middle Atlantic states, which have a stable population, to the Mountain states where mobility out of the region is high and there is a considerable loss of leaders (60 per cent), with almost complete mobility out of the region by men born in the region (0.94). The West North Central states should also be noted. While the region's productivity in business leaders is moderate (1.00), this region loses three fourths of its native leadership to other regions (ratio of 0.76).

A somewhat special case is that of the New England states. Although retention is only moderate, as given in the left column of Table 22, and although loss of future leaders to other regions is large, the average ratio of mobility out of the region is low (0.41). As will be seen in a later analysis, this low ratio of average movement out of New England is due to the fact that movement out of New England is almost wholly into the Middle Atlantic states, and the low mobility into more distant regions depresses the average.

As the comment on New England indicates, the movement between regions by future business leaders is not random but takes place in definite patterns. Men born in certain regions are more likely to assume business leadership in certain other regions. These interactions between regions are given in Table 23.

The basis of calculation of Table 23 is similar to that used in the analysis of occupational mobility in the preceding chapter. The distribution of business leaders by region of birth is given in the column on the left of Table 23. If none of the business leaders had left his region of birth, all the men now located in New England would have been born in New England and the vertical column under New England would read 0.00 throughout. The same would be true of the other vertical columns. If, however, all business leaders were geographically mobile, and were no more likely to arrive in one region than another, then 10 per cent of the New England–born business leaders would now be in New England, about 10 per cent of the Middle Atlantic–born business leaders would be in New England, and so on for each region. The vertical column would read 1.00 throughout in that case. The ratios are then a measure of the extent to which men born in a given region moved to another region.

In the first row, the ratio of 0.90 under Middle Atlantic indicates the degree to which men who are born in New England and become business leaders are finally located in the Middle Atlantic states. Men born in New England also move into the South Atlantic states to some extent (ratio of 0.50), but there is relatively little movement in directions other than down the Atlantic seaboard.

Men born in the Middle Atlantic states tend on the whole not to

Table 23. Geographical Mobility Ratios: 1952 Business Leaders' Movement out of Region of Birth into Region of Present Business *

Region of Birth	Distribution by Region of Birth	Region of Present Business									Average Mobility out of Region
		New England	Middle Atlantic	East North Central	West North Central	South Atlantic	East South Central	West South Central	Mountain	Pacific	
New England	10%		0.90	0.40	0.30	0.50	0.40	0.20	0.30	0.30	0.41
Middle Atlantic	28	0.61		0.42	0.25	0.50	0.21	0.32	0.18	0.32	0.35
East North Central	26	0.35	0.53		0.77	0.27	0.38	0.42	0.50	0.62	0.48
West North Central	14	0.36	0.57	0.86		0.43	0.29	0.86	1.50	1.21	0.76
South Atlantic	8	0.38	0.75	0.38	0.50		1.75	0.75	0.25	0.38	0.64
East South Central	4	0.50	0.50	0.75	0.75	1.50		2.25	0.50	0.50	0.91
West South Central	4	0.25	0.50	0.25	0.75	0.50	0.75		1.50	0.75	0.66
Mountain	2	0.50	1.00	1.00	0.50	0.50	0.00	0.50		3.50	0.94
Pacific	4	0.25	0.50	0.50	0.25	0.25	0.25	0.50	1.25		0.47

* Random movement into a region = 1; mean = 0.62.

leave the region, although a number move into the New England states (0.61). The two northeastern regions tend to form a unit in terms of geographic mobility, and there is a fair amount of reciprocal spatial movement between them. The East North Central states appear on the whole to occupy a central and strategic position in these respects, with some movement into all regions but with no single marked interaction. The highest mobility from these states is into the adjoining West North Central states, and there is also considerable movement into the Middle Atlantic states.

The relatively high geographic mobility rate of men born in the West North Central states has been noted. From Table 23 it appears that the primary movement out of these states has been westward. A substantial proportion of the present-day business leaders of both the Mountain and Pacific regions were born in the West North Central region.

The southeastern regions, South Atlantic and East South Central, have relatively high mobility rates into all regions. Interregional mobility is very often a concomitant of occupational mobility for men born in these regions. Movement is most marked into adjoining southern regions, with a very large proportion of future business leaders from the East South Central states moving into the West South Central region.

With respect to the western states, the Mountain and Pacific regions, the Mountain region is of particular interest because of the high mobility out of that region. This mobility tends to be in two directions. As might be expected, most is westward into the Pacific region; the other direction of movement is into the East North Central and Middle Atlantic states.

On the basis of this analysis the regions of the United States can be roughly grouped in terms of their characteristic production of, and retention of, business leaders.

Types of Regions in Terms of Production and Retention of Potential Business Leaders

I. More than a proportionate share are born in the region; high retention of leaders.
  1. Middle Atlantic
  2. East North Central
  3. Pacific

II. More than a proportionate share are born in the region; low on retention of business leaders.
1. New England

III. A proportionate share are born in the region; low on retention of business leaders.
1. West North Central
2. Mountain

IV. Less than a proportionate share are born in the region; moderate on retention of business leaders.
1. South Atlantic
2. West South Central

V. Less than a proportionate share are born in the region; low on retention of business leaders.
1. East South Central

The Occupations of the Fathers in Each Region

The question of representation in American business leadership may at this point be examined in terms of two variables. The role of occupation in mobility to business leadership and the influence of the region of birth are not independent factors. Given the differences between mobility rates for sons of white-collar workers and for sons of farmers, for example, what differences exist in mobility rates between the northern-born son of a white-collar worker and the southern-born son of a farmer?

The distribution of the 1952 business elite by the occupation of the father and by the region of birth is given in Table 24. The regions examined earlier have been further combined. As used in Table 24, North includes the New England and Middle Atlantic states; Midwest includes the East and West North Central states; South includes the South Atlantic and East and West South Central states; West,

Table 24. Distribution, by Occupation of Father and by Region of Birth,
of Native-Born 1952 Business Leaders

Occupation of Father	Region of Birth				All Regions
	North	Midwest	South	West	
Laborer	6.6%	6.0%	1.5%	0.8%	14.9%
White-collar worker	4.4	5.0	1.9	0.5	11.8
Business executive or owner	20.4	19.4	6.9	3.5	50.2
Professional man	5.3	5.1	2.7	1.2	14.3
Farmer	1.5	4.3	2.4	0.6	8.8
Total	38.2	39.8	15.4	6.6	100.0

Occupational Mobility

the Mountain and Pacific states. The matrix of frequencies in Table 24 sums to 100 per cent, and each category may be compared with every other. Thus, 6.6 per cent of the 1952 business elite are sons of laborers and were born in the North.[3]

In order that the productivity of each of the four geographic regions in terms of occupational groups may be studied, comparable data for the 1920 census are presented in Table 25. As in previous analyses, the ratios of the percentage distributions in Table 25 to those in Table 24 will provide a measure of the relative representation of each occupational group by region among the present-day business elite.

The ratios as given in Table 26 make it possible to compare each of the regional-occupational groups with every other group. The productivity of business leaders by occupational background ranges from a ratio of 6.69, for sons of midwestern businessmen, to 0.15 for sons of southern laborers. That is, given their proportions in the population,

Table 25. Distribution, by Occupation and Region, of the U.S. Male Adult Population in 1920

| Occupation | Region of Residence | | | | All Regions |
	North	Midwest	South	West	
Laborer	17.7%	15.4%	9.7%	4.3%	47.1%
White-collar worker	4.0	3.8	2.2	1.1	11.1
Business executive or owner....	3.1	2.9	1.8	0.9	8.7
Professional man	1.3	1.2	0.8	0.5	3.8
Farmer	2.8	10.1	13.6	2.8	29.3
Total	28.9	33.4	28.1	9.6	100.0

Table 26. Regional and Occupational Sources of 1952 Business Leadership: Ratio of Proportion of Population to Proportion of Business Leaders

| Occupation of Father | Region of Birth | | | | All Regions |
	North	Midwest	South	West	
Laborer	0.37%	0.39%	0.15%	0.19%	0.32%
White-collar worker	1.10	1.31	0.86	0.45	1.06
Business executive or owner ...	6.58	6.69	3.83	3.89	5.77
Professional man	4.08	4.25	3.38	2.40	3.76
Farmer	0.54	0.43	0.18	0.21	0.30
All occupations	1.32	1.19	0.55	0.69	

[3] Some error is introduced into Table 24 by the fact that the occupation of the father as given in the questionnaire is not necessarily the same as that at the time of his son's birth, as the table and subsequent analysis imply.

between six and seven sons of midwestern businessmen move into the business elite at the present time for every one expected under conditions of random movement, while between one and two of southern laborers move into the business elite for every ten expected on the basis of their proportion in the population.

Northern businessmen are proportionately similar to midwestern businessmen as sources of business leaders (6.58), with midwestern and northern professional men also major sources (ratios of 4.25 and 4.08). Fathers who were western and southern businessmen and southern professional men were next in order of representation, followed by western professional men.

Two regional-occupational groups in addition to these business and professional fathers are represented by sons in the business elite in proportions greater than their proportion in the population. These are sons of white-collar men in the Midwest and North (ratios of 1.31 and 1.10). In the more urban regions the white-collar occupations are sources of future business leaders in substantial proportion. Vertical occupational mobility from this occupational group in the North and Midwest is more frequent than would be expected on the basis of their proportion in the population.

The remaining groups are all underrepresented in the business elite. Sons of southern or western laborers or farmers have a proportional disadvantage of no less than one to five in mobility into the business elite. The wide disparity between farm groups by region should be noted. In the North, and to a lesser degree the Midwest, sons of farmers move to business leadership in substantially greater proportions than in the South and West. This is no doubt due in some degree to mobility in the farm hierarchy itself, the able and ambitious farmer in the South and West moving up in farming. This possibility would not seem to account for the regional differences in mobility into urban occupational hierarchies, however.

On the broader regional level, Table 26 reveals that the tendency to greater productivity in business leaders in the northern and midwestern states is not confined to a predominance in these regions of fathers who are business leaders and whose sons become business leaders. While the groups with greatest representation, business and professional men, are in the North and Midwest, the advantage of these two regions, in terms of movement of sons into elite business positions, extends to all occupational groups, sons of white-collar workers, laborers, and farmers as well.

It might have been expected that the observed tendency for the South and West to be less productive of business leaders was partly the function of the fact that the lower occupational groups in these regions are filled in large measure by Negroes and other racial minorities who, by virtue of discrimination in American business, have no opportunity to move into business leadership. As a result it might be expected that men from the upper occupational levels in the South, sons of business and professional men, would enjoy a substantial advantage and would show a markedly higher representation in business leadership than the sons of lower occupational groups. Table 26 indicates that, on the contrary, the general underrepresentation in positions of business leadership of southern-born men extends through all occupational levels, with the difference in proportional representation about as great, between higher and lower occupations, in the southern as in the northern states.

State and Regional Mobility

Mobility from one geographic region of the United States to another is only one of a wide range of territorial moves involved in the total process of mobility. To examine further the meaning of territorial movement in relation to occupational mobility, the responses of the native-born 1952 business leaders were grouped into four categories.

1. Business leaders whose state of birth and state of residence are the same, and who were born in communities of over 2500 population. This group is identified in subsequent analyses by the term "intrastate" mobility.

2. Business leaders whose state of birth and state of residence are the same, but who were born in communities of less than 2500 population. This group is termed "intrastate, rural to urban."

3. Business leaders whose state of birth and state of business are different but within the same region. This group is termed "interstate, intraregion."

4. Business leaders whose region of birth and region of business are different. This group is termed "interregion."

By the use of these categories the business leaders are grouped along a continuum of territorial mobility, each group representing a point on the continuum from relatively stable (urban birthplace in state of present business) to relatively highly mobile (movement between regions).

The scale points are only approximations of real differences in territorial mobility, and err in the conservative direction in estimating total territorial movement. They should not be taken to represent precise points on a scale, but rather should be viewed as rough groupings, by the use of which the relative functions of territorial mobility may be examined. Clearly most of the men in group 1, intrastate mobility, are less mobile territorially than most of the men in group 2, intrastate mobility, rural to urban. And so for groups 3 and 4. Not all the men in group 1, however, are stable: for example, the first group includes men who have moved from smaller cities to large cities; men who in the course of their careers, either in attending school, early in their business careers, or at some other point, left the state in which they were born, but have subsequently returned to it; and men who have moved from one city to another within a state — as from Los Angeles to San Francisco within California, or Cleveland to Cincinnati within Ohio.

To summarize the categories used, it is safe to say that all the men in group 4, interregion mobility, have been territorially mobile — more so than the men in the other groups. However, many men in the other groups were undoubtedly geographically mobile in their lifetimes. Differences among the four groups will tend to be minimized by these facts. If it were possible to isolate "pure" groups in these terms, the differences among the groups in subsequent analysis would undoubtedly be greater than they are seen to be.

The proportions of 1952 business leaders in these groups are given in Table 27. Forty-five per cent of the men studied are included in the group that is mobile between geographical regions. An additional 15 per cent are now in business in a state different from that in which they were born, but in the same geographical region. Only 40 per cent of the business elite are now located in the same state in which they were born, and many of these men have moved from the farms and small towns to the city. A very high rate of territorial mobility characterizes this group of men. A measure of the difference between this group and the general population in these respects is provided by census data. At this writing, figures are not available for the 1950 census. In 1940, however, 77 per cent of the native-born U.S. population were born in their state of residence. This may be compared with the 40 per cent of the business elite as given in Table 27. The percentage of business elite who are territorially mobile in this definition is almost twice as high.

The meaning of territorial mobility becomes clearer from an examination of territorial mobility in relation to the size of birthplace, given in Table 28. It is clear that in good measure this mobility is closely related to the movement to the large city. Over half the men in the study who were born in the larger cities are now located in the state in which they were born. On the other hand, over half the men born in the smaller towns (population 2500–25,000) have moved out of the region in which they were born. It may be inferred from Table 28 that a major force in this territorial mobility is a function of the need to move to larger cities to conduct a business career.

A further inference seems justified on the basis of Table 28. It has

Table 27. Geographical Mobility of U.S.-Born 1952
Business Leaders

Type of Mobility	Percentage of Business Leaders Who Moved
Intrastate	33
Intrastate, rural to urban	7
Interstate, intraregion	15
Interregion	45
Total	100

Table 28. Geographical Mobility and Size of Birthplace of 1952 Business Leaders

| Type of Mobility | Size of Birthplace | | | | | All Groups |
	400,000 and Over	100,000– 400,000	25,000– 100,000	2500– 25,000	Under 2500	
Intrastate	58%	49%	39%	32%	0%	33%
Intrastate, rural to urban	0	0	0	0	28	7
Interstate	12	12	15	17	18	15
Interregion	30	39	46	51	54	45
Total	100	100	100	100	100	100

been assumed that geographical mobility is a necessary step in occupational and social mobility, that movement through social space and the implied break with the family and the class of orientation require sheer physical distance. Certainly the extent of mobility of the business elite would support this assumption.

In following this argument, it may be held that the relatively low territorial mobility rate of the city-born person (cities of over 100,000 population) is a function of the fact that within the confines of the complex modern community of large size a relatively short geographic distance will place an enormous social distance between the mobile individual and his social and physical antecedents. In every sense except the number of miles, the distance from Halsted Street in Chicago's South Side to Lake Forest in the northern suburbs is greater than the distance from Lake Forest to Philadelphia's Main Line.

This interpretation is supported by the analysis of territorial mobility and the occupation of the father as given in Table 29. As would be expected, the sons of farmers are territorially the most mobile of the men studied. The most stable group, territorially, is the occupational group that is also most stable occupationally — sons of major executives or owners of large businesses. The sons of laborers are more stable territorially than the men of other urban occupational backgrounds.

Of special interest are the sons of ministers. The deviation of this group with respect to territorial mobility was so great from the mean of all other sons of professional men that it is given separately in Table 29. More than any other group of men studied, the sons of ministers are territorially mobile. Two thirds of the sons of ministers are engaged in their business careers in a region other than that in which they were born. A total of 81 per cent are now located in states other than those in which they were born. As with the other data collected, it would be helpful to know at what point in the careers of these men the moves took place. For example, the families of ministers may move from one community to another more frequently while the children are young. In the absence of such data, it is possible to speculate that the kinds of restrictions and expectations that the community holds for the sons of ministers often require them, when they engage in business careers, to place a good deal of distance between themselves and their point of origin.

Table 29. Occupational Background and Geographical Mobility of 1952 Business Leaders

Type of Mobility	Occupation of Father							
	Farmer	Minister	Professional Man, except Minister	Owner of Small Business	White-Collar Worker	Laborer	Major Executive or Owner of Large Business	All Groups
Intrastate	7%	9%	29%	31%	33%	34%	49%	33%
Intrastate, rural to urban	23	10	5	7	6	8	4	7
Interstate	14	15	15	17	16	16	12	15
Interregion	56	66	51	45	45	42	35	45
Total	100	100	100	100	100	100	100	100

Circulation of the Elite

The Contributions of Big Cities and Small Towns to Business Leadership

The region of birth has been established as an important variable in the origins of business leaders. Another aspect of territorial origins concerns the size of the community in which the individual is born. Like the problem of occupational origins of business leaders, the question of the relationship between the size of the community lived in and occupational mobility has been the subject of some controversy. American folklore has often portrayed the mobile man in his ideal type as the product of the small town or the countryside; in a presidential campaign, the "barefoot boy from Wall Street" phrase satirized the mythology. Less lyric support of the idea has been given by sociologists. Their argument is based on the relative status homogeneity of the city neighborhood as compared with the status heterogeneity of the small town. Thus it has been maintained that the product of a lower status urban neighborhood does not have higher status models available with whom to identify and from whom to learn goals and behaviors appropriate to higher status positions. On the other hand, the small-town boy is seen as being in more intimate contact with, or at less social distance from, the professional and business men of the community, from whom — given the motivation and skill — he may acquire the techniques necessary for subsequent mobility.

To obtain data bearing on this question of the influence of the size of the community on occupational mobility, the 1952 questionnaire included an item on the size of birthplace. Responses were given in five categories of population as follows:

1. Rural or less than 2500
2. 2500 to 25,000
3. 25,000 to 100,000
4. Over 100,000 (or a suburb of a city this size)
5. New York, Chicago, Philadelphia, Baltimore, St. Louis, Boston, or Pittsburgh (or a suburb of one of these cities, which were 400,000 or over in 1900)

Preliminary use of the questionnaire (see Chapter VIII) established that the businessmen were able to differentiate these categories with some accuracy but that the use of a greater number of categories noticeably increased the probability of error in response. Perfect accuracy of recall and response would not, of course, be expected, but it seems likely that, given the size of the categories, the errors were restricted to errors of one scale point in size and would cancel out for the group. The final category of large cities listed them by name to achieve maximum reliability of response to the two large-city categories, which we find to be potentially the most difficult to discriminate between and recall accurately.

The distribution of business leaders by the size of the birthplace is given in Table 30. About a quarter of the 1952 business leaders were born in the seven metropolitan areas, each of which in 1900 had a population exceeding 400,000. An equal proportion were born in rural areas. As with earlier data, these proportions must be compared with the appropriate proportions in the population for their meaning to be gauged.

The distribution of the U.S. population by the size of the community at the mean birth year of the business leaders is given in the second column of Table 30. (Both distributions, the business leaders and the U.S. population, are confined to native-born populations.) The ratio of the two distributions provides a measure of the relative importance of each community-category as a source of business leaders. The ratios are given in the column on the right of Table 30.

As the ratios indicate, there is a marked size gradient. The larger communities are the primary source of future business leaders, while the smaller communities decline in importance with the size of the community. At the extremes, the largest cities are represented two to two and one-half times more frequently in business leadership than their proportion of the U.S. population would indicate, while the rural areas are represented less than half as frequently as would be expected.

When the size of the community and the region of birth are considered together, the question of the territorial origins of the business elite takes on greater complexity. With the regions combined into four categories once again, the distribution by size of birthplace for each region is given in Table 31. The categories of size of birthplace are reduced to three because of the limited number of categories used in the 1900 census.

Table 31 presents a comparison of the distribution, by region of birth and size of birthplace, of the native U.S. population in 1900 and of the native-born 1952 business elite. While 50 per cent of the business leaders born in cities with a population of 100,000 or more were born in the North, the northern states included in 1900 over 50 per cent of the large-city population. While only 6 per cent of the business leaders born in large cities were born in the West, an even smaller proportion — 4 per cent — of the U.S. native population in large cities was located in the West.

Table 30. Size of Birthplace of 1952 Business Leaders and Size of Community of Residence of 1900 U.S. Population

Size of Community	Percentage of Business Leaders Born in Community	Percentage of 1900 U.S. Population Living in Community	Ratio of Business Leaders to Population
400,000 and over	26	11	2.36
100,000–400,000	14	8	1.75
25,000–100,000	12	7	1.71
2500–25,000	22	14	1.57
Under 2500	26	60	0.43
Total	100	100	

Table 31. Distribution, by Region of Birth and Size of Birthplace, of 1952 Business Leaders and, by Region and Size of Community of Residence, of 1900 U.S. Population

Region	Community of 100,000 or More		Community of 25,000 to 100,000		Community under 25,000	
	U.S. Population of 1900	Business Leaders	U.S. Population of 1900	Business Leaders	U.S. Population of 1900	Business Leaders
North	53%	50%	47%	36%	20%	28%
Midwest ..	33	35	25	36	36	44
South	10	9	20	19	39	21
West	4	6	8	9	5	7
Total ..	100	100	100	100	100	100

Table 32. Region and Size of Community as a Factor in Occupational Mobility: Ratio of Proportion of Population to Proportion of Business Leaders

Region	Community of 100,000 or More	Community of 25,000–100,000	Community under 25,000
North	0.94	0.77	1.40
Midwest	1.06	1.44	1.22
South	0.90	0.95	0.54
West	1.50	1.12	1.40

Occupational Mobility

For more convenient study, the ratios of the distributions of Table 31 were computed, and these are presented in Table 32. The large cities of the Midwest and West — cities of 100,000 or more — are the birthplace of proportionately more business leaders than the large cities of the North and South; the smaller cities, with populations of 25,000 to 100,000, in the Midwest and West produce proportionately more business leaders than this group in the South; while the medium-sized cities of the North produce proportionately the fewest business leaders in this group.

In terms of regional productivity, care in interpreting Table 32 should be exercised. The rows cannot be accurately compared across unless adjustments are noted. Thus, the ratio of 1.40 for the rural North and West indicates that, in comparison with rural areas in other regions, the northern and western rural areas are productive of business leaders. This does not mean that in comparison with communities in other regions and of different sizes, the rural North and West are highly productive of business leaders; it means simply that the discrepancy between different sized communities within the North and West is not as great as in other regions in the proportions of business leaders born in them. The major gap in this respect is, as noted, in the South. It may be said with some accuracy that men living in the rural South simply did not move into positions of business leadership. When the occupational data on the farmer are recalled, it becomes clear that southern farmers are by all odds the group least likely to break into the business hierarchy. This is a source of manpower that, for whatever reason, is simply not utilized by American business; it does not have access to higher level positions in American business and industry.

The census data required for joint consideration of the size and region of the place of birth and the occupation of the father are not available for the time periods in question. Some indication of the relationships among these three factors may be seen in Table 33, where three types of communities — northern large city, northern small town and rural, and southern small town and rural — and the occupations of the fathers of business leaders born in each of the three types are presented.

Men who move to business leadership from northern large cities tend to be sons of laborers, white-collar workers, or big business men.

88

Circulation of the Elite

Table 33. Occupations and Types of Communities of Fathers
of 1952 Business Leaders

Occupation of Father	Type of Community		
	North, over 100,000	North, under 25,000	South, under 25,000
Laborer	21%	18%	10%
Owner of small business	13	24	17
White-collar worker	24	17	16
Major executive or owner of large business..	26	17	16
Professional man	13	14	19
Farmer	3	10	22
Total	100	100	100

(The small percentage of farmers in this group no doubt results from cases of the father moving into farming following the birth of the son. It should be recalled that the father's occupation is given at the time the business leader became self-supporting, while the other data on region and size of birthplace are for a period some 20 years earlier.) The sons of owners of small businesses appear in greater proportion from northern small-town and rural backgrounds, along with sons of farmers. The difference between the northern small town and the southern small town is most striking in the smaller proportion of sons of laborers, the increase in sons of professional men, and the increase in sons of farmers in the South. All these proportions must be evaluated in terms of the probable occupational distributions in each type of community. If the data on occupations were available, it would seem likely that for the southern small-town background the proportion of sons of laborers and professional men, as well as of big business men, would seem very high indeed, and that the proportion of sons of farmers would be seen to be very low in relation to their proportion in the population.

The Foreign-Born

The analysis of the relationship between territorial origins and the business elite of 1952 has been confined thus far to those born in the United States. The 1952 questionnaire asked if the business leader, his father, and his father's father were born in the United States.

Occupational Mobility

Table 34. Nativity of 1952 Business Leaders and U.S. Population in 1940

Nativity	Percentage of Business Leaders	Percentage of U.S. White Population in 1940
Leader foreign-born	5.3	9.6
Leader U.S.-born	19.7	19.5
Father and leader U.S.-born	20.2 ⎫	70.9
Paternal grandfather, father, and leader U.S.-born	54.8 ⎭	
Total *	100.0	100.0

* Thirteen out of 7500, or 0.2 per cent, failed to answer.

Responses were classified into four groups, as presented in Table 34.[4] About 5 per cent of the 1952 business leaders are foreign-born; about 20 per cent are U.S.-born sons of foreign-born fathers; the remaining 75 per cent are no less than third-generation Americans.

Comparable figures for the most recent census available are given for the white U.S. population in the column on the right. Nearly 10 per cent of the population in 1940 was foreign-born, a proportion almost twice as great as that in the business elite. (The difference would be somewhat less, presumably, if more recent census figures were the basis of comparison.) However, the proportion of U.S.-born sons of foreign-born fathers in the two groups is almost identical, 19.7 of the business elite and 19.5 of the U.S. white population. In a generation, the disadvantage of foreign birth in movement into the top positions of the business hierarchy disappears — a powerful testimonial to the efficiency of the American "melting pot."

Table 35, presenting the occupations of the fathers for each of the four nativity categories, provides an additional basis for exploring the relationship between nativity and the recruitment of the business elite. The occupations of the fathers of foreign-born business leaders clearly present a special case. Immigration regulations as well as the job market play a role in determining the distribution by father's occupation. A relatively high proportion of fathers of foreign-born business leaders were professional men or farmers; proportionately few were in business executive positions.

The remaining nativity categories present a more definite curve of occupational frequency. Beginning with those business leaders whose fathers were foreign-born and continuing across the columns to those

[4] See Appendix III, p. 261.

Table 35. Occupational Mobility and Nativity: Occupations of the Fathers of 1952 Business Leaders in Four Nativity Categories

Occupation of Father	Leader Foreign-Born (5% of Total)	Leader U.S.-Born (20% of Total)	Father and Leader U.S.-Born (20% of Total)	Father's Father, Father, and Leader U.S.-Born (55% of Total)	Percentage of All 1952 Business Leaders
Unskilled and semiskilled laborer..	5%	9%	5%	3%	4%
Skilled laborer	16	15	13	7	10
Owner of small business	20	24	18	15	17
Clerk or salesman	9	8	9	9	8
Minor executive	9	11	11	10	11
Major executive	8	9	15	17	15
Owner of large business	9	9	9	8	8
Professional man	14	8	11	17	15
Farmer	8	5	6	11	9
Other	2	2	3	3	3
Total	100	100	100	100	100

business leaders whose paternal grandfathers were U.S.-born, the trend is to higher occupational status. Compared with sons of U.S.-born fathers, a larger proportion of the sons of foreign-born fathers who move to business leadership are sons of laborers: 24 per cent of the foreign-born fathers were laborers; 18 per cent of the U.S.-born fathers were laborers; and in only 10 per cent of the cases in which the father's father was U.S.-born were the fathers laborers. The proportion of fathers who were owners of small businesses declines from 24 to 15 per cent.

Almost half, 48 per cent, of the foreign-born fathers were either laborers or small business men. Only a quarter of the "old American" group, whose fathers' fathers were U.S.-born, were sons of laborers or owners of small businesses. The proportion of fathers in white-collar positions remains fairly constant for the three groups, as does the proportion of fathers who were owners of large businesses. However, the proportion of fathers who were farmers or major executives increases sharply.

Certainly Table 35 introduces the distinct possibility that a disproportionate share of the vertical occupational mobility in American business is accomplished by men who are subject to the presumed disadvantage of comparatively recent ethnic origins. The test of this hypothesis can be made only by turning again to census data in order to compare proportions, for it is also clear that more of the foreign-born fathers than of U.S.-born fathers in the total population would be laborers and small business men.

To make this comparison, it is necessary to exclude from the sample the 1952 business leaders who are foreign-born. The comparison is between the U.S.-born and foreign-born fathers of 1952 business leaders, in terms of occupation, on the one hand, and of the 1920 male adult working force divided into the two comparative groups.

Without regard to occupation, Table 36 indicates that the proportion of foreign-born fathers whose sons become business leaders is slightly less than the proportion of foreign-born male adults in the 1920 working force. The difference is minor, however, and the impression remains that nativity in general had little effect on movement into top business positions by sons of foreign-born men.

Table 37 provides the basis for the comparison in terms of the father's occupation. The first column on the left presents the distribution by occupation of the foreign-born fathers of present-day business leaders. The second column presents the distribution by occupation of foreign-born adult males in 1920. While a large proportion of foreign-born fathers of business leaders were laborers (24 per cent), two thirds of the total foreign-born male population were laborers in 1920. It was not possible to divide the census data further, so minor and major executives and owners of small and large businesses are combined into the category called "business owner or executive" in this table. The columns on the right present the comparison, by occupation, of U.S.-born fathers of business leaders and the U.S.-born male adult working force.

On the basis of the ratios derived from Table 37, the question may be posed again: Is there more vertical occupational mobility by sons of foreign-born fathers or by sons of U.S.-born fathers? As the ratios in Table 38 indicate, there is a slight but consistent tendency among lower status occupational backgrounds for proportionately more sons

Table 36. Nativity of the 1952 Business Leaders' Fathers and of 1920 U.S. Male Adults

Nativity	Fathers of 1952 Business Leaders	U.S. Male Adult Working Force in 1920
U.S.-born	76.2%	75.0%
Foreign-born	23.8	25.0
Total	100.0	100.0

Table 37. Distribution by Nativity and Occupation of 1952 Business Leaders' Fathers and of 1920 U.S. Adult Males

	Foreign-Born		U.S.-Born	
Occupation	Fathers of Business Leaders	U.S. Adult Males in 1920	Fathers of Business Leaders	U.S. Adult Males in 1920
Unskilled or semiskilled laborer ..	8	48	3	24
Skilled laborer	16	19	9	17
Clerk or salesman	8	5	9	12
Business owner or executive	51	12	52	11
Professional man	10	3	16	5
Farm laborer, owner, tenant	5	12	9	30
Other	2	1	2	1
Total	100	100	100	100

Occupational Mobility

Table 38. Place of Birth as a Factor in Occupational Mobility: Ratio of
Proportion of 1920 Adult Males in Occupation to Proportion
of Fathers of Business Leaders in Occupation,
by Two Nativity Groups *

Occupation	Foreign-Born	U.S.-Born
Unskilled and semiskilled laborer	0.17	0.13
Skilled laborer	0.84	0.53
Clerk or salesman	1.60	0.75
Business owner or executive	4.25	4.73
Professional man	3.33	3.20
Farmer	0.42	0.30

* Proportional representation = 1.00.

of foreign-born men than sons of U.S.-born men to move into positions of business leadership. The differential is substantial in the case
of sons of foreign-born white-collar workers, who are represented in
substantially greater proportion in the business elite than sons of
U.S.-born white-collar workers. It is clear that if the category "business owner or executive" could be further differentiated into major
and minor executive, and owner of large or small business, the differential would be even greater. Occupational rigidity is greater and
vertical occupational mobility less in those groups in the population
that have been established in American society for longer periods of
time.

The Education of the Business Elite

Grade School and College Men in the Business Elite

FORMAL education, as everyone knows, has become increasingly important in American life. Instead of starting within an industry and working their way up, more and more men use a college education to launch their careers. Technical and business school training is taken today more often than in the last generation by men ambitious to succeed. Since the mean age of those successful men in our study is slightly over fifty, their decisions about going to college were made around thirty years ago. How many of them chose then to go to college? How many did not go to college but chose the hard way to reach the top? How do the proportions of the 1952 business leaders at each level of educational advancement compare with the proportions in the general population?

An overwhelming majority of the 1952 business leaders went to college (76 per cent). Most of them graduated (57 per cent); some did not (19 per cent), but an equal percentage took advanced graduate study, often in one of the better colleges or universities (19 per cent). In brief, three fourths of all the business elite attended college; some graduated, some did not, and some went on to higher degrees. (See Table 39.)

How much education did all these men have? Did they have more than men of their own age in the present population? Did a smaller proportion of them stop in high school and grade school than did others of their age?

Only 4 per cent, fewer than 1 out of 20, had less than high school training; 9 per cent went to high school but did not finish; and 11 per cent graduated from high school but did not enter college.

Occupational Mobility

Table 39. Education of 1952 Business Leaders and of the General Population in 1950

Education	U.S. Adult Males (30 years and over) in 1950	1952 Business Leaders
Less than high school	55%	4%
Some high school	16	9
High school graduation	16	11
Some college	6	19
College graduation	7	57
Total *	100	100

* No answer was made by 16 out of 7500.

The differences in the proportions of college and non-college men, while dramatic enough, become even more so when they are compared with the proportions of adult males (30 years and over) in the general American population (see Table 39). (Holding the level down to 30 years for the general group rather than using the older age of the men in our sample favors an *increase* of men at the college level in the general population because of the increase in college education since 1920.) Whereas 76 out of every 100 of the business elite (76 per cent) had gone to college, only 13 out of 100 males in the general population had college training. Fifty-seven out of every 100 business leaders had graduated from college, as compared with only 7 men (30 years or over) from the general population.

Comparisons at the lower educational levels are perhaps even more forceful. Well over half of the grown males in the general population had not gone to high school, compared with only 4 per cent of the elite. There were about 14 times more men of meager education in the general population than in the elite. A glance down the two columns of Table 39 tells the story. Men of the lowest educational level were eight times more frequent in the general population than were college graduates; on the other hand, men of the highest educational attainment (college graduates) were 14 times more frequent in the business elite than those at grades below the high school level.

College education and the careers of the business elite are closely associated; the high proportion of college men among the elite and the low proportion in the general population are at first glance most impressive. But given the value placed on higher education, the almost magical belief in a college degree, the long association of high

96

educational attainment and high social position, as well as many other similar evaluations in this culture, perhaps the most extraordinary facts are that, at mid-century in America, 24 per cent of the most successful men in American business had never entered college, and 4 per cent had not even gone to high school, some having failed to complete the eighth grade.

Are these the men who belong to the older American tradition, who started at the bottom and worked their way up? Or did they come from well-placed families whose fathers had already arrived and who, being so favored, found no need for college education to compete successfully? What kind of men got a college education? Which business leaders climbed the hard way, and which rested easily on their fathers' occupational and educational accomplishments?

Who Gets Educated?

Educated men come from the higher occupational backgrounds in larger proportions than from the other levels (see Table 40). Nearly three fourths of the business leaders who were sons of professional men had a college degree; nine out of ten had gone to college (89 per cent). The sons of business leaders closely followed them: 88 per cent had been to college and seven out of ten were college graduates. About a third of the sons of laborers who had risen to the elite had graduated from college, and approximately five out of ten had attended college. The percentage of college men increases step by step from the laboring level: 57 per cent of the sons of small owners, 50 per cent of the sons of farmers, and 50 per cent of white-collar workers were college graduates.

The highest percentage of men with only grade school education came from the laboring classes: 14 per cent of the sons of unskilled workers and 9 per cent of skilled. These were followed by the farmers (6 per cent), white-collar workers (5 per cent), the small owners (4 per cent), the professional men (2 per cent), and the sons of big business men (1 per cent).

All occupational levels, except big business men and professional men, were above or at the average educational level of the total group of business leaders for sons who had some high school training or had graduated from a secondary school (see Table 40). All occupational levels except big business and professional men were below or at the

Table 40. Occupational Mobility and the Education of 1952 Business Leaders

Occupation of Father	Less Than High School	Some High School	High School Graduation	Some College	College Graduation	Total
Unskilled or semiskilled laborer ..	14%	18%	16%	16%	36%	100%
Skilled laborer	9	16	20	21	34	100
Small owner	4	9	12	18	57	100
White-collar worker	5	11	14	20	50	100
Major executive or large owner ..	1	4	7	18	70	100
Professional man	2	3	6	17	72	100
Farmer	6	9	15	20	50	100
All occupations in sample	4	9	11	19	57	100

average for sons who were college graduates. The men from higher origins get the most education, and the ones from the lower, the least. Although this statement is true, obviously significant, and important, it should be remembered that these are not categorical differences.

Perhaps an even more important generalization about the business elite and their education is that all levels — unskilled workers and big business men, farmers and white-collar men — furnished a higher proportion of sons at the level of college graduate than at any other level of educational achievement. The men who achieve and advance themselves in business most often are the kind of men who achieve and advance themselves in school. Their ambitions drive them upward step by step to higher educational levels just as they push them upward in business. As the eye moves across the table "down" from the college graduate level to the men with less than high school education there is a steady drop in the proportion for each occupational background, the only exception being the unskilled workers; yet, in general, they too fit this configuration.

The men of all levels of the elite tend to seek and get higher education; over half at any level have had some college education, those from the higher levels more often doing better than those from below. These facts tell us that a substantial number — but now a minority — do come up the hard way. A third of all the sons of laborers did not even get through high school. Education is vitally important, but "uneducated" men still get to the top!

What Were the Educational Levels of the Business Leaders' Families?

The educational attainment of the family is an important factor in determining the educational achievement of the children; yet many Americans advance beyond the educational level of their parents. Did these men climb higher in school than their fathers? Did some advance more than others? Table 41 helps to answer these questions. The three vertical columns give the educational levels of the 1952 business leaders, the schooling of their fathers, and the percentage of each educational level in the U.S. adult male population (55 years and over) in 1940. (It would have been better to have had the educational level for adult males of 1920 who were of the average age of the business leaders' fathers. This was not possible. The figures given are the

Occupational Mobility

Table 41. The Education of Fathers of the 1952 Business Leaders, as Compared with Their Sons and U.S. Adult Males in 1940

Education	U.S. Males, 55 Years and Over, in 1940	Fathers of 1952 Business Leaders	1952 Business Leaders
Less than high school	78%	38%	4%
Some high school	8	16	9
High school graduation ...	7	18	11
Some college	3	10	19
College graduation	4	18	57
Total	100	100	100

Table 42. The Education of 1952 Business Leaders and the Education of Their Fathers

Education of Business Leader	Education of Father			All Business Leaders
	Less Than High School	High School	College	
Less than high school ...	8%	1%	1%	4%
High school	29	19	8	20
College	63	80	91	76
Total	100	100	100	100

nearest approximation; they err on the side of increasing the proportion of men with higher education in the general population.)

The percentage of business leaders' fathers with less than high school education (38 per cent) was half that for men in the general population, and the percentage who were college graduates or had gone to college (28.7) was four times that for American males of comparable age levels in 1940. Still their sons far outstripped them. The percentage of college graduates among the sons was three times as great, and the percentage of those who failed to go beyond grammar school was only about one ninth the percentage of the fathers. Although these general figures tell us much about similarities and differences in the education of the fathers and sons, they do not answer our questions.

Are the sons of educated men the most likely to go on to college? Are the sons of "uneducated" men least likely to achieve advanced training in school? Table 42 provides the answers to these important questions. In general the sons of men with college training were more likely to go to college than others were, yet the important story in

100

this table is not so much this point as the fact that the sons of men of all educational levels — grammar school, high school, and college — were highly represented at the college level. It is true that 91 per cent of the business leaders with college-educated fathers were also college educated — an overwhelming number — yet 63 per cent of the business leaders who had fathers with no more than grammar school education also advanced to college study, as did 80 per cent of those whose fathers had been to high school. Only 1 per cent of the men having fathers with a college education and 8 per cent of those having fathers with low schooling had only a grammar school education; only 8 per cent of those having college-educated fathers and 29 per cent having fathers of low schooling went no farther than high school. Clearly the education of the father is important but far from sufficient to explain or determine who goes to college.[1]

We have learned about the relation, in the business elite, of the father's occupational background and educational achievement to his son's education. Although, after the earlier inspection of the occupational and educational origins of these men, the results are no more than would be expected, it seems worth our time to learn how great is the disparity in the cultural origins of the two classes of men — those born to the position and those who achieved it. Such an inference is possible since the occupational and educational levels of the parents, when combined and viewed as the kind of environment from which the business leaders came, are good indicators of cultural differences. Table 43 provides a significant story. It demonstrates that many of these men came a long, long distance and still "made good." Eighty-two per cent of the fathers who were in the professions and 37 per cent of those in big business were college men; on the other hand, 83 per cent of the fathers who were unskilled laborers and 67 per cent who were skilled laborers had less than a high school education. Ninety-three per cent of the unskilled laborers had not graduated from high school. Relatively speaking, many of these men came from very limited environments.

[1] When four categories of educational level are employed rather than the three reported above to analyze the education of the business leaders in terms of that of their fathers, the pattern of results is not changed. Thus, using four categories, we obtain the following proportions: 14 per cent of the sons of college graduates get some college training and 78 per cent graduate from college; 19 per cent of the sons of fathers with grammar school backgrounds go to college without graduating, while 44 per cent graduate.

Table 43. The Occupations and Education of the 1952 Business Leaders' Fathers

			Education of Father			
Occupation of Father	Less Than High School	Some High School	High School Graduation	Some College	College Graduation	Total
Laborer, unskilled or semiskilled ..	83%	10%	5%	1%	1%	100%
Laborer, skilled	67	18	11	3	1	100
Small owner	46	18	19	10	7	100
White-collar worker	38	19	24	11	8	100
Major executive or large owner ..	22	15	26	14	23	100
Professional man	6	5	7	13	69	100
Farmer	60	16	11	8	5	100
All occupations in sample	38	16	18	10	18	100

Table 44. Education, by Region, of 1952 Business Leaders as Compared with Adult Males in 1950

	North		Midwest		South		West	
Education	Business Leaders	Adult Males	Business Leaders	Adult Males	Business Leaders	Adult Males	Business Leaders	Adult Males
Less than high school	4%	47%	4%	50%	4%	59%	4%	39%
High school	19	38	20	36	19	29	19	41
College	77	15	76	14	77	12	77	20
Total	100	100	100	100	100	100	100	100

Education of the Business Elite

Region, Nativity, and Education

Although it might be assumed that there would be considerable difference in the educational levels of big business men among the several regions of the United States, the differences seem to be few and of little consequence. Table 44, which divides the United States into four major regions, shows this clearly. Every region shows only 4 per cent with less than high school; the regions vary from 19 to 20 per cent for those at the high school level, and from 76 to 77 per cent for those at the college level. Some may ask whether differences might appear if the school levels were divided (into "some high school" and "high school graduation," and "some college" and "college graduation") and the regions re-divided into the nine previously described (see Figure 1 in Chapter III) instead of four. The variations are still small. For those with less than high school they range from 5 per cent for the Middle Atlantic and East South Central to 2 per cent for New England. Yet most regions show some 3 to 4 per cent in this category of education. The New England region has a higher percentage of college graduates and postgraduates (those with advance study beyond the bachelor's degree), and the southern regions, smaller percentages in these categories. When the postgraduates and college graduates are combined the New England and Mountain states lead the others.

It is not until the proportions of college-trained businessmen are compared with the proportions of college-educated men in the population of each region that the significance of college training in the lives of the businessmen of the several regions becomes most apparent. While the education of business leaders is largely the same whatever their region of birth, as shown in Table 44, there are substantial differences between the regions as to the educational achievements of their adult male populations. Well over half of the men living in the South have less than high school education, although only 4 per cent of the business leaders born in the South failed to attend high school. In other words, while there are important variations in the general level of educational training between one region and another, business leaders have about the same level of formal education, whatever their region of birth. A major factor in the limited mobility of men from certain sections of the country is clearly the low level of education available to men born in those regions. Since educational facilities are limited, occupational mobility into the business elite is correspondingly limited.

The educational scores of the several generations of American-born men, compared with the foreign-born, demonstrate that education operates more often to the advantage of the old Americans than of those more recently arrived. On the whole, those men whose fathers' fathers were born in the United States have more college education than those from all other generations of Americans accounted for in this study. Table 45 presents the evidence for the relation between ethnic background and educational achievement. Three categories of educational advancement are listed and four generations of Americans accounted for, including men whose fathers' fathers (and possibly more distant ancestors) were born in the United States. Those businessmen who were foreign-born were much less likely than native Americans to attend college, and more frequently did not attend high school. The average level of education increases as foreign backgrounds become more distant. Those of the elite whose grandfathers were American-born have the most college education (81 per cent), and almost none (2 per cent) failed to enter high school.

The averages for all these categories of education—grammar school, high school, and college—for those men whose fathers were born in the United States are exactly the same as those for the entire group. The men with foreign background, born here or born abroad, average less education than those with a longer ancestry here.

Although we have emphasized the differences among those with varying foreign and American backgrounds, the important and significant facts are that 6 out of every 10 business leaders who were

Table 45. Nativity and Education of 1952 Business Leaders

Education	Business Leader Foreign-Born	Business Leader U.S.-Born	Business Leader and Father U.S.-Born	Business Leader, Father, and Father's Father U.S.-Born	All Groups
Less than high school	11%	7%	4%	2%	4%
High school	29	26	20	17	20
College	60	67	76	81	76
Total	100	100	100	100	100

foreign-born and 7 out of 10 with foreign-born parents acquired a college education. The old American averaged high, 8 out of 10; yet this is but one or two more points than his culturally disadvantaged competitors.

The men born abroad are changing cultures and social places as they move from one society to another. Meanwhile they and other mobile men are changing social and occupational positions from lower to higher status. Each uses education to help him transform himself culturally and to provide many of the necessary skills for functioning in the higher realms of management and ownership.

The fact that men of different cultural backgrounds find college education accessible and attainable helps to demonstrate that this society is flexible. Thus this society permits some of those socially most distant from the top to equip themselves with the important skills needed for competing successfully with all others for the prizes and high statuses present in American life. It also demonstrates that, despite difficulties, these men must be given strong and meaningful encouragement to educate themselves to become not only successful businessmen but persons who are American in culture.

The differential effects of college and grammar school education on the mobility of American businessmen, particularly those who start at the bottom, are indicated by Tables 46 and 47. Table 46 presents the territorial movement of big business men who have risen from the lower to the higher occupational ranks. Those included are men whose fathers' occupations were laborer, clerk, salesman, and farmer. The column on the left gives a measurement of movement from the place of birth to the present location. It is a rough measurement, yet in the large it tells a fairly accurate story.

The places of birth have been divided into rural and urban;[2] movements within the state of birth are distinguished from those which took a man from one state to another. Careful sampling shows that, generally, the movements between states are longer and socially more important than those within a state. This arrangement of the evidence, when related to the educational level of the business elite, provides one kind of answer to several important questions.

Some of these vital questions may now be asked. Since one large and important segment of the business elite consists of men in motion,

[2] See p. 85ff for definitions.

Occupational Mobility

Table 46. The Education and Geographical Mobility of 1952 Business Leaders of the Lower Occupational Origins *

Place of Birth and Type of Geographical Mobility	Less Than High School	High School	Some College	College Graduation	Total
Urban: intrastate	10%	35%	19%	36%	100%
Rural: intrastate	9	32	19	40	100
Urban: interstate	6	28	18	48	100
Rural: interstate	5	24	22	49	100
All business leaders of lower occupational origins	7	29	20	44	100

* Father's occupation was farmer, laborer, clerk, or salesman.

Table 47. The Education and Geographical Mobility of 1952 Business Leaders of the Higher Occupational Origins *

Place of Birth and Type of Geographical Mobility	Less Than High School	High School	Some College	College Graduation	Total
Urban: intrastate	2%	15%	19%	64%	100%
Rural: intrastate	5	20	20	55	100
Urban: interstate	2	12	17	69	100
Rural: interstate	2	16	19	63	100
All business leaders of higher occupational origins	2	15	18	65	100

* Father's occupation was executive, business owner, or professional man.

who have come up the long distance from the bottom, and another segment consists of those energetic men who continue to be active at the same high occupational level as their fathers, one can first ask how much these men have moved territorially, in order to learn something about how the two elites have circulated in the forty-eight states while moving in the American business hierarchy. Chapter III gave some of the answers to such a question. We may now ask this question: How are the several levels of educational advancement related to territorial movement? Hypothetically, mobile men should move territorially more than nonmobile men. The evidence bore out this hypothesis. Hypothetically, men who have moved upward through college education should move territorially more than those with less education — this on the grounds that the well-educated man is equipped to fit more kinds of business situations, whereas the less well educated, coming up from the bottom, is more likely to stay in one familiar place which he has learned to understand through daily experience.

The facts show that there is a general tendency in this direction. Table 46 presents the evidence. The percentages for each level of education for all business leaders of lower occupational origins are given at the bottom of the table. It will be noted that both urban and rural men who are college graduates are above the average for movement beyond the boundaries of their native states (48 and 49 per cent) and below average for staying within those boundaries (40 and 36 per cent). On the other hand, the mobile men with less than high school education tended to stay within their home states: they are below the mobility average of 7 per cent for both urban and rural interstate movements (6 and 5 per cent) and above the average for staying within their native states (10 and 9 per cent). The same holds true for the high school group: 35 per cent of the urban and 32 per cent of the rural intrastate people are high school men (the average for high school being 29 per cent), whereas the interstate movements of urban and rural high school men are slightly below average.

It might be assumed that the effect of birth in a high status (professional and business leader) would alter the situation. Table 47, set up in the same way as Table 46, presents the evidence for this group. The averages for all business leaders born of fathers of professional or business leader status are presented at the bottom of the table. A comparison of those from rural or urban backgrounds who remain within their states of origin with those who have moved beyond their birth states shows that urban college men are more likely to move beyond the state (69 per cent) than to stay home (64 per cent). Furthermore, those from rural backgrounds are more likely to go farther from home (63 per cent) than to stay within the state of origin (55 per cent). Furthermore, men from urban backgrounds who have no more than high school education stay placed (15 per cent) more often than they move elsewhere (12 per cent). This also holds true for those of rural origin; 20 per cent "stayed home," but 16 per cent went away. Of the men at the grammar school level and with rural background two and a half times more (5 per cent) stay home than move (2 per cent). It should be noted that men of rural background for all levels of education are more likely to stay home than move.

Most of these differences point in the same general direction. College tends to propel men over greater distances; it attracts and pulls them away from home in the first place and gives them some of the mental luggage to continue their journeys to still greater social and geographic distances.

Education of the Elite in 1928 and 1952

Businessmen today are much more highly educated than they were a generation ago. Table 48 makes this abundantly certain. Although there has been an increase of college men in the general population, there has been a far greater increase among business leaders. In 1928 about a third of the business leaders had graduated from college and some 45 per cent had either attended or graduated; in 1952 about 6 out of 10 had graduated and 76 per cent had at least attended. It will be remembered that 4 per cent of the present leaders had not advanced beyond grammar school; in 1928, 27 per cent were at this low level, about seven times as many. More and more, the business career is believed to demand, and very often does require, college preparation. Increasingly, technical and business school training is necessary.

The evidence covered on the education of the 1928 and 1952 groups has not accounted for the changes that have taken place in the education of the men from the several occupational levels. Which levels show the greatest change and which the least? Who gets educated now that didn't in 1928? Did some groups lag behind while others advanced? These and similar questions are answered by Table 49 on

Table 48. Education of Business Leaders of 1928 and 1952

Highest Stage of Schooling Completed	1928 Business Leaders	1952 Business Leaders
Less than high school	27%	4%
High school	28	20
Some college	13	19
College graduation	32	57
Total	100	100

Table 49. Occupational Background and Education of Business Leaders in 1928 and 1952

Occupation of Father	Education of Business Leaders							
	Less Than High School		High School		Some College		College Graduation	
	1928	1952	1928	1952	1928	1952	1928	1952
Unskilled or semiskilled laborer	57%	15%	31%	36%	4%	15%	8%	34%
Skilled laborer	56	10	27	35	6	21	11	34
Owner of small business	34	4	33	23	11	17	22	56
Clerk or salesman	38	6	33	27	9	19	20	48
Minor executive	32	5	33	24	11	20	24	51
Major executive	8	0	22	8	18	18	52	74
Owner of large business	13	1	28	14	19	19	40	66
Professional man	15	2	23	9	15	16	47	73
Farmer	35	5	29	23	12	20	24	52
All occupations	27	4	28	20	13	19	32	57

the education of the elite of 1928 and 1952 coming from different occupational backgrounds. There have been enormous changes. The reader should first examine the column of figures on the left, which presents the percentages for men with grammar school education in 1928 and 1952.

In 1928 the group of sons of professional men and large business men had the smallest percentage of men with the lowest educational attainment — the professional with 15 per cent, owners with 13 per cent, and major executives with 8 per cent. But in 1952 only 10 per cent of the sons of skilled laborers and 15 per cent of the unskilled had failed to acquire more than grammar school training; yet these occupations, in 1952 as in 1928, had the highest percentage of men with low educational attainment. In other words, the lowest ranked occupation in 1952 had no more men who had failed to go beyond the eighth grade than the highest ranked occupation in 1928.

Several other statistics in the column need inspection. The farm and rural people tend to drop out of school earlier than city people, yet in 1952 only 5 per cent had less than high school education whereas in 1928, seven times as many were at this low level (35 per cent). Although all groups made notable advances, the sons of small business men and farmers made the most.

In examining the college graduates for the two periods, let us recall that in 1928 only about a third at all occupational levels were graduates, compared with close to six out of ten in 1952. In 1928 six occupational levels were below the low average for that time: skilled and unskilled workers, clerks, owners of small businesses, minor executives, and farmers. Today not only are all these groups above their 1928 averages, but each is above the average for *all* of the elite for 1928. Although it is the same groups today that fall below the general average, each — including the two laboring classes — more closely approximates the average than it did in 1928. For example, in the former period the general average was four times the average for unskilled laborers (8 per cent); today it is less than twice that for unskilled laborers (34 per cent). The occupational groups that have made the great gains in the number of men with college training are the unskilled laborers, four times more than in 1928; the skilled, some three times; and the owners of small businesses and farmers. But all classes advanced. For all occupations except laborers the percentage of those with only high school education dropped. The laboring classes increased, showing again a net increase in their educational equipment.

The education of the mobile and birth elites moves steadily to higher levels, the lowest occupation today having as high a proportion of college men as the highest did in 1928. Present indications make it seem likely that today's young men who will be the business leaders of tomorrow will be even more highly educated.

It might be supposed that the increased effort to prepare for a business career by going to college and even doing postgraduate work would constitute all that might be attempted. But the statistics tell a different story. All categories of these men continue in appreciable numbers to equip themselves through adult education with the special knowledge necessary for their further advancement. They do this either by taking comprehensive courses and business school training or by taking commercial training in a college or university. After the 1952 business leaders had said whether they had attended college and specified what degrees they had taken and the colleges they had attended, they were asked how much formal business training they had (see Table 50). Inspection of the returns shows that most of their formal business training was in and beyond the work done for degrees and that a distinction was made between the two categories of education, college and formal business training.

In 1928 some 71 per cent of the business elite had no extra business training; in 1952 about 42 per cent stated they had not. (See Table 51.) In 1928 only 7 per cent reported commercial training in a college

Table 50. Education and Formal Business Training of 1952 Business Leaders

		Formal Business Training		
Education	None	Correspondence Courses, Public School, or Business College	Commercial Training in College or University	Total
Less than high school ..	42%	56%	2%	100%
Some high school	38	60	2	100
High school graduation	33	64	3	100
Some college	35	24	41	100
College graduation	49	11	40	100
Postgraduate work	42	7	51	100
All groups	42	25	33	100

Table 51. Occupational Background and Formal Business Training of Business Leaders in 1928 and 1952

Occupation of Father	No Formal Business Training		Correspondence Courses, Public School, or Business College		Commercial Training in College or University	
	1928	1952	1928	1952	1928	1952
Unskilled or semiskilled laborer	59%	32%	36%	41%	5%	27%
Skilled laborer	63	31	30	40	7	29
Owner of small business	64	41	28	24	8	35
Clerk or salesman	72	40	24	29	4	31
Minor executive	71	36	22	31	7	33
Major executive	79	50	14	13	7	37
Owner of large business	72	47	20	20	8	33
Professional man	78	51	16	17	6	32
Farmer	66	40	25	30	9	30
All occupations	71	42	22	25	7	33

or university, compared with 33 per cent in 1952 — less than one in ten in 1928, and in 1952 one in three. Correspondence, public school, or business college courses in 1928 were taken by 22 per cent; in 1952 this proportion had advanced only to 25 per cent. Business education is increasingly a function performed by colleges and universities. Table 50 shows that most men below the college level take special business training through correspondence and business school courses, but that college men rely on commercial training provided by institutions of higher learning.

Although some differences exist between college and non-college men in taking additional business training, it will be noted that equal proportions of college postgraduates and men with only grammar school education (58 per cent) have taken additional work.

These ambitious men, highly motivated and driven by the need to succeed, spend their energies in this as well as in any other way that will push them on toward their goals. The highly educated seem to feel the need of this support almost as much as those with much less education. It remains to be seen if the birth elite are as energetic and active in their field of training as their mobile competitors. Table 51 supplies the evidence to answer this question and shows the changes for each level since 1928.

When the two right-hand columns for each occupational level for 1952 are added, it becomes clear that the men who are the sons of business leaders or of the professional classes took less outside educational training than men from other occupational origins. About 7 out of 10 of the 1952 elite who were sons of unskilled and semiskilled laborers and 6 out of 10 of the sons of clerks, small owners, and farmers took special training courses as compared with 5 out of 10 of the sons of the higher levels. Perhaps to give a measurement of those who had *no* special training would make this clearer. It will be noted that the average for all groups who had *no* training is 42 per cent. Only the sons of major executives, large owners, and professional men were above the average for *no* formal business training, meaning that the sons of those at the lower levels more often made this kind of extra effort. Yet about half of the men born to these high positions — 50 per cent of the sons of major executives, 53 per cent of the sons of large owners, and 49 per cent of the sons of professional men — reported they had taken formal business training.

113

Occupational Mobility

All occupational levels show a definite drop, from 1928 to 1952, in the number of those who had no formal business training, whereas all occupations show great increases in the percentages of those taking commercial training in colleges or universities. The changes from 1928 to 1952 for formal business training outside the colleges are at first less clear, but when viewed along with the increases in training in college, they reinforce the story about the increasing reliance on higher education.

The average for those in all occupational levels taking business training outside the colleges rose from 22 to 25 per cent. While several occupational levels remained about the same or fell slightly, others gained from 5 to 9 per cent. In general, the higher occupational levels remained about the same while the lower ones increased, with the exception of the small business owner category, which fell from 28 to 24 per cent. Other evidence indicates that owners of small businesses are increasingly following the lead of the big business men in sending their sons to college or using college for special training to help their sons get ahead.

American business leaders are educated far beyond the average population. They are growing more and more into a professional class where formal preparation is felt necessary and commendable, so that the educated man has the advantage. Education is now the royal road to success and to the positions of power and prestige at the higher rungs of big business. On this road all men can travel; that it is open to many is given ample testimony in our sample by the large number of educated men from the lowest occupational levels.

CHAPTER V

Business Careers and the Business System

The Career Patterns of Business Leaders

Occupational mobility in American business has been studied thus far in the broadest context, that of mobility from occupation and location of father to present position of son. It may also be defined as the movement from occupation to occupation within the lifetime of the individual himself.

To study the career patterns of the business elite, we asked respondents for "the occupation you engaged in when you first became self-supporting," "five years later," "ten years later," and "fifteen years later." ("Twenty years later," included on an early draft of the questionnaire, was dropped as it became evident that the majority of the men studied had achieved their present positions by about that time. The timing of the career is examined in detail later in this chapter.) The list of occupations provided for this item on the questionnaire was the same as that for occupation of father, except that doctor and minister were deleted from the professions, and the category "formal training program in a business" was added. This last was employed to meet the increasing importance of company training programs as a selecting and training ground for potential business executives.

The occupational sequences of 1952 business leaders are shown for the group as a whole in Table 52. Certain fairly well defined sequences appear from one occupation to another, and these may be expected to vary systematically with the occupational and educational level of the individual in question. More than a third of the entire group are included in the lower white-collar occupations at the time of first employment — the category "clerk or retail salesman." When the additional white-collar groups — "salesman" and "minor executive" — are

115

Occupational Mobility

Table 52. Career Sequence of 1952 Business Leaders

Occupation of Business Leader	First Occupation	Five Years Later	Ten Years Later	Fifteen Years Later
Unskilled or semiskilled laborer.	11%	1%	0%	0%
Skilled laborer	3	2	1	0
Clerk or retail salesman	34	15	4	1
Salesman	9	10	4	2
Foreman	1	4	3	1
Minor executive	9	35	43	25
Major executive	1	6	26	57
Business owner	1	2	3	3
Engineer	9	8	4	3
Lawyer	6	5	4	3
Other profession	9	8	6	4
Military career	2	2	1	1
Government service	1	1	1	0
Training program	3	0	0	0
Other occupation	1	1	0	0
Total	100	100	100	100
No answer (percentage of 7500)	3	4	6	10

added to this, the total in white-collar occupations at the beginning of their careers comprises more than half of the entire group (52 per cent). The professions include an additional 24 per cent, with engineering the first occupation for 9 per cent and law for 6 per cent. A number of men in the category "other professions" began their careers as accountants, with a wide range of other professions also included, making a total of 9 per cent.

No more than 14 per cent of the businessmen studied began their careers in the "laborer" or "foreman" categories. The office, rather than the shop, provides the background for most of these executives. It should also be noted that 1 per cent of the men studied began their careers as owners of businesses.

Looking across Table 52 at the changes in occupations over fifteen years, we find that the general and overwhelming trend is for the business leaders to move through the white-collar groups, with all other occupational categories decreasing in size rather rapidly. Few of the business elite remained long in the laboring occupations. Movement out of the lower white-collar positions is also prompt, and is generally into lower managerial white-collar positions. Movement out of the professions into business is fairly rapid. Within fifteen years of becoming self-supporting, more than half of the men studied were major executives and a quarter were minor executives.

There is no indication, on the basis of Table 52, that either the military services or the government furnishes a substantial number of men to top-level business positions. The business training programs for future executives provided the first jobs for 3 per cent of the men studied. This proportion may be expected to increase as these programs are more widely adopted and accepted by big business.

Turning to the question of the influence of occupational background on first occupations, we find data in Table 53. The first column presents the distribution, by first occupation, of the entire 1952 business elite. Succeeding columns present the first occupations of men from each of six occupational backgrounds.

Sons of laborers began their careers in laboring positions in 24 per cent of the cases. An additional 46 per cent were first employed as clerks or retail salesmen. Less than 10 per cent of the sons of laborers began their careers in higher level white-collar positions, and a total of only 14 per cent began in the professions. It may be assumed that these latter individuals are sons of laborers who have made the most intensive use of education in shaping their later careers.

Sons of white-collar workers or of owners of small businesses show a similar distribution by first occupation. About 25 per cent were first employed in the professions, with engineering of particular importance. Like the sons of laborers, the majority of the sons of white-collar workers and owners of small businesses were employed in white-collar positions initially, with the distribution ranging higher up the white-collar scale into the "minor executive" positions.

The sons of major executives or owners of large businesses are also spread through a wide range of initial occupations. Their careers were more likely to begin in the upper reaches of the white-collar hierarchy, with 19 per cent first employed as minor executives and 2 per cent in positions of major executive rank at the time of first employment. At the same time, about 12 per cent of these men began their careers as laborers. The proportion of sons of big business men who enter the professions and later move into business leadership is below the average of all business leaders, except for those who entered law. The proportion of sons of big business and professional men first engaged in business training programs (4 per cent) is somewhat higher than that

Table 53. Career Pattern and Father's Occupation: First Occupation of 1952 Business Leaders

First Occupation of Business Leader	All Business Leaders	Occupation of Father					
		Laborer	White-Collar Worker	Owner of Small Business	Major Executive or Owner of Large Business	Professional Man	Farmer
Unskilled or semiskilled laborer	11%	18%	11%	9%	9%	9%	12%
Skilled laborer	3	6	4	3	3	2	4
Clerk or retail salesman	34	46	39	35	27	22	32
Salesman	9	5	9	9	12	11	7
Foreman	1	1	1	1	1	1	0
Minor executive	9	4	5	10	19	9	4
Major executive	1	0	0	0	2	1	1
Business owner	1	1	1	2	2	1	0
Engineer	9	5	11	10	8	13	12
Lawyer	6	1	4	5	6	12	5
Other profession	9	8	9	10	4	11	13
Training program	3	2	3	3	4	4	3
Other occupation	4	3	3	3	3	4	7
Total	100	100	100	100	100	100	100

for men from other backgrounds (3 per cent). Thirty-six per cent of the sons of professional men began their careers in the professions, with 12 per cent first engaged as lawyers.

The distribution of sons of farmers by first occupation is similar to that of sons of white-collar workers, with about 16 per cent first employed as laborers and almost a third first employed as clerks. The importance of education and professional training for mobility from the farm into business is indicated by the high proportion of sons of farmers who are first engaged in engineering and other professional pursuits. While few sons of farmers are first employed as lawyers, almost a third are first engaged in one of the professions. The high figure in "other occupations" for sons of farmers is a result of the inclusion of farming in that category. Some 4 per cent of the sons of farmers are first employed in farm work.

The occupations of future business leaders, by occupational background, for the period five years after becoming self-supporting are given in Table 54. As remarked in the examination of the career pattern of the entire group, movement out of the lower level occupations is rapid. As Table 54 indicates, this movement is most marked in the case of sons of major executives or owners of large businesses, of whom 44 per cent are minor executives and 13 per cent major executives within five years of beginning their business careers.

Sons of professional men who are first employed in nonprofessional positions show a similar pattern of rapid movement through the occupational hierarchy. A very large proportion of those sons of professional men who go to the professions initially, however, are still engaged as professional men five years after beginning their careers (36 per cent initially, and 31 per cent five years later).

More than a third of the sons of laborers continue in laboring or clerical occupations five years after beginning their careers. It should also be noted that the proportion of sons of laborers in professional pursuits increases from 14 to 19 per cent during this period, which is a further indication of the role of education and specialized training in the total mobility process.

Tables 55 and 56 provide the data on occupations by occupational background for the ten- and fifteen-year career points. The progression noted in Tables 53 and 54 continues through these time periods. By the tenth year in business, 80 per cent of the sons of major execu-

Table 54. Career Pattern and Father's Occupation: Occupation of Business Leaders Five Years after Becoming Self-Supporting

Occupation of Business Leaders Five Years Later	All Business Leaders	Occupation of Father					
		Laborer	White-Collar Worker	Owner of Small Business	Major Executive or Owner of Large Business	Professional Man	Farmer
Laborer	3%	9%	3%	3%	1%	2%	5%
Clerk	15	26	20	13	7	10	15
Salesman	10	7	13	9	10	8	11
Foreman	4	5	6	4	4	4	4
Minor executive	35	27	29	37	44	33	30
Major executive	6	2	3	5	13	5	2
Business owner	2	1	1	3	4	2	3
Engineer	8	7	9	8	5	12	8
Lawyer	5	2	4	6	5	10	5
Other profession	8	10	9	9	3	9	11
Other occupation	4	4	3	3	4	5	6
Total	100	100	100	100	100	100	100

Table 55. Career Pattern and Father's Occupation: Occupation of Business Leaders Ten Years after Becoming Self-Supporting

Occupation of Business Leaders Ten Years Later	All Business Leaders	Occupation of Father					
		Laborer	White-Collar Worker	Owner of Small Business	Major Executive or Owner of Large Business	Professional Man	Farmer
Laborer	1%	2%	0%	0%	0%	0%	1%
Clerk	4	7	6	3	1	2	4
Salesman	4	5	5	4	3	3	5
Foreman	3	5	4	2	1	1	4
Minor executive	43	46	46	43	39	41	44
Major executive	26	17	21	27	41	24	18
Business owner	3	2	2	4	5	3	3
Engineer	4	4	4	5	2	7	5
Lawyer	4	1	3	4	4	9	4
Other profession	6	8	7	6	2	7	9
Other occupation	2	3	2	2	2	3	3
Total	100	100	100	100	100	100	100

Table 56. Career Pattern and Father's Occupation: Occupation of Business Leaders Fifteen Years after Becoming Self-Supporting

Occupation of Business Leaders Fifteen Years Later	All Business Leaders	Occupation of Father					
		Laborer	White-Collar Worker	Owner of Small Business	Major Executive or Owner of Large Business	Professional Man	Farmer
Laborer	0%	0%	0%	0%	0%	0%	0%
Clerk	1	2	2	1	0	1	1
Salesman	2	2	3	2	1	1	2
Foreman	1	2	1	1	1	0	2
Minor executive	25	32	30	24	15	23	27
Major executive	57	48	52	57	71	55	48
Business owner	3	2	2	4	5	3	4
Engineer	3	3	3	4	2	6	4
Lawyer	3	2	2	3	3	5	4
Other profession	4	6	2	3	1	4	7
Other occupation	1	1	1	1	1	2	1
Total	100	100	100	100	100	100	100

tives or owners of large businesses hold the positions of minor or major executives in business. Movement into the business hierarchy of sons of professional men accelerates during this stage of their careers. A substantial proportion of sons of farmers who become business leaders work out their careers in the professions. The sons of laborers show a consistent time lag, as would be expected, in their movement to business leadership.

A further point may be noted from these data. If any question remains concerning the role of entrepreneurships in occupational mobility, it is clear from this analysis that independent ownership of business is not an important avenue of mobility to business leadership in the lifetime of these individuals; the largest proportion in business leadership from any occupational background is only 5 per cent in the case of sons of major executives and owners of large businesses. As has been shown, the small entrepreneur is an important category in over-all occupational mobility as a transition point in the mobility process over three generations.

The association between education and career pattern is even closer than that between occupational background and job sequence. Table 57 compares the first occupations of 1952 business leaders from four educational levels. The column on the left is the distribution of the entire group by first occupation. The succeeding columns provide the

Table 57. Career Pattern and Education: First Occupation of 1952 Business Leaders

First Occupation of Business Leader	All Business Leaders	Education of Business Leader			
		Less Than High School	High School	Some College	College Graduation
Unskilled or semiskilled laborer.	11%	27%	15%	13%	8%
Skilled laborer	3	4	4	4	3
Clerk	34	54	57	41	22
Salesman	9	6	8	11	9
Foreman	1	0	0	1	1
Minor executive	9	3	6	9	11
Major executive	1	1	1	1	1
Business owner	1	2	1	2	1
Engineer	9	0	1	4	15
Lawyer	6	0	0	0	10
Other profession	9	2	4	8	11
Training program	3	0	1	2	5
Other occupation	4	1	2	4	3
Total	100	100	100	100	100

distribution by first occupation for men whose formal education was discontinued before high school, men who attended high school, men with some college training, and men who are college graduates.

Almost a third of the group who did not attend high school were first employed as laborers. The proportion diminishes steadily with education, and only 11 per cent of the college graduates were first employed as laborers. Conversely, 36 per cent of the college graduates were first engaged in the professions. More than half of the men with less than college education were first employed in clerical positions. Only 22 per cent of the college graduates were first employed in lower level white-collar positions, while proportionately more were employed in positions of minor executive status. The company training programs are largely confined to college-trained men also.

Tables 58, 59, and 60 present the distribution of business leaders by first occupation and by education for the three succeeding time periods studied. The considerable impact of college training on the over-all occupational sequence is clear from these data, and the trends suggested by the distribution according to first occupation are borne out.

A further analysis of the career patterns of 1952 business leaders is available in Table 61. Changes through time in the pattern of occupational mobility within the career of business leaders can be approximated by comparing business leaders by present age. The group has been divided, in Table 61, into men who are under fifty years of age, between fifty and sixty years of age, and sixty years of age and over. The distribution by first occupation is given for these three age categories.

The comparisons from Table 61 must be viewed with considerable caution, since age is related in this population to occupational background and education. Thus the trends shown in the table are not for age alone, but are combined to some degree with other factors already examined. In general, important differences in first occupation are not evident in Table 61. The pattern of first occupation is similar for all three age groups, with modifications in certain directions. Fewer of the younger men were first employed as laborers, while the proportion first employed in white-collar occupations remains fairly constant. The proportion first engaged as engineers is smaller among the younger men, while the proportion in law and other professions increases. A marked increase occurs in the proportion first engaged in formal busi-

Table 58. Career Pattern and Education: Occupation of 1952 Business Leaders Five Years after Becoming Self-Supporting

Occupation of Business Leader Five Years Later	All Business Leaders	Education of Business Leader			
		Less Than High School	High School	Some College	College Graduation
Unskilled or semiskilled laborer.	1%	5%	2%	1%	0%
Skilled laborer	2	9	4	4	1
Clerk	15	35	31	18	7
Salesman	10	13	12	12	8
Foreman	4	5	6	5	4
Minor executive	35	20	30	36	37
Major executive	6	3	3	6	7
Business owner	2	4	4	2	2
Engineer	8	1	2	4	12
Lawyer	5	0	0	1	9
Other profession	8	2	4	8	9
Other occupation	4	3	2	3	4
Total	100	100	100	100	100

Table 59. Career Pattern and Education: Occupation of 1952 Business Leaders Ten Years after Becoming Self-Supporting

Occupation of Business Leader Ten Years Later	All Business Leaders	Education of Business Leader			
		Less Than High School	High School	Some College	College Graduation
Laborer	1%	3%	2%	1%	0%
Clerk	4	14	9	4	1
Salesman	4	11	6	4	2
Foreman	3	5	5	4	1
Minor executive	43	39	50	45	34
Major executive	26	12	18	27	28
Business owner	3	8	4	3	2
Engineer	4	2	1	3	5
Lawyer	4	0	0	1	15
Other profession	6	4	4	6	9
Other occupation	2	2	1	2	3
Total	100	100	100	100	100

Table 60. Career Pattern and Education: Occupation of 1952 Business Leaders Fifteen Years after Becoming Self-Supporting

Occupation of Business Leader Fifteen Years Later	All Business Leaders	Education of Business Leader			
		Less Than High School	High School	Some College	College Graduation
Laborer	0%	1%	0%	0%	0%
Clerk	1	4	3	1	0
Salesman	2	6	3	2	1
Foreman	1	1	2	1	0
Minor executive	25	34	34	26	21
Major executive	57	40	49	58	60
Business owner	3	9	4	3	3
Engineer	3	1	1	2	5
Lawyer	3	0	0	1	5
Other profession	4	3	3	4	4
Other occupation	1	1	1	2	1
Total	100	100	100	100	100

Table 61. Career Patterns, Past and Present: The First Occupations of 1952 Business Leaders and Their Present Age

First Occupation of Business Leader	Under 50 Years of Age	50–59 Years of Age	60 Years of Age and Over
Unskilled or semiskilled laborer	10%	11%	13%
Skilled laborer	3	4	4
Clerk	32	35	34
Salesman	10	10	7
Foreman	1	1	1
Minor executive	10	9	9
Major executive	1	1	1
Business owner	1	1	2
Engineer	8	9	12
Lawyer	7	4	5
Other profession	10	8	7
Military career	1	2	1
Government service	0	1	1
Training program	5	3	2
Other occupation	1	1	1
Total	100	100	100

ness-training programs. In general, this examination of time trends in career patterns reflects the increased role of education and specialized training in career patterns in business.

The Number of Companies in the Leader's Career

Another aspect of the business career closely related to mobility from one occupation to another is the movement of business leaders from one business firm to another. The extent of interfirm mobility among the men studied is presented in Table 62. One quarter of the 1952 business elite have been with the same firm throughout their business careers, while 30 per cent have been with four or more business firms during their careers. Typically the business leader is associated with two or more firms in the course of moving to business leadership.

In examining the meaning of interfirm mobility in the careers of the business leaders, a first question arises as to the point in the career where such mobility occurs. Is the move from one company to another a shifting about prior to achieving an executive position? It might be assumed that mobility to a top position in a firm is most effectively executed in those cases where, after receiving training and acquiring the skills and habits necessary for a top position, the individual moves into another hierarchy at a higher position, severing the connections with the past position, acquaintances, and duties.

As Table 63 indicates, about half of the men studied moved from one firm to another after becoming executives; that is, they have been associated as executives with more than one firm. Further analysis of the questionnaire responses indicated that movement from firm to firm would be expected to be an integral part of the whole complex of social and spatial mobility.

Table 64 presents interfirm mobility in relation to occupational background. Among the business leaders who have made frequent moves between companies the proportion of sons of laborers is greater than among men who remained with the same business firm. Sons of major executives or owners of large businesses comprise 32 per cent of the men who have worked for a single business firm and only 18 per cent of the men who have worked for four or more firms. This relationship does not hold for the sons of professional men or the sons of farmers, who are equally distributed in relation to interfirm mobility.

Table 62. Number of Companies Business Leaders Have
Been Associated with during Career

Number of Companies	Percentage of Respondents *
1	25
2	23
3	22
4	13
5	7
6	5
7 or more	5
Total	100

* No answer was given by 24 of 7500.

Table 63. Number of Companies Business Leaders Have
Been Associated with as Executive

Number of Companies	Percentage of Respondents *
1	48
2	26
3	14
4	6
5	3
6 or more	3
Total	100

* No answer was given by 74 of 7500.

Interfirm mobility is also related to education, as shown in Table 65. College graduates make up 63 per cent of the men who have worked for a single firm and only 52 per cent of those who have worked for four or more firms. The individual with more formal training is most likely to achieve business success without moving between companies. The individual with less formal training is more likely to move from one firm to another in the course of his career.

An examination of the relationship between career pattern of the business leader and interfirm mobility did not indicate any substantial differences among the various groups. Men who worked through their careers in a single firm, and those who were employed by two or more firms during their careers, experienced the same general sequence of occupations; and men who began their careers as laborers

Occupational Mobility

Table 64. Interfirm Mobility and Occupational Mobility

Occupation of Father	Number of Companies Business Leader Has Been Associated with			
	1	2	3	4 or More
Laborer	12%	14%	16%	18%
White-collar worker	16	21	21	20
Owner of small business ..	17	17	19	20
Major executive or owner of large business	32	24	22	18
Professional man	14	15	14	15
Farmer	9	9	8	9
Total	100	100	100	100

Table 65. Interfirm Mobility and Education

Education of Leader	Number of Companies Business Leader Has Been Associated with			
	1	2	3	4 or More
Less than high school	3%	4%	4%	5%
High school	17	18	21	22
Some college	17	17	20	21
College graduation	63	61	55	52
Total	100	100	100	100

were as stable in this respect as men who began their careers as professional men.

In summary of interfirm mobility, the business elite are highly mobile in this as well as in other ways. Only a fourth of the men studied worked for a single firm throughout their careers; this mobility from one company to another took place throughout the business career — after they became executives as well as earlier. Men from lower status occupational backgrounds tended to move from one firm to another more frequently than those from business backgrounds, and college graduates were less likely to move between firms as they went on to top business positions than men with less formal education.

The Leader's Achievement Time and Occupational Background

A chronological portrait of the typical career of the 1952 business leader may be derived in its rough outlines from the several questionnaire items relating to age and time factors in the business career The average age of the 1952 business elite is 53.7 years. The average business leader entered business at the age of 21.4 years and entered his present business firm 7.2 years later. He has been with this firm for 24.1 years. From the time of entering business, the average time required to assume his present business position was 23.9 years. The typical business leader has held this position for 6.7 years. (Appendix V presents more detailed distributions of the total population studied for each of these time variables.)

The data on the timing of the business leaders' careers provide a tool both for the further examination of the career and for estimating the effects of background and training on the career. In the analyses following, the number of years required to achieve the present business position is employed as a measure of the effect upon the business career of occupational background, education, and other factors.

The effect of occupational background on the careers of business leaders is given in Table 66. Three time factors are presented: the average age of entering business, the average number of years in business before attaining a position of business leadership, and the average present age. These are given, according to the occupation of the father, in ten occupational groupings.

Sons of laborers enter business (i.e., become self-supporting) at an earlier age than men of any of the other occupational backgrounds — before they are nineteen, on the average. Sons of major executives and of professional men do not enter business, on the average, until they are nearly twenty-two. The sons of farmers occupy a somewhat unex-

Table 66. Occupational Mobility and Speed of Career

Occupation of Father	Age Leader Entered Business	Years to Achieve Position	Present Age
Laborer	18.7	26.0	53.7
Clerk or salesman	19.7	24.8	53.5
Minor executive	20.1	25.0	53.4
Owner of small business	21.1	22.6	54.2
Owner of large business	21.1	21.2	53.2
Major executive	21.6	20.6	50.6
Professional man	21.9	22.5	53.2
Farmer	21.6	25.1	56.3
All business leaders	21.4	23.9	53.7

129

pected position in the rank order of Table 66. The average age of the sons of farmers at the time of entering business is 21.6 years, or as high as that of the sons of major executives. This no doubt results in part from the fact that a few sons of farmers entered business subsequent to their first full-time occupation, which was farming. The rather high percentage of the sons of farmers who prepare for, and enter, the professions is also reflected in this average. Although no data are available, the largest single influence may be a somewhat later movement through the educational institutions for sons of farmers than for other groups — with a higher average age of completion of education.

Whatever the result of the variations in the age at which the sons of farmers enter business, the expected rank order in column two of Table 66 obtains. The length of the business career before achieving a top business position was longest for the sons of laborers — 26 years — and shortest for sons of major executives — 20.6 years. Apart from the advantages already noted, in terms of representation in business leadership, the time difference of some five and one half years may be taken as an index of the advantage of birth (and its attendant qualifications for an executive position). In this distribution of the time required to achieve the present business position, the sons of farmers as a group fall closest to the sons of laborers, with a time period of 25.1 years on the average.

Present age, as given in column three, may be taken as a summary measure of the two factors that are presented in columns one and two. The youngest business leaders, on the average, are sons of major executives; the oldest, sons of farmers. With these two exceptions at the extremes, however, the differences among the other groups are not great, and all are near the average of 53.7 years for the entire sample.

In the light of the discussion of the findings concerning the educational backgrounds of the business elite, the summary of columns one and two takes on added interest. Men from higher occupational backgrounds enter business at relatively older ages. They achieve business leadership in relatively less time thereafter than do men from the lower status occupational backgrounds. When the two factors are combined, however, the differences are not great. That is, the total life span involved in movement to business leadership is approximately the same for all groups except the two noted, the sons of farmers and the sons of major executives. Education is a large factor in the later age at which members of the higher occupational groups enter business. From this age data, however, it would appear that a similar period of education in an informal setting is involved in the case of the sons of laborers. The net effect is that all the men, whatever their occupational backgrounds, move into business leadership at about the same age.

Table 67. Education and Speed of Career

Education	Age Leader Entered Business	Years to Achieve Position	Present Age
Less than high school	15.3	31.0	60.5
Some high school	17.0	30.6	58.0
High school graduation	18.7	27.9	56.5
Some college	20.3	24.5	52.9
College graduation	22.3	22.9	52.8
Postgraduate work	23.4	19.9	49.8
All business leaders	21.4	23.9	53.4

Age data for 1952 business leaders, classified according to education, is given in Table 67. The average age of entering business, the average years in business before attaining the present business position, and the average present age of respondents are given for each of the six educational categories available.

In Table 67, the column on the right (present age) presents the results of two factors working together, and should be noted first. The average age of business leaders decreases as the amount of formal education increases. The average age of men who have less than high school education is 60.5 years. At the other extreme, the average age of men who have had postgraduate work at colleges or universities is 49.8 years. This wide variation in age, when looked at in terms of the amount of education, is first of all due to the fact that education in the population as a whole has been increasing rapidly, and that in any population, therefore, the older group would have had less formal education. In this population the age-education relationship is also a result of the fact that the business career is materially lengthened in those cases where education is relatively limited.

The first two columns show that the expected relationship between

131

age of entering business and education obtains. Men with relatively little formal education became self-supporting at very early ages, the average for men with less than high school education being 15.3 years. The group with the greatest amount of education, postgraduate study at college, entered business at an average age of 23.4 years. A negative relationship is observed between "years to achieve present business position" and education. While men with little or no formal education required on the average 31 years to achieve their positions, the time period for college graduates was a little over 20 years.

When the effects of education on the business career are measured only in terms of the number of years required on the part of each educational group from time of entering business to time of achieving business leadership, education appears to have a very large effect on the subsequent career pattern. This single measure fails, however, to take account of the fact that men with less education begin their careers at an early age, and in effect are educated on the job. Combining the two sets of figures to obtain a measure of the length of the total career before achieving business leadership substantially reduces the apparent impact of education on the career. By combining columns one and two for men with less than high school education, a sum of 46.3 years before achieving the present position is obtained. For men who graduated from colleges or universities, the sum is 45.2 years.

The conclusion can only be that, given the prerequisites to mobility — motivation, skill, opportunity, and the rest of an undetermined complex — the occupationally mobile man may obtain the necessary skills outside the boundaries of formal education. The total time required for this more difficult process does not greatly exceed that involved in the usual conventional approach to training and experience. This is true, of course, only for those rare few with little formal education who filter through and appear in this study.

With an index based on the number of years it took to achieve the present business position, the several spatial mobility variables presented thus far can be examined in their effects on the business career. Table 68 presents the average number of years taken to achieve their present position for business leaders in four categories of geographical mobility — men who are now located in the state in which they were born (intrastate mobility), men who have moved to another state

Business Careers and the Business System

within their region of birth (interstate), men who have moved between regions from their place of birth to their place of present business, and the foreign-born who have moved to the United States. As indicated in Table 68, territorial mobility is related to length of the career in that it appears to lengthen somewhat the time required to achieve business leadership. The difference is not great, however, and it will be recalled that the categories are far from clear-cut.

The effects of nativity on the time required to achieve business leadership are somewhat more sharp, as shown in Table 69. Consistent but slight differences obtain for the three categories of U.S.-born business leaders, with movement to business leadership most rapid on the part of the men whose fathers and paternal grandfathers were U.S.-born. It will be recalled that this category includes not only the higher occupational groups in large proportion, but also a considerable proportion of farmers. The differences cannot be assigned to occupational background alone. A substantial difference in achievement time between the foreign-born and the American-born is shown in Table 69. The average time taken to achieve the present position is 23.9 years, while for foreign-born business leaders the time required is 26.6 years.

Interfirm mobility, as given in Table 70, does not make for more

Table 68. Geographical Mobility and Speed of Career

Type of Mobility	Median Years to Achieve Present Position
Intrastate	23.4
Interstate	24.4
Interregion	24.0
Foreign nation to U.S.	26.6
All business leaders	23.9

Table 69. Nativity and Speed of Career

Nativity	Mean Years to Achieve Present Position
Business leader foreign-born	26.6
Business leader U.S.-born	24.5
Father U.S.-born	23.9
Father's father U.S.-born	23.4
All business leaders	23.9

133

Occupational Mobility

Table 70. Interfirm Mobility and Speed of Career

Number of Companies Business Leader Has Been Associated with	Years to Achieve Position	Years before Entering Present Organization
1	22.4	0.0
2-3	24.0	9.4
4-6	25.3	15.3
7 or more	27.7	20.0
All business leaders	23.9	7.2

rapid movement into top business positions. On the contrary, men who have been associated with larger numbers of firms during their careers require longer periods of time to achieve business leadership than the other men. The 27.7-year period for men who have been with seven or more firms considerably exceeds that for men from any given occupational background.

The column on the right of Table 70 gives the average number of years the leaders spent in business before entering their present organization, for those in each of the categories of interfirm mobility shown. It will be seen from a comparison of the two distributions of years that movement into top positions is relatively rapid for men who have been with a number of firms once they become associated with their present organization.

In summary, examination of the timing of the business career and its relation to territorial mobility leads to the general conclusion that territorial mobility operates to retard the career, on the whole. Territorially mobile men, whatever the spatial dimension examined, move into positions of business leadership later than do territorially stable men. This analysis cannot examine further the questions of territorial mobility and the career: for example, would territorially mobile men have been occupationally mobile at all without spatial mobility?

The 1928 study of business leaders provides several points of comparison with 1952 in the matter of age characteristics. Table 71 presents the distributions by age at the time of the study of the 1928 population and the 1952 population of business leaders. The pattern of the two distributions shows decided changes over the intervening twenty-four years. The general effect has been in the direction of a higher average age for business leaders. This increase in average age

Business Careers and the Business System

Table 71. Age of Business Leaders at Time of Study
in 1928 and 1952

Age at Time of Study	1928	1952
Under 30	1%	0%
30–34	4	1
35–39	10	4
40–44	13	10
45–49	16	18
50–54	17	20
55–59	16	21
60–64	12	15
65–69	7	7
70–74	3	3
75 and over	1	1
Total	100	100

Table 72. Number of Years in Position Held at Time of
Study in 1928 and 1952

Number of Years in Present Position	1928	1952
Less than 10	51%	66%
10–19	30	22
20 and over	19	12
Total	100	100

is a result of a decrease in the proportion of 1952 business leaders in the age categories under 45 years, while the proportion in the categories for 65 years and over has not increased. The net result is an increase in the proportion of business leaders between the ages of 45 and 65. In 1928, 61 per cent of the men studied were included in this age range, as compared with 74 per cent in 1952. The conventional retirement age of 65 seems to be as effective in limiting business careers now as in the past.

The data for 1928 and for 1952 on the number of years in the present position, as given in Table 72, are consistent with the data on age at the time of the study. While the retirement age appears to have remained fixed at about 65 years of age for most businessmen, the age of entrance into positions of business leadership has increased from

Occupational Mobility

1928 to 1952. As a result not only has there been an increase in the average age of the men studied but also the business leaders of 1952 have been in their present positions for shorter periods of time than the 1928 leaders. Two thirds of the 1952 business leaders have held their present positions for less than ten years, while 51 per cent of the 1928 business leaders had held their positions for less than ten years at the time of the study.

Tables 71 and 72, on present age and time spent in present position, would seem to present an example of a delay in the accommodation of institutions to changes in the wider culture. As shown earlier, increased educational requirements and lengthened periods of preliminary training delay the entrance of future leaders into business careers. At the same time it would appear that business institutions have not moved the upward age limits of the business career to adjust for the longer training period. The net effect appears in Table 72, where the business leaders are seen to hold their positions for shorter periods of time. In effect, the business hierarchy is losing in this process a substantial proportion of the total leadership potential of its men.

A comparison of the average age of entering business in 1928 with that of 1952 is given in Table 73. For sons of laborers and farmers, the age of entering business has not changed substantially since 1928. As in 1928, the sons of farmers in 1952 business leadership show a late average age of entering business. Again, the change through time is not great. For the remaining occupational groups, there has been an increase in the age of entering business — an average of about one

Table 73. Occupational Mobility and Average Age of Entering Business for Business Leaders in 1928 and 1952

Occupation of Father	Age in 1928	Age in 1952
Unskilled or semiskilled laborer	18.5	18.3
Skilled laborer	18.9	18.9
Farmer	21.7	21.4
Clerk or salesman	18.4	19.8
Minor executive	18.9	20.1
Owner of small business	19.5	20.4
Major executive	20.9	21.6
Owner of large business	20.2	21.3
Professional man	20.8	22.0
All occupations	20.4	21.4

year. This may be attributed in large part to the observed increase in education between the two time periods.

The effect of occupational background on the length of business career, for business leaders of 1928 and of 1952, is given in Table 74. The columns on the left compare the 1928 and 1952 leaders as to the average age of assuming their present business position. (It should be noted that this is average age, not average number of years. The previous measure employed was average years to achieve — age of assuming position minus age at entering business.) The average age of assuming the present position has increased substantially from 1928 to 1952, for all occupational backgrounds.

Table 74. Occupational Mobility and Age of Achieving Leadership of Business Leaders in 1928 and 1952

Occupation of Father	Average Age of Assuming Position Held at Time of Study		Advantage of Sons of Major Executives in Achieving Leadership (in Years)	
	1928	1952	1928	1952
Unskilled or semiskilled laborer ..	38.4	44.9	0.4	2.6
Skilled laborer	40.9	45.3	2.9	3.0
Farmer	41.3	47.0	3.3	4.7
Clerk or salesman	39.3	44.8	1.3	2.5
Minor executive	40.2	44.9	2.2	2.6
Owner of small business	40.0	45.5	2.0	3.2
Major executive	38.0	42.3	...	...
Owner of large business	38.3	42.9	0.3	0.5
Professional man	40.4	44.9	2.4	2.5

The columns on the right give the difference, in the age of assuming the present position, between the sons of major executives and sons from other occupational backgrounds. Since in both 1928 and 1952 sons of major executives moved into top positions at an earlier age than any other group, all differences shown in the columns on the right of Table 74 are positive for both time periods. In general, the time advantage of the sons of major executives has increased from 1928 to 1952. The increase in the number of years required before they can assume their business position has been slight in the case of the sons of professional men and the sons of owners of large businesses, and substantial in the case of laborers, clerks, and farmers.

Occupational Mobility

Occupational Mobility and Business Expansion

The analysis of occupational mobility and the business elite has proceeded thus far on the implicit assumption that the business world and the business hierarchy are homogeneous entities sociologically. The assumption is not correct, of course. American business and industry, far from being a hierarchical or functional unit, is a far-flung system of loosely bound and widely differing institutions and activities. Not only are the component types of business and industry widely variant, but the stage of development, the organization, and the complexity of the many firms within a given type vary widely.

In the following analysis, American business and industry are examined in further detail in terms of occupational mobility along three variables:

1. The expansion of the industry and firm in which the business leader holds his present position.

2. The type of business or industry in which the business leader holds his present position.

3. The position in the business hierarchy held by the business leader.

These subcategories of business by no means exhaust the possible analytic variables by means of which the business community may be studied. They are three critical variables, however, and comprise the dimensions along which occupational mobility is commonly discussed.

In the exhortative literature on business success, most notably in commencement addresses, the expansion of American business is treated as an important dimension in occupational mobility. The common phrase "the new frontiers of American business" refers to those types of business and business firms that have in recent years shown most spectacular growth. Whether these rapidly expanding businesses do in fact provide for greater occupational mobility is an unresolved question, and the point admits of argument in both directions. On the face of it, increased opportunity for advancement is offered in a firm where rapid expansion is under way, as new positions are opened. It may be argued, however, that the rapidly expanding firm or industry is one that most needs access to capital offered by men of higher status backgrounds, and therefore can least afford to deny itself the possible advantages of filling executive positions with these men.

Table 75 presents the basis for an empirical examination of the

Business Careers and the Business System

Table 75. Occupational Mobility and Business Expansion

Expansion of Firm			Occupation of Father				Total
	Laborer	White-Collar Worker	Owner of Small Business	Major Executive or Owner of Large Business	Professional Man	Farmer	
Slow Expansion of Type of Business or Industry							
Slow	13%	22%	15%	23%	19%	8%	100%
Moderate ...	16	18	19	23	16	8	100
Rapid	15	23	19	21	12	10	100
Moderate Expansion of Type of Business or Industry							
Slow	15	19	16	29	13	8	100
Moderate ...	15	17	19	29	11	9	100
Rapid	16	20	20	17	14	13	100
Rapid Expansion of Type of Business or Industry							
Slow	13	19	18	24	19	7	100
Moderate ...	16	21	17	23	16	7	100
Rapid	16	21	17	20	17	9	100
All businesses	15	20	18	24	14	9	100

question. The 1952 business leaders are categorized by the rate of expansion of the business or industry in which they hold their positions, and by the growth of the firms with which they are associated. (For a discussion of the categories employed, see Appendix V, p. 284.) The distinctions between the industry or business and the firm are somewhat arbitrary, but they offer an adequate basis for the consideration of the role of business expansion in occupational mobility. Table 75 gives the population of the present study in terms of six categories of occupational background.

If the assumption of accelerated mobility in expanding business is accurate, Table 75 should provide an approximation of a nine-point scale, from the slowly expanding firm in a slowly expanding type of business, to the rapidly expanding firm in a rapidly expanding type of business, with amount of mobility correlated directly with the scale of expansion. An examination of the columns of Table 75 indicates that the expected relationship is present in rough form; only to a moderate degree may it be said that occupational mobility is greater in expanding businesses.

Occupational Mobility

Within each type of business or industry, more sons of laborers are present in leadership in the rapidly expanding firms than in the slowly expanding firms. Conversely, proportionately fewer sons of major executives or owners of large businesses are in the rapidly expanding firms. This latter relationship is also true, to a lesser degree, for the sons of professional men. No consistent relationship with the rate of expansion of the firm is apparent for the sons of white-collar workers. The sons of farmers appear in larger proportions in rapidly expanding firms within each type of business than in slowly expanding firms.

When Table 75 is examined for each type of firm within each type of business or industry, the results in terms of occupational mobility are more obscure. Thirteen per cent of the leaders in slowly expanding firms in slowly expanding types of business are sons of laborers. If industrial expansion increases occupational mobility, a higher proportion of leaders of such stable firms in rapidly expanding industries would be sons of laborers. However, an identical proportion, 13 per cent, of the leaders in slowly expanding firms in rapidly expanding types of business are sons of laborers. A similar relationship obtains for the sons of major executives and owners of large businesses.

In summary of Table 75, occupational mobility is somewhat greater in rapidly expanding firms than in slowly expanding firms. The differences are consistent but not great. Sons of laborers, farmers, and white-collar workers are present in leadership of rapidly expanding firms in greater proportions than they are in slowly expanding firms. However, the expansion of the type of business in which the firm is located does not appear to be so important a factor, on the basis of Table 75, as the expansion of the firm. The two factors together do not operate in an accumulative and consistent fashion.

From the fact that only a limited relationship exists between business expansion and occupational mobility, as given by father's occupation, the conclusion should not be drawn that business expansion is an inconsiderable factor in the selection and distribution of the business elite. It is observed that stable firms, and stable types of business and industry, do recruit leaders from all occupational backgrounds in much the same proportions as do rapidly expanding firms and types of business.

When the process of recruitment is studied, however, it becomes clear that the mobility into leadership in stable types of business operates in a manner different from that in expanding ones, in terms of the training of the individual. Table 76 presents the results of an analysis of the education of business leaders in the several types of industry and business.

Table 76. Education and Business Expansion

Expansion of Firm	Education of Leader			Total
	Less Than High School Graduation	High School Graduation and Some College	College Graduation	
Slow Expansion of Type of Business or Industry				
Slow	6%	27%	67%	100%
Moderate	10	27	63	100
Rapid	14	32	54	100
Moderate Expansion of Type of Business or Industry				
Slow	9	32	59	100
Moderate	13	32	55	100
Rapid	23	38	39	100
Rapid Expansion of Type of Business or Industry				
Slow	10	24	66	100
Moderate	13	31	56	100
Rapid	22	34	44	100
All businesses ...	13	30	57	100

When types of business are categorized by their rate of growth over the past decades, and individual firms by their expansion during the career of each business leader, major and consistent differences among these categories appear in terms of the amount of formal education of the leaders. Two thirds of the elite in slowing expanding firms in slowly expanding types of business are college graduates. Only 6 per cent have education amounting to less than high school graduation. On the other hand, only 44 per cent of the business leaders of rapidly expanding firms in rapidly expanding types of business have had college educations, and 22 per cent have not graduated from high school.

The comparison given between the two extreme types of business is, on the whole, consistent through the range of types analyzed. Within each type of business — slow, moderate, or rapid in its relative rate of expansion — a much higher proportion of college graduates direct

141

the more slowly expanding firms and many more of the leaders of rapidly expanding firms have relatively little formal education. Thus the expansion of the firm appears to be a critical variable in the selection of the business elite, with formal education at a high level much more frequent in the more stable firms.

Expansion of the type of business or industry has a similar, but lesser, relationship with the amount of formal education possessed by its leaders. Those characterized as slowly expanding have a higher proportion of college graduates than those categorized as moderate or rapid in expansion. More men with relatively little formal education are in positions of leadership in the types of business where expansion has been moderate or rapid. There is little difference, in terms of this factor, between the types whose expansion has kept pace with the over-all expansion of the economy and those rapidly expanding ones that have outgained the economy.

From the consideration of the effects of business expansion on the recruitment of the business elite, two general conclusions appear. One, the disadvantaged occupational groups are not represented, on the whole, more frequently in rapidly expanding types of business than in the stable ones. The "frontier" of business, where opportunity is golden, is something of a myth in terms of occupational background. However, when education is considered, rapidly expanding types of business do indeed offer more substantial opportunities to men with less formal education. These men make up a much larger proportion of the leadership of these "frontier" sectors in the business community.

At this point the question of the relationship of occupational background and education arises. We have noted that a relatively high formal education is evident in the more stable business sectors, and less education common in expanding types of business. It might be expected, for example, that the son of a laborer or farmer would balance the disadvantage of birth by advanced education in order to achieve mobility in a stable industry. Formal education at the college level might be seen as a matter of relative indifference to the son of a business or professional man.

The proportion of college graduates from each occupational level is given in Table 77 for types of business and industry that have expanded slowly and firms that have expanded slowly or moderately. This is contrasted with the proportion of college graduates from each

Business Careers and the Business System

Table 77. Occupational Mobility, Education, and Business Expansion

Occupation of Father and Education of Business Leader	Slow Type of Business or Industry Expansion; Slow or Moderate Firm Expansion	Rapid Type of Business or Industry Expansion; Moderate or Rapid Firm Expansion	Total
Laborer			
Less than college graduation .. 49%	51%	100%
College graduation 59	41	100
White-collar worker			
Less than college graduation .. 41	59	100
College graduation 59	41	100
Owner of small business			
Less than college graduation .. 48	52	100
College graduation 59	41	100
Major executive or owner of large business			
Less than college graduation .. 48	52	100
College graduation 57	43	100
Professional man			
Less than college graduation .. 49	51	100
College graduation 56	44	100
Farmer			
Less than college graduation .. 49	51	100
College graduation 58	42	100
All occupations			
Less than college graduation .. 47	53	100
College graduation 58	42	100

occupational level for those types of business where expansion has been rapid and for firms where expansion has been moderate or rapid.

As the two types of business in Table 77 illustrate, the proportion of college graduates is independent of occupational background. For all business leaders in the slowly expanding group, the proportion with less education than college graduation is 47 per cent, which approximates the proportion for each of the occupational groups. Whatever the occupational background, about half the business leaders who are not college graduates are in rapidly expanding types of business.

Conversely, whatever the occupational background, the majority of leaders in slowly expanding types of business are college graduates.

Mobility for the man with limited formal education most frequently occurs in those sectors of American business undergoing rapid growth. Business leaders are college graduates in high proportion in those sectors where growth of the type of business and of the firm is slow. Business expansion facilitates the occupational mobility of the individual whose formal training, whatever his occupational background, is relatively limited. Since a much higher proportion of college graduates than others are leaders of stable businesses, it may be inferred that the formal prerequisites of recruitment are exaggerated in these stable organizations. It should be further noted that the factor of formal education operates in a similar fashion for all individuals regardless of occupational origins.

Differences in the proportion of business leaders born in the various regions were examined in detail in Chapter III. There have been important changes in the geographic locations of businesses over the past decades, especially the movement of large industrial organizations out of the Northeast to the South and West. The rapid development of other industries — petroleum and aircraft, for example — has occurred in some of these areas. As a result business expansion might be expected to affect mobility in these regions.

Table 78 presents the territorial origins of business leaders in the nine groups of firms categorized by expansion of the type of business or industry and of the firm. It would appear that business growth does increase the proportion of men born in the South who move to business leadership, while reducing the proportion of leaders born in the North. The most important factor in this respect appears to be

Table 78. Territorial Origins and Business Expansion

Expansion of Firm	Region of Leader's Birth				Total
	North	Midwest	South	West	
Slow Expansion of Type of Business or Industry					
Slow	43%	42%	10%	5%	100%
Moderate	40	42	12	6	100
Rapid	36	44	13	7	100
Moderate Expansion of Type of Business or Industry					
Slow	39	40	13	8	100
Moderate	33	40	19	8	100
Rapid	32	42	20	6	100
Rapid Expansion of Type of Business or Industry					
Slow	45	33	18	4	100
Moderate	41	35	17	7	100
Rapid	33	40	19	8	100
All businesses ...	38	40	16	6	100

the growth in size of the firm. A consistent differential exists in the proportions of northern-born business leaders, with the larger proportion of these men in stable firms; whereas the larger proportion of southern-born business leaders is in rapidly expanding firms. A somewhat greater proportion of business leaders born in the Midwest also appears in the expanding than in the stable firms. The proportions for the Far West seem little affected by business expansion.

In the further examination of the role of business expansion in occupational mobility, special attention was paid to new firms, defined in the questionnaire as those firms established since 1928–29. Six per cent of the men studied were with such firms. The occupation of the father was not related to the age of the firm in any consistent fashion. Five per cent of the sons of major executives and 7 per cent of the sons of professional men are in new firms. At the same time, 5 per cent of the sons of laborers studied are in these recently established firms, along with 7 per cent of the sons of farmers. It would appear that the age of the business firm bears no relationship to occupational origins. Tabular presentation of the relationship between leadership in new business firms and other variables in this study is provided in Appendix V.

Careers in the Several Industries

Expansion is only one dimension in the total complexity of American business. While the many differing types of business activities and business firms may be grouped together as representing a sector of the nation's total organization, business itself is made up of widely varying types of activities covering the whole range of economic institutions. When the 1952 questionnaires were received, each was coded to the type of business of the respondent's company. The classification of the census publications was used in order to make comparison possible. A total of forty-four categories was employed, and in preliminary analysis these were grouped into the eight conventional broad types: mining, construction, manufacturing, trade, finance and insurance and real estate, transportation, communications and public utilities, and services.

The census classification did not prove useful in the sociological analysis of occupational mobility, however. For a discussion of the basis for classification by type of business, see Appendix V. For more

Table 79. Occupational Mobility and Types of Business

Type of Business of Leaders	Occupation of Father					
	Major Executive, Owner of Large Business, and Professional Man	Owner of Small Business	White-Collar Worker	Laborer	Farmer	Total
All types of business	38%	18%	20%	15%	9%	100%
Brokers and dealers	58	14	18	8	2	100
Paper and allied products	43	21	19	13	4	100
Real estate	42	22	16	10	10	100
Metals and their products	42	15	19	17	7	100
Glass, stone, and clay products	42	16	19	17	6	100
Trade, wholesale and retail	41	19	16	15	9	100
Miscellaneous transportation	41	10	29	12	8	100
Business services	41	21	18	15	5	100
Textiles and apparel	40	21	18	15	6	100
Printing and publishing	40	17	22	16	5	100
Banking and miscellaneous finance.	40	18	19	14	9	100
Miscellaneous manufacturing	39	22	17	17	5	100
Chemicals and allied products	39	22	18	11	10	100
Construction and engineering	39	20	18	14	9	100
Personal services	38	17	20	20	5	100
Machinery (except electrical)	37	22	20	12	9	100
Wood products and furniture	37	20	19	18	6	100
Insurance	36	15	27	10	12	100
Food and tobacco	35	18	21	14	12	100
Transportation equipment (manufacturing)	33	18	22	17	10	100
Public utilities and communication.	31	19	23	16	11	100
Mining	31	18	24	13	14	100
Railroads	30	11	22	23	14	100
Highway transportation	30	12	23	25	10	100
Oil and gas	28	24	20	14	14	100
Electrical machinery	26	19	23	22	10	100

meaningful study, the respondents were grouped according to twenty-six types of business, as given in Table 79, which appeared to represent the maximum useful grouping. The occupational origins of leaders in each type of business are given for five occupational groups.

Table 79 lists types of business in rank order according to the proportion of sons of big business and professional men in each. Sons of major executives, owners of large businesses, and professional men comprise nearly 60 per cent of the leadership of the first category of business listed, brokers and dealers. This compares with an average of 38 per cent for all other types of business studied. No other type of business has its leadership so confined to a single level of occupational background. Several types of business are low in this respect: less than a third of the business leaders in public utilities, mining, railroads, highway transportation, oil and gas industries, and electrical-machinery manufacturing are sons of big business and professional men.

With the exception of transportation — railroads, highways, and other transportation — where their proportions are consistently low, sons of owners of small businesses are rather evenly distributed throughout all types of business and industry. In this respect as well as many others, the small entrepreneur background provides access into all sectors of the economy. The white-collar group is distributed in similar fashion, with a high proportion of sons in positions of leadership in insurance.

The strongest contrast with the proportions from big business and professional backgrounds is provided by the sons of laborers and farmers. Both groups make up only a small proportion of leadership among brokers and dealers and in the paper industry. Few sons of laborers are leaders in the insurance business. However, the proportion of sons of laborers in railroads, highway transportation, and electrical machinery is relatively high. A high proportion of leadership in mining, railroads, and the petroleum industry is made up of sons of farmers.

In the relationship between education and the type of business, as given in Table 80, a somewhat similar ordering of the types of business is observed. In two types of business — brokers and dealers, and the paper industry — where the proportion of college graduates is over 70 per cent, the proportion of sons of big business and professional men in leadership positions was also high. Railroads and highway transpor-

Occupational Mobility

Table 80. Education and Types of Business

Type of Business	College Graduate	High School Graduation and Some College	Less Than High School Graduation	Total
		Education of Business Leader		
All types of business	57%	30%	13%	100%
Chemicals and allied products	77	18	5	100
Paper and allied products	72	21	7	100
Brokers and dealers	71	21	8	100
Public utilities and communication	69	23	8	100
Glass, stone, and clay products	68	22	10	100
Construction and engineering	65	26	9	100
Machinery (except electrical)	64	28	8	100
Insurance	64	28	8	100
Oil and gas	63	28	9	100
Electrical Machinery	59	28	13	100
Transportation equipment (manufacturing)	59	30	11	100
Miscellaneous manufacturing	58	30	12	100
Mining	58	33	9	100
Metals and their products	58	29	13	100
Banking and miscellaneous finance	57	29	14	100
Textiles and apparel	57	29	14	100
Business services	56	33	11	100
Miscellaneous transportation	56	32	12	100
Printing and publishing	55	32	13	100
Personal services	52	29	19	100
Food and tobacco	50	37	13	100
Trade, wholesale and retail	49	35	16	100
Wood products and furniture	45	42	13	100
Real estate	44	38	18	100
Railroads	39	35	26	100
Highway transportation	34	44	22	100

tation, where sons of laborers and farmers made up a substantial proportion of business leadership, are low in the proportion of college graduates in elite positions.

As would be expected from the study of business expansion and occupational mobility, however, the relationship of education and occupational origins to the type of business is an imperfect one. In certain industries — including chemicals, utilities, and construction — professional skills may be assumed to be of substantial importance for admission to leadership positions. In these groups, although occu-

Business Careers and the Business System

Table 81. Territorial Origins and Type of Business

Type of Business	Region of Birth				Total
	North	Midwest	South	West	
All types of business	38%	40%	16%	6%	100%
Brokers and dealers	60	20	9	11	100
Personal services	52	25	12	11	100
Paper and allied products	50	40	4	6	100
Printing and publishing	49	39	8	4	100
Electrical machinery	49	40	8	3	100
Textiles and apparel	47	25	22	6	100
Insurance	45	33	17	5	100
Miscellaneous manufacturing	43	46	10	1	100
Metals and their products	43	44	10	3	100
Chemicals and allied products	42	35	17	6	100
Glass, stone, and clay products	42	44	8	6	100
Construction and engineering	38	33	18	11	100
Public utilities and communication	38	37	17	8	100
Mining	37	32	26	5	100
Machinery (except electrical)	36	47	12	5	100
Banking and miscellaneous finance	36	39	18	7	100
Transportation equipment (manufacturing).	36	49	9	6	100
Trade, wholesale and retail	34	39	19	8	100
Business services	34	44	13	9	100
Miscellaneous transportation	32	40	20	8	100
Real estate	30	45	15	10	100
Oil and gas	29	34	24	13	100
Food and tobacco	27	54	14	5	100
Railroads	27	43	25	5	100
Highway transportation	27	47	12	14	100
Wood products and furniture	13	57	24	6	100

pational mobility is relatively high, the proportion of college graduates is also high. In certain others, e.g., wholesale and retail trade and real estate, occupational mobility is moderate to low while the proportion of the elite with high amounts of formal education is also low.

The proportion of leadership in each type of business, according to region of birth, is shown in Table 81. The types of business are listed in the order of the diminishing proportion of leadership born in the northern states. The northern states are the birthplace of half of the business leaders in the types of business designated as brokers and dealers, personal services, paper, printing, and electrical machinery. Less than a third of the leaders in transportation, real estate, petroleum, food and tobacco, and wood products were born in the North.

As would be expected, given the concentration of industry there, the midwestern states are a major source (approximately one half) of leadership in food, transportation, equipment, and wood products. The South is an important source of leadership in the textile industry, mining, the petroleum industry, railroads, and lumber and wood products.

Consistent with its more recent population expansion, the West is high in providing leaders in real estate and in the construction industry. More than the expected proportion of men born in the West also makes up the elite in highway transportation, the petroleum industry, personal services, and brokers and dealers. As would be expected, the proportion of men born in the West who are leaders in manufacturing industries tends to be low, but the proportion might be expected to increase in the future.

From the analysis of occupational and territorial origins, and educational background of American business leadership, certain types of business emerge as characteristic of the extremes of representation. Thus, brokers and dealers represent the extreme of exclusion as it has been seen in the total economy. Business leaders in this group are typically sons of big business or professional men, college graduates, born in the North. At the other extreme are railroads and highway transportation, where the groups that are least represented in the business elite find most ready access to business leadership — sons of laborers and farmers, with relatively little formal education, born in the South and West. It might be noted too that railroads and highway transportation are far removed from each other with respect to age and stability — the long-established, stable, and well-entrenched railroad business, contrasted with the new, dynamic, rapidly changing bus line and trucking businesses.

It is clear from the two preceding attempts to clarify the role in mobility of the firm and the type of business or industry in which it operates that each firm, as well as each sector of the business world, has its own separate and different history, conditions, and organizational type, all of which affect the nature of mobility. It is beyond the scope of this study to examine all these variations.

The Size of the Business and the Positions Achieved

Another dimension of differentiation within the business community is the magnitude of the position held by the business leader. While it

Business Careers and the Business System

is probable that all the men studied are business leaders in terms of the entire economy, they show wide variation in the kind of position held. For the study of occupational mobility into different levels of business positions, two measures are available from the questionnaire.

The respondents provided a measure of the size of the company in terms of the gross income or annual sales in 1952. Thus the size of the business firm may comprise one factor in the ranking of respondents by the magnitude of the position held. The other factor available is the title of the position held. These two factors, title of position and size of firm, will be analyzed jointly. Respondents are grouped by the size of the business into those whose firms' income or annual sales were (1) less than 10 million dollars per annum, (2) 10 million to 250 million dollars per annum, and (3) over 250 million dollars per annum. Business position is grouped into (1) chief executive — owners, partners, presidents, chairmen of the board; (2) vice presidents; and (3) other positions — secretary, treasurer, controller, general manager, and others.

From the combination of these factors, a roughly hierarchical arrangement of the 1952 business elite into nine levels of business position is made possible. Table 82 presents the occupational origins of the business leaders in each of these nine categories. The first column on the left presents the distribution by father's occupation of all the business leaders studied. Succeeding columns to the right give the distribution by father's occupation of business leaders according to company size and business position.

It might be anticipated that the sons of laborers, farmers, and white-collar workers would be represented in smaller proportions in large companies than in small ones, and in higher positions than in lesser ones. The relationship is not of this order, however. In the first row of Table 82, sons of laborers are present in smaller proportions in the chief executive position than in other business positions. However, there is no consistent relationship with size of business.

Conversely, a smaller proportion of the sons of major executives and owners of large business are leaders in the larger firms. Occupational mobility rates are substantially higher in the larger firms. However, within each size category, a larger proportion of men in the higher positions than of those in lower positions are sons of big business men.

Table 82. Occupational Mobility and the Business Hierarchy: Occupation of Father, Business Position, and Size of Business (in Millions of Dollars) of 1952 Leaders

Occupation of Father	All Groups	Chief Executive			Vice President			Other Position		
		Less Than 10	10-250	More Than 250	Less Than 10	10-250	More Than 250	Less Than 10	10-250	More Than 250
Laborer	15%	9%	11%	9%	14%	15%	17%	24%	22%	21%
Owner of small business	18	17	17	20	20	19	17	15	18	16
White-collar worker	20	15	16	16	17	22	22	16	22	24
Major executive and large owner	24	37	35	30	25	22	17	25	15	14
Professional man	14	14	13	16	16	14	17	9	14	13
Farmer	9	8	8	9	8	8	10	11	9	12
Total	100	100	100	100	100	100	100	100	100	100

Table 83. Education and the Business Hierarchy: Education, Business Position, and Size of Business (in Millions of Dollars) of 1952 Leaders

Education of Leaders	All Groups	Chief Executive			Vice President			Other Position		
		Less Than 10	10-250	More Than 250	Less Than 10	10-250	More Than 250	Less Than 10	10-250	More Than 250
Less than high school graduation	13%	14%	14%	16%	11%	12%	13%	15%	13%	12%
High school graduation	11	10	10	9	10	11	10	16	15	13
Some college	19	17	19	13	21	19	17	24	20	20
College graduation	57	59	57	62	58	58	60	45	52	55
Total	100	100	100	100	100	100	100	100	100	100

152

Business Careers and the Business System

Table 83 presents the business hierarchy and education. The proportion of college graduates is greatest in the larger firms and in the higher positions. Sixty-two per cent of the chief executives of the largest firms are college graduates, while only 45 per cent of the men holding "other positions" in the smaller firms are college graduates. On the basis of this analysis, it would appear that the giant business firms, instead of closing off opportunity for sons of men in lower status occupations, are areas of considerable occupational mobility in American business. It is the smaller, less complex firm where mobility is less frequent. It would appear, however, that the enormous business structures place more emphasis than do the smaller ones on college education as a requisite to business leadership.

Some data are available in this area by which to compare the influence of business size and business position on occupational mobility in 1928 with that of 1952. The size categories used in the 1928 study are discussed in Chapter VIII. Five categories were employed in that study, from A, the largest, through E, the smallest. Comparable groupings for 1952 have been made and the comparison of 1928 and 1952 with respect to occupational mobility is given in Table 84. The trend evident in 1952, of somewhat greater occupational mobility in larger than in smaller businesses, does not appear in the 1928 data. The proportion of sons of big business men remains fairly constant in all size categories and is lowest in the smallest, in 1928. About one third of the leaders in each category are sons of big business men. In

Table 84. Occupational Mobility and Size of Business * for 1928 and 1952 Leaders

Occupation of Father	A		B		C		D		E	
	1928	1952	1928	1952	1928	1952	1928	1952	1928	1952
Laborer	11%	14%	10%	16%	11%	16%	11%	15%	13%	13%
White-collar worker .	13	21	13	22	12	19	10	19	12	16
Owner of small business	17	18	19	17	20	17	24	18	22	19
Major executive or owner of large business	32	20	33	22	33	23	32	27	25	29
Professional man ...	16	18	14	14	12	16	11	14	13	14
Farmer	11	9	11	9	12	9	12	7	15	9
Total	100	100	100	100	100	100	100	100	100	100

* See pp. 234–35 for the size of businesses here indicated by A, B, C, D, and E.

153

the 1952 business elite, 20 per cent of the leaders of the largest businesses are sons of big business men, while the proportion is 29 per cent in the smaller firms studied.

With respect to business position, the 1928 study divided the business elite into an owner-partner group, chief executives, and other positions. While the number of owners and partners in the 1952 study is of course much smaller, a comparison of occupational mobility into business positions for 1928 and 1952 is given in Table 85.

On the whole, in 1928 as in 1952, occupational mobility is proportionately greater into lesser business positions. In both time periods, sons of laborers, farmers, and white-collar workers make up the larger proportion of the men in lesser positions. Further, the differences by business position have increased. In 1928, 35 per cent of the owners or partners, 33 per cent of the chief executives, and 27 per cent of the men in "other positions" were sons of major executives or owners of large businesses. In 1952, the pattern is 36, 34, and 20 per cent. That is, occupational mobility takes place from lower status backgrounds at a higher rate into lesser positions, and at a lesser rate into higher positions.

These data must be viewed with some caution. It is hardly necessary to point out that the "owner or partner" category is much smaller in 1952 than in 1928. Further, the increasing division of labor in the top hierarchy of business has expanded and divided the "other positions" category. The total effect has been to raise the relative rank of the "chief executive" group, and to insert a new category between "other positions" and "chief executive." It would be expected, if this has been the case, that mobility into chief executive positions from the lower status occupational backgrounds would take place at a somewhat reduced rate, as has been observed in Table 85.

The role of education in mobility into the several positions in the business hierarchy is presented in Table 86. The percentages in the table give the proportion of college graduates in each category. The columns on the extreme right present the proportions of college graduates in each size category, and the row on the bottom presents the proportions of college graduates in each type of business position.

The over-all impression gained from Table 86 is that of an enormous increase in the proportion of college graduates at all levels of the business hierarchy. The proportion of college graduates in the business

Business Careers and the Business System

Table 85. Occupational Mobility and Business Position for
1928 and 1952 Leaders

Occupation of Father	Owner or Partner		Chief Executive		Other Position	
	1928	1952	1928	1952	1928	1952
Laborer	10%	10%	10%	11%	13%	17%
White-collar worker ...	12	14	11	16	15	20
Owner of small business	20	18	20	18	20	18
Major executive or owner of large business	35	36	33	34	27	20
Professional man	14	17	13	12	13	16
Farmer	9	5	13	9	12	9
Total	100	100	100	100	100	100

Table 86. The Business Hierarchy and College Graduates among
Leaders in 1928 and 1952

Size of Business	Owner or Partner		Chief Executive		Other Position		All Positions	
	1928	1952	1928	1952	1928	1952	1928	1952
A	55%	62%	46%	62%	40%	60%	43%	60%
B	37	57	35	64	31	61	34	61
C	32	40	29	57	31	59	30	59
D	26	61	26	52	30	55	27	54
E	25	62	26	55	28	54	26	56
All grades.	33	61	31	57	32	58	32	58

elite as a whole has increased, between 1928 and 1952, from 32 to 58
per cent. This increase has taken place throughout the business hierarchy, and educational differences by size of business have been sharply reduced. Thus, in both 1928 and 1952 more college graduates are
in the largest businesses (category A) than in the smallest; but in 1928
the difference was 17 per cent (43 per cent of the leaders in the largest
businesses were college graduates, as against 26 per cent in the smallest) whereas in 1952 the difference between the largest and the smallest
businesses is only 4 per cent (from 60 per cent to 56). This same tendency to an equalizing of the amount of general education is true with
respect to business position as well as with respect to the size of the
business.

Another facet of business position is the number of firms of which
the business leader is a director. Table 87, presenting the proportion

of 1952 business leaders by the number of directorships held, under-estimates the numbers for this population. It is clear that in those cases where the directorships held were with subsidiary or affiliate companies, the respondent usually did not indicate the directorships, but merely noted their exclusion from his reply. Nearly 75 per cent of the 1952 business leaders are directors of one or more business firms, and the number of directorships held may be taken as a further index of business position.

The relationship between occupational origins and the number of directorships held is given in Table 88. A much higher proportion of the men holding multiple directorships, compared with those holding no directorships, are sons of major executives or owners of large busi-

Table 87. Directorships Held by 1952 Business Leaders

Number of Directorships	Percentage of Business Leaders *
0	27
1	29
2	14
3	9
4	7
5	4
6	3
7	2
8	1
9 or more	4
Total	100

* No answer was given by 3 per cent of 7500.

Table 88. Occupational Mobility and Directorships

Occupation of Father	Number of Directorships				All Business Leaders
	0	1	2 or 3	4 or More	
Laborer	20%	15%	13%	12%	15%
White-collar worker	24	18	19	15	20
Owner of small business.	18	19	19	17	18
Major executive or owner of large business	14	24	28	33	24
Professional man	15	15	14	14	14
Farmer	9	9	7	9	9
Total	100	100	100	100	100

nesses. Sons of laborers or white-collar workers make up a much smaller proportion of the men holding multiple directorships.

Like other aspects of business position, the number of companies in which executive power is wielded is related to occupational origins. Within the business hierarchy, entrance to which is markedly influenced by occupational origins, relative position is also determined to a considerable degree by occupational origins.

CHAPTER VI

A Man's Family and His Career

Birth Status and Achieved Status

In many societies men are born to their occupational as well as their social status. They are trained by their fathers and others to learn how to function in the position they inherit. The principles of achieved status, compared with those of birth status, maximize competition, heterogeneity of career lines, and variety of experience in the careers of those who strive for position. They may place more emphasis on economic than on social criteria for determining who shall succeed or fail. Or social factors, including the family and friendship groupings, may greatly reduce the force of the strictly economic factor of the market place. Ability alone may not decide; a father in the firm, friends on the job, financial assistance from wealthy friends or relatives at crucial moments in the career may play important parts in the successful advance of many men.

Common knowledge and experience tell us that both the influences of the family and birth status and those of achieved status operate in America. Birth status may be *directly* inherited; or its influence may be exerted *indirectly* by the family's position in our social and economic life. The relations within the immediate family of parents and children, in particular the relations of fathers and sons, have had a considerable and sometimes a decisive influence on the careers of some of our business leaders. The power of the family is felt by them not only in their choice of occupation but in the development and advancement of their careers after the choice is made. The mobile men, rejecting the occupations of their fathers while seeking advantages elsewhere, seem less influenced by the family than the sons of the

158

elite — in fact many not only have positively aspired to higher status but have rejected the entire world of their fathers and the ways of life provided by their families of birth. Yet our evidence shows that the careers of some men from all levels have been partly controlled by family factors. Many questions that are crucial for our scientific understanding arise out of these considerations, and the answers seem to be of great importance to this country. Let us ask some of them.

How does the family influence occupational succession? When it does, in what ways are such influences expressed? Do certain social institutions, such as families and friends, rather than economic ones, increase the likelihood of some occupational groups advancing themselves more than would be expected if such factors as skill, ability, and the like were the only ones involved in occupational advancement? What kinds of men do and do not receive help? Are those men with relatives in the firm advantaged or disadvantaged? Do such men climb to the top more rapidly than others or are there no differences? Do those with connections reach higher positions more often than those less well placed? How does 1952 compare with 1928 in regard to the social and family influences that impede or expedite the development of a business career?

It is the task of this present chapter to consider these and other questions having to do with this difficult and at times controversial area of business life. The mobile men have pushed forward not only from different economic backgrounds but also from different social backgrounds. The ways of life are different; the social worlds they inhabit provide varying prestige, supply their members with increased or decreased amounts of social honor, and equip them poorly or admirably for their chosen careers. From some sources, perhaps malicious and cynical, one hears it is not *what* you know but *whom* you know that counts in getting ahead. Others cry that in the tough competition of today, when shirt sleeves to shirt sleeves in three generations is more than ever true, no business can afford to hire and advance men who cannot compete successfully with the strongest and most ruthless competitors.

For the purpose of learning what kinds of influence might operate, the questionnaire included items about personal friends, business acquaintances, and relatives; their intention was to find out whether the business leader had entered business through relatives or friends and whether he now was in a firm where such close connections were present.[1] (See Chapter VIII for the phrasing of the questions.)

Table 89, which is on the relation of the number of years consumed to reach business leadership to the kind of influential friends and relatives present in the firms, tells a significant story.[2] There is little or no difference in the time taken by those men with *no* relatives and friends in the firm (Type I, 1 and 2) and by the several types in whose cases personal friends were involved. Briefly, there is little or no difference between the advancement of a man with friends and those without them in his business. The old adage of businessmen that "friendship may get you in the firm but after that you're on your own" seems to be well borne out by the breakdown of the two types of men, those with and those without friends in the organization.

This point is more strikingly demonstrated by the considerable difference in time for achievement between the types who have relatives in the firm and those who do not. On the average, men with relatives in the firm took 19 to 20 years, well below the average for all types (23.8 years), while the others approached or were well above the average.

The nine categories listed in Table 89 were reduced to four general ones partly for ease in presentation and partly to sharpen the meaning of the several categories of influence. The division of the nine categories into four is also shown in Table 89: Type I, no friends or relatives in the first or present firm (categories 1 and 2); Type II, friends in one or both firms (categories 3, 4, and 5); Type III, relatives in the first, but neither friends nor relatives in the present firm (category 6); and Type IV, relatives in the present firm or in both (categories 7, 8, and 9).

The percentage of men reporting no influential connections, neither relatives nor close friends in the same firm, is in direct relation to the rank of the father's occupation: the lower the rank, the higher the percentage of those who were on their own; the higher the rank, the higher the percentage of those with kinsmen. Table 90 shows that the

---

[1] By the use in the questionnaire of the term "business acquaintance" as contrasted with "friend," an effort was made to separate people in a business or economic relationship from those who were friends in a more personal and social sense. The distinction is a difficult one to make in a questionnaire. Where the two terms are employed in the following analysis they should be considered as no more than approximations of the underlying difference in social relations.

[2] The procedures used in the following analysis are described in Appendix VI.

Table 89. Years to Achieve Business Leadership and Influential Connections

Influential Connections *	Mean Years to Achieve Leadership
Type I: No connections	
1	24.8
2	26.8
Type II: Friends	
3	25.4
4	23.5
5	24.7
Type III: Relatives (first firm)	
6	25.0
Type IV: Relatives (present firm)	
7	20.1
8	18.9
9	18.9
Average for all	23.8

* Categories of influential connections are as follows:

Type I.

1. No connections in first or present firm. No connections in present firm; business acquaintances in present firm. No connections in first (and only) firm 3,705
2. Business acquaintances in first and present firm. Business acquaintances in present firm; no connections in first firm. Business acquaintances in first (and only) firm 1,210

Type II.

3. Friends in first firm; business acquaintances in present firm. Friends in first firm; no connections in present firm 311
4. Friends in first and present firm. Friends in present firm; relatives in first firm. Friends in first (and only) firm 485
5. Friends in present firm; business acquaintances in first firm. Friends in present firm; no connections in first firm 366

Type III.

6. Relatives in first firm; business acquaintances in present firm. Relatives in first firm; no connections in present firm 332

Type IV.

7. Relatives in first and present firm. Relatives in present firm; friends in first firm 347
8. Relatives in first (only) firm 549
9. Relatives in present firm; business acquaintances in first firm. Relatives in present firm; no connections in first firm 195

Total 7,500

Table 90. Influential Connections and Occupational Mobility

Occupation of Father	Type I, No Connections	Type II, Friends	Type III, Relatives in First Firm	Type IV, Relatives in Present Firm	Total
Unskilled or semiskilled laborer...	85%	10%	2%	3%	100%
Skilled laborer	87	9	2	2	100
Clerk or salesman	77	15	3	5	100
Owner of small business	71	15	5	9	100
Minor executive	73	17	4	6	100
Major executive	33	15	6	46	100
Owner of large business	39	16	9	36	100
Professional man	62	25	4	9	100
Farmer	82	12	2	4	100
All occupations	66	15	4	15	100

overwhelming mass of workers and farmers were without such help but that the sons of business leaders who had no influential connections in the firm were a minority of that occupational class: a third of the sons of executives and about two fifths of the sons of large owners were in this minority. Let us examine the figures for relatives in the same firm. All occupational backgrounds have a small representation (2 to 9 per cent) except business leaders; 46 per cent of the sons of executives and 36 per cent of the sons of large owners were in firms where they had close relatives.

Another way of finding out whether influential connections helped the careers is to examine the several positions in the business hierarchy in relation to influential connections. The right-hand columns of Table 91 list the several categories of influence; the column to the left divides the business positions into chief executive, vice president, and other positions below it. Half of all those who belonged to Type IV (relatives in the present firm) were chief executives, whereas less than a sixth of those in the lower positions — those below the vice-presidential level — had kindred in either the first or the present firm. On the other hand, only about a fifth of the chief executives were in firms without friends or relatives. In general, the percentages of chief executives rise from Type I, without friends or relatives (21 per cent), through friends (29 per cent), and relatives in the first firm (35 per cent), to relatives in the present firm (50 per cent). The percentages for vice presidents drop (54 per cent to 37 per cent), as they do also for the lower positions (25 per cent to 13 per cent). Since the proportion of chief executives with relatives in their present firm is more than double that for chief executives without connections, and the proportion of those in lower statuses with relatives in the present firm is about half that in the category without relatives or friends in the present firm, it appears that high position in the hierarchy is positively connected with the presence of kindred.

Table 92 gives the percentage of business leaders with or without influential connections according to the size of the business enterprise. The general configuration indicates that, as the size of the firm increases, fewer leaders have influential friends or relatives present. For example, in about a third of the firms with incomes or sales under 10 million dollars, leaders have relatives in the present firm, whereas in only 9 per cent of firms with incomes or sales over 250 million dollars is this a characteristic. Furthermore, in firms with incomes or sales under 10 million dollars the proportion of leaders having relatives in the present firm was twice as high as the proportion of those without connections. On the other hand, for those firms with incomes or

Table 91. Influential Connections and Business Position of Leaders

Business Position	Type I, No Connections	Type II, Friends	Type III, Relatives in First Firm	Type IV, Relatives in Present Firm
Chief executive	21%	29%	35%	50%
Vice president	54	52	50	37
Other position	25	19	15	13
Total	100	100	100	100

Table 92. Influential Connections and Size of Business of Leaders

Size of Business (Gross Annual Income or Sales)	Type I, No Connections	Type II, Friends	Type III, Relatives in First Firm	Type IV, Relatives in Present Firm
Under $10 million ...	14%	17%	19%	32%
$10–250 million	64	64	62	59
Over $250 million ...	22	19	19	9
Total	100	100	100	100

sales of over 250 million dollars, the proportion of those without connections (22 per cent) was twice as high as for those with relatives in the present firm (9 per cent).

It might be expected that the presence or absence of influential friends or relatives in the firm would make a difference in the age of reaching top managerial status; however, the age of rising to this status was 45.0 years for those with connections, and 45.6 years for those without them (see Table 93). The difference in age at reaching the top is very small. This holds true for all sizes of business, the difference in age for the two categories at each level being small. In 1928 the difference in chronological age was about two years, those with connections being 39.4 years and those without, 41.2 years. Again, the difference was not great.

Table 93. Influential Connections and Achievement Time of Leaders in 1928 and 1952 *

Size of Business †	Average Age of Assuming Position for Leaders with Connections		Average Age of Assuming Position for Leaders without Connections	
	1928	1952	1928	1952
A	42.8	47.5	45.0	48.1
B	41.3	46.3	43.0	46.3
C	40.1	45.5	42.3	46.8
D	37.5	44.7	40.1	43.9
E	36.8	42.7	37.8	43.1
All sizes	39.4	45.0	41.2	45.6

* For 1928, and thus for 1952 also, the sample here is limited to those men who received no financial aid, who completed college, and who had no formal business training.

† See pages 234–35 for the annual income or sales of businesses here indicated by A, B, C, D, and E.

Fathers and Sons: Business Leaders in the Same Firm

It will be recalled that 23.4 per cent of all the elite studied were the sons of major executives or owners of large businesses (see Table 1). Almost 10 per cent (9.5 per cent) of *all the leaders* were in firms where their fathers were either owners or major executives (see Table 95). This amounted to 43 per cent of all the business elite who were *sons of business leaders* (see Table 94). This figure has decreased slightly from 1928 when 45 per cent were in the same firms as their fathers. Placing the sons of large owners and the sons of major executives in

A Man's Family and His Career

Table 94. Sons of Executives or Owners in the Same Firms as Their
Fathers, 1928 and 1952, Classified According to Size of Business

Size of Business	Sons of Major Executives in Same Firm as Father		Sons of Owners of Large Businesses in Same Firm as Father		Sons of Major Executives and Owners of Large Businesses in Same Firm as Father	
	1928	1952	1928	1952	1928	1952
A	36%	23%	17%	9%	28%	18%
B	49	40	35	13	43	30
C	57	50	49	27	53	42
D	50	64	48	34	49	52
E	39	64	46	70	43	66
All sizes ..	49	40	41	60	45	43

one category obscures certain important facts. In 1928, 49 per cent of the sons of major executives and 41 per cent of the sons of large owners were in the same firms as the fathers. By 1952 only 40 per cent of the sons of major executives were in the same firms, a decrease of 9 per cent, whereas the sons of owners in the same firms had advanced to 60 per cent, an increase of 19 per cent (see Table 94).The sons of major executives go elsewhere in increasing numbers for their careers; the sons of owners tend to stay in the fathers' firms.[3]

In Table 94 the size of the firm is on the left, and the percentage of sons in the same firm as their fathers, to its right, is redivided into sons of major executives and large owners. To the far right both are combined. All columns are arranged so that 1928 and 1952 may be compared. Under 1952, it will be noted that there is a steady increase in the percentage not only of owners' sons but of managers' sons, too, as the size of the business decreases from Grade A, the very large type of industry, to Grade E. For the sons of managers, the figure rises from 23 per cent for Grade A to 64 per cent for Grade E (below 10 million dollars); for the sons of owners, from 9 per cent to 70 per cent. Clearly circumstances and the nature of the small enterprise seem to foster the "inheritance" of the father's position; conversely, very large enterprises are less favorable environments. A comparison of the sons of managers and owners at the different levels brings out another set

[3] The region of birth of the business leader, and the region of present business, have little or no relationship with the proportion of men in their fathers' firms.

of generalizations. At the highest levels (A and B) the sons of managers are approximately three times more frequent than sons of owners, and about twice as frequent in the next highest levels; but they drop behind in the last (E). In the lowest three grades of industry half or more of the sons of major executives are in the same firm as their fathers, but it is only in the fifth and smallest that the sons of owners predominate, the proportion jumping from 34 per cent in D to 70 per cent in E.

Significant and important trends embodying certain social principles are immediately apparent when one compares the figures for 1928 and 1952. We have already shown that the over-all percentage of managers' sons has declined and that the percentage of owners' sons has increased since 1928. An examination of the several sizes of business reveals much more than these general figures about what is happening to American business. The percentage of leaders who were sons of major executives and large owners actually decreased for most size-types of business from 1928 to 1952. Only in the smallest was there an increase, but it was sufficient to more than offset the decreases. The percentage of sons of managers decreased in the three larger size groups of firms, but increased in the two smaller groups, from 50 to 64 per cent for D, and from 39 to 64 per cent for E.

The percentage of sons in the father's business varies considerably according to the type of enterprise, ranging from the retail and wholesale trade with the most (19.1 per cent) to public utilities and communication (0.0 per cent). In Table 95, the several categories of businesses are ranked and divided into three general classes according to fathers and sons in the same firms, the highest including those above average (9.5) and the lowest, those with less than 5 per cent. It will be noted that the first five include real estate, wood and coal products, personal services, and security and commodity brokers. Those with the least, in addition to the one mentioned, are oil, gas and coal products, the railroads, other transportation (including air and water), banking and finance, electrical machinery, chemicals, and stone, clay, and allied products.

Some of the factors involved have to do with traditions within an industry: the degree of feeling against nepotism, the strength of the feeling that every man who is capable should be hired regardless of kinship, the family feeling that the son should learn his father's busi-

A Man's Family and His Career

Table 95. Sons of Executives or Owners in the Same Firms as Their Fathers,
Classified According to Type of Business

Type of Business	Percentage of Business Leaders in Same Firm as Father
All 1952 business leaders	9.5
High	
Retail and wholesale trade	19.1
Real estate	17.5
Wood and wood products	14.8
Personal services (including hotels, amusements)	12.4
Security and commodity brokers and dealers	12.0
Other manufacturing (including rubber and leather products)	11.8
Textiles, apparel, and other finished products	11.1
Metals and their products	10.2
Business services	10.1
Printing and publishing	10.0
Moderate	
Paper and allied products	9.2
Food and tobacco products	9.1
Construction and engineering	8.8
Mining, coal, and metal	8.3
Machinery (except electrical)	8.3
Transportation and equipment	5.9
Insurance	5.6
Highway transportation	5.1
Low	
Chemicals and allied products	4.9
Stone, clay, and glass products	4.8
Electrical machinery	3.4
Banking and finance	3.4
Railroads	3.1
Other transportation (including air and water)	2.2
Oil, gas, and oil, gas, and coal products	1.7
Public utilities and communication	0.0

ness and continue making a success of a family enterprise. Further, some types of business are too new to give sufficient time for sons to inherit or acquire high positions through family influence.

The fact that the smaller of the important firms included in this study are generally characterized by a much higher level of inheritance of position than are the largest business firms in America is a finding of broad significance. It has long been held that the giant corporation, often exercising a near monopoly in its sector of the economy, represents a considerable danger to the democratic recruitment of economic leadership. In this view the giant corporation represents a final form of plutocracy, the control of important areas of the society by a small financial and industrial elite. These data demonstrate the error of this view. It is the smaller firms in which caste-like occupational succession predominates; it is the largest firms in which recruitment to business leadership most frequently occurs from all levels of the occupational system.

The general cause appears to lie in the extent of the trend to rationalization of the giant firm. Recruitment of leadership is rationalized along with production, distribution, and financing. The separation of ownership as represented by stock holdings from the active management of these huge firms, the heightened impersonalization of relationships within the firm, increased specialization of the occupational role at all levels of status in the firm — these and other phenomena of the social organization of the large corporation contribute to the results noted in this study. It is in the less-rationalized smaller firm that familial relationships play a more important role in executive recruitment. Given access to education and training by men from all levels of the society, there is nothing in the nature of the "monopolistic" giant corporation to dictate oligopolistic executive recruitment. On the contrary, the formalized structure and rationalized procedures of these corporations work to accelerate occupational mobility in the business system.

While the proportion of sons of business owners and executives with the same firm as their fathers has declined from 1928 to 1952, Table 96 indicates that of those men who are with the same firm as their fathers a higher proportion occupy the upper echelon positions. In 1928, 64 per cent of the men studied were chief executives. Sixty-seven per cent of the sons of executives in the same firm as their fathers were chief executives. In 1952, 28 per cent of all men studied were chief executives, but 57 per cent of the sons of executives in the same firms as their fathers were chief executives. In other words, while this kind of occupational inheritance is less frequent today than it was a generation ago, insofar as it takes place, the effects are to substantially elevate rank within the business firm. Nepotism is less common than previously but more effective where and when it takes place.

The stronghold of the inherited position in America today is in the

A Man's Family and His Career

Table 96. Sons of Executives or Owners in the Same Firms as Their Fathers, 1928 and 1952, Classified According to Business Position

Business Position	Sons of Major Executives or Owners of Large Businesses in Same Firm as Father		All Business Leaders	
	1928	1952	1928	1952
Owner or partner	9%	7%	11%	5%
President or chairman of the board ..	58	50	53	23
Vice president	15	31	21	53
Other	18	12	15	19
Total	100	100	100	100

smaller enterprises; the freest and most open positions are in the largest enterprises. The bigger the business the freer it is for the ambitious and for those who start from the bottom to seek their fortunes and to make their successful advance into the places of business prestige and power.

What Happens to Those Who "Inherit" Their Positions

We have established that in 1952, despite many changes in occupational succession between 1928 and 1952, a substantial minority of men were in an elite where they and their fathers occupied high positions in the same firm. It is time to ask what happens to their careers. Do they simply fill an important office on their first arrival on the job or must they, too, devote a substantial period of their lives to attaining high status? How long does it take them? Table 97, called, significantly, "Acceleration of Career," answers some of these questions and is a good indicator of the answers to some of those not directly asked. The first column lists the sons of minor and major managers and of small and large owners, and indicates whether they were in the same firm as the father or a different one; the second indicates the years taken to achieve the position by the different categories of men.

The careers of all categories of men who are the sons of highly placed fathers in their firms are considerably advantaged. Their careers are accelerated from two and a half to six years over those of men not in their fathers' firms. The degree of difference between sons of managers and sons of owners, however, is great. The sons of both

Occupational Mobility

Table 97. Acceleration of Career of the Sons of Executives or Owners in the Same Firms as Their Fathers

Background and Firm	Years to Achieve Position (Mean)
Son of minor executive	
Same firm as father	22.1
Different firm from father	24.6
Son of major executive	
Same firm as father	19.1
Different firm from father	21.6
Son of owner of small or medium business	
Same firm as father	18.7
Different firm from father	24.6
Son of owner of large business	
Same firm as father	15.7
Different firm from father	21.9
Business leaders from all other occupational levels	24.7

minor and major executives, if they are in the father's firm, average a speed-up of two and a half years, but the sons of owners, large or small, gain about six years. The mean number of years to achieve their positions for mobile men from all other occupational levels is 24.7 years. Several types of sons so favorably placed, when compared with the men least advantaged at the start of their careers, were even more benefited than first appears. The sons of large owners who are in their fathers' firms gain nine years over the men from all other occupational levels; the sons of major executives, five and one half years. The sons of minor executives and lesser owners whose fathers are in different firms take about the same time as all others to advance.

Other advantages also are given these favorably placed members of the elite. To indicate how this particular group of men who are in the same firm are privileged it will be necessary to anticipate for a moment what properly belongs to the next section, their financial aid. Most contemporary business leaders received little or no direct financial aid in their careers (6.1 per cent, see Table 98). Twenty-eight per cent of those in the same firm as their fathers were given financial assistance; 5 per cent of the sons of executives whose fathers were in other firms were so benefited. Only 3 per cent of all *other* business leaders received this help. Thus, the proportion of business leaders with the same firm as their fathers who received financial assistance is six times that of sons of executives not with the same firm, and nine times the percentage of all other business leaders. These several measurements of advantages should be compared with the data in the next section in this chapter, on financial aid and influential connections, to see the contrastive differences between the mobile men from the bottom and those who were born to the elite.

The Influence of Financial Aid: Gifts, Loans, and Inheritances

Most of the men presently occupying high positions of prestige and authority in the business elite came up the hard way. As we said above, few of them received financial aid as loans or gifts from friends or relatives or had the good fortune to inherit money from their kindred. A small segment did — some 6 per cent (see Table 98). Although numerically few, they are an important and significant group in the business life of America. Let us begin our inquiry by finding out who and what they are.

More sons of major executives and large owners received aid than those from any other occupational background (see Table 99); 17 per cent of these men enjoyed these benefits, three times the percentage of

Table 98. Sources of Financial Aid for 1952 Business Leaders

Source	Percentage of 1952 Leaders Receiving Aid
Inheritance	3.0
Relatives	2.8
Friends	0.3
Total receiving such aid	6.1

Table 99. Financial Aid and Occupational Mobility for 1952 Leaders

Occupation of Father	Percentage of Leaders Receiving Financial Aid
Laborer	0.6
White-collar worker	1.6
Owner of small business	2.9
Major executive or owner of large business	17.0
Professional man	6.2
Farmer	2.5
All backgrounds	6.1

171

the sons of professional men (6.2 per cent), the next ranking group in this respect. The latter had more than double the proportions of the sons of small business men (2.9 per cent) and of farmers (2.5 per cent), who outranked the white-collar men (1.6 per cent) and the sons of laborers (0.6 per cent). Approximately thirty times more sons of the elite than sons of working men were given a financial boost and had their careers thus accelerated. Despite this and other aids given their highly placed competitors, men from all other levels advanced in considerable numbers to these top positions.

Who were the people who gave these men financial assistance and how was it done? Most of it came from relatives, either while they were living or as inheritance at their deaths. Only 6 per cent of all those receiving aid received it from friends, whereas 46 per cent were helped by living relatives and 48 per cent by inheritance (see Table 100). Only 2 per cent of the sons of the elite who received aid were helped by friends, 49 per cent of the sons of the elite were aided by inheritance, and an equal proportion by loans and gifts from relatives. About 59 per cent of the sons of professional men (the only other sizable group in this category) who received aid were helped by inheritance, 35 per cent by relatives, and some 6 per cent by friends.

Comparisons between 1928 and the present time record a decided diminution of the percentage of those receiving financial help. In 1928 some 13 per cent were so benefited (see Table 101); at the present, only 6 per cent receive such help. In the earlier group, 6 per cent received an inheritance, compared with 3 per cent today. In 1928, 7 per cent were helped by friends or relatives; today, only 3 per cent have been helped. In general, the percentages in all occupational levels drop. Noteworthy, however, is the decline from 14 per cent to 9 per

Table 100. Sources of Financial Aid for 1952 Sons of Big Business Men and of Professional Men

Source	All Business Leaders	Sons of Major Executives or Owners of Large Businesses	Sons of Professional Men
Inheritance	48%	49%	59%
Relatives	46	49	35
Friends	6	2	6
Total	100	100	100

cent and from 14 per cent to 7 per cent in inheritances received by the sons of major executives and of large business owners respectively, and a drop in the same categories of from 17 to 7 per cent and 16 to 8 per cent in those receiving financial help from friends or from relatives. The other losses are sometimes proportionately greater but the percentage figures are far smaller.

Understanding of the general lessening of financial aid from 1928 to 1952 is further sharpened by an examination of the percentages for sons of those in all major positions in the several grades of business enterprise. Table 102 provides such information for those aided by gifts or loans from friends or relatives (see right-hand column). Those in all grades of business from A through E are severely cut, but those who suffered the greatest loss were the sons of owners of the larger enterprises (A, B, and C). In 1928, 14 per cent of the sons of owners of the largest enterprises were aided, compared with only 8 per cent in 1952; in 1928, 16 per cent at the C level were helped, while today help is received by only 3 per cent, less than one fifth of the previous proportion. Fewer and fewer of the sons of those in top positions and greatest power are being aided.

The sons of owners at the D and E levels, however, have not lost but have held their own. These two categories of men, the sons of owners of big businesses below the 50-million-dollar mark, are the only exceptions to the general trend of decreasing financial help at all levels of position and size of business. The sons of men from smaller enter-

Table 101. Financial Aid and Occupational Mobility in 1928 and 1952

Occupation of Father	Percentage of Those Receiving Aid by Inheritance		Percentage of Those Receiving Aid from Friends	
	1928	1952	1928	1952
Unskilled or semiskilled laborer ..	0	0	1	0
Skilled laborer	0	1	2	0
Clerk or salesman	2	1	2	1
Minor executive	2	1	4	1
Owner of small business	3	1	4	2
Major executive	14	9	17	7
Owner of large business	14	7	16	8
Professional man	6	4	5	2
Farmer	2	1	2	1
All occupations	6	3	7	3

Occupational Mobility

Table 102. Leaders of 1928 and 1952 Receiving Financial Assistance * in Business
Careers, Classified According to the Size of the Business and the Position Held

Size of Business	Subordinate Executive		Chief Executive		Partner or Owner		All Positions	
	1928	1952	1928	1952 ·	1928	1952	1928	1952
A	3%	2%	5%	4%	14%	8%	5%	2%
B	5	2	8	6	15	5	7	2
C	4	2	7	4	16	3	7	2
D	6	2	9	7	13	13	9	4
E	4	3	9	6	7	7	8	5
All sizes	4	2	8	6	13	7	7	3

* Inheritance as a source of aid is not included.

prises hold this kind of competitive advantage while the proportions
of the sons of all other owners, as well as of those from all other categories who receive such aid, have been greatly reduced. In general the
power of money, although very much present in the careers of many
men, is of decreasing significance in the competitive world of those
who strive for position among the business elite.

The relation of financial aid to the power of close social and family
connections in the firm shows several things: (1) that the overwhelming majority of those receiving financial assistance belonged to that
category of men with *relatives* in the firm, (2) that friends were of
little importance, (3) that those without friends or relatives received
very little monetary aid. Whereas one fourth (23 per cent) of all men
with relatives in the firm were aided, only 6 per cent of those with
friends and 2 per cent of those with no connections were benefited.
Financial assistance and influential connections in the firm go together;
yet three fourths of all men with kindred in the same business organization received no direct monetary aid from them.

We have learned of the enormous part higher education has played
in the lives of a substantial percentage of these men. In the lives of
many, education has provided the social power which their families
have been unable to give them. Those not born to position may achieve
it by the power of an acquired education which is believed to fit them
for higher occupation and social position. Yet men born to the elite
go to college more than all others; they too believe higher education
fits them for higher things. Education works to advance lowly placed

174

mobile men, and to help them compete with men born to the status to remain there. Since highly placed families are more apt to send their sons to college as well as to provide financial assistance during their careers, this question arises: How are financial aid, influential connections, and education related? A further question is as follows: Are there differences between the previous generation of business leaders (1928) and those of today? Table 103 indicates some of the relations among the several factors in the career. Those with no influence or aid were divided from those with one or both. All in turn are resorted by the amount of education they received.

In 1952, 5 per cent of all business leaders enjoyed both financial aid and influential connections in their firm, 47 per cent had one or the other, and 48 per cent neither. In 1928 a larger percentage had the advantage of both influence and financial help (8 per cent), a smaller percentage had one or the other (31 per cent), and a larger proportion had neither (61 per cent). Only college men received financial aid and also had influential connections (5 per cent of the total). It will be noted that from 1928 there is a decrease in this category at all levels of education.

In 1952 more than a third (37 per cent) of those with either financial aid or influential connections were college men, about one out of ten (9 per cent) were high school graduates, and but 2 per cent were

Table 103. Influential Connections, Financial Aid, and Education for 1928 and 1952 Business Leaders

Education	Both Influential Connections and Financial Aid	Either Influential Connections or Financial Aid	Neither Influential Connections nor Financial Aid
Less than high school			
1928	1%	6%	20%
1952	0	2	3
High school			
1928	2	8	18
1952	0	9	11
College			
1928	6	17	23
1952	5	37	34
Total			
1928	8	31	61
1952	5	47	48

from the lower educational ranks. The percentage of men with college in this category in 1952 is more than double that of 1928 (17 per cent), but the percentages for those of lowest educational status decrease. Much of this is due to the increase of college men in contemporary business leadership.

For those with neither influence nor aid there has been an increase among college men from 23 per cent in 1928 to 34 per cent in 1952; a decrease among high school graduates from 18 per cent in 1928 to 11 per cent in 1952; and among those with less than a high school education, a decrease from 20 per cent to 3 per cent. While the proportion of college men in the business elite increased greatly, the proportion of those who combined aid and influence declined, indicating that fewer men today are as much advantaged by birth as previously. More men went to college and on to a successful career in 1952 than in 1928, but more men now have been benefited by *either* financial aid *or* influential connections than in 1928.

The special influence of the family and friends of the family is present. Some men are benefited by financial aid. Gifts and inheritance advantage the more highly placed men. The man from farther down has a longer and a harder way to travel than those born to fathers in the business elite. Yet the chronological ages of both groups are very similar despite the fact that those with influential connections take less time. More of the latter start later, having devoted more time to higher education.

Since 1928 there has been a strong trend away from the influences of the family and an increasing emphasis upon competitive achievement. Birth status does not assure a son of the elite permanent position there. More and more the factors involved in achieved status influence occupational succession into the business elite.

The Marriages of the American Business Elite

The Women They Marry

IN ALL previous chapters, we have examined the relations of fathers and sons to occupational succession, thus learning how the family and the patrilineal line influence, and are influenced by, the economic and occupational world in which these men operate. We must now determine the status and occupational origins of the women who marry members of the business elite. To gather the evidence, we inquired about the occupations of the fathers of the wives, and these occupations were typed in the same way as those of the men under study. Then it was possible to discover how free the choices of the men were and to what extent status operated in the selection of the women they married. This chapter asks and answers several important questions, the first of which is as follows: What is the occupational status of the wife's family? Or, stated another way, at what economic level did she originate?

Many more detailed questions about this matter are involved: Do these men marry above or below themselves? Did these highly successful men of ambition seek and find women to marry from higher social and economic positions, very much in the style in which they sought and acquired their present high position in the business elite? Did they marry the daughters of big business men or those from the much esteemed professional elites? Or did some mobile men marry at the lower levels of their own origin and fashion a lifetime career of continuing to advance from there to higher levels, a career in which their wives shared, fighting to maintain for themselves and their children the pace set by their husbands? Was the wife a partner with her

177

husband in the difficult task of unlearning old ways and learning new patterns of living? The way the mobile business leader relates to his children as well as to his wife, his satisfactions and frustrations, the ease with which he translates economic and pecuniary success into social achievement, "what he brings to the job" every morning and goes home to at night, will vary enormously according to the choice he makes in the status of the woman he marries.

In many respects it is more important to ask of two or more generations of powerful and prestigeful men whether they marry into or outside their own class. Marriages to women from families enjoying an equivalent status strengthen and increase the rigidity of the social-class lines since marriage is one of the principal methods by which women advance their status. The daughters of men from the lower levels may then face impossible barriers to their upward advancement. The children of men who married women of their own high rank would have to go outside the intimate bonds of their families and beyond their circle of highly placed friends to experience what those from other social and economic levels are as social beings. They would learn to recognize all people of lower ranks as outsiders.

But, should the men of the business elite who are born to fathers of similar status choose wives from the lower ranks, the effect on the status system would be to help keep it loose and flexible. Their children would be socially nearer those of lower station; distance being reduced, the relations of the family to the larger American community would be very much different from those where the women are of the same high level as the husbands.

To learn about the crucial matter of marriage for the upward mobile male or his non-mobile competitor in the business elite, we asked each of them to tell us the occupation of his wife's father (see p. 3 in the questionnaire, which is reproduced on p. 244 of this volume). It would have advanced our understanding to learn the occupational status of the *father* of the wife's father and thus to match by generation the occupational information we had about her husband. Preliminary inquiry led us to believe that such information derived from a questionnaire sent to her husband might be unreliable.

Virtually all these men married during their careers. The percentage of the businessmen studied who listed their wife's father's occupation was 92.9; since some did not answer the question, less than 7 per cent

The Marriages of the American Business Elite

of these men remained unmarried. What were the occupational backgrounds of the wives of the business elite?

Half (51 per cent) of the wives were from business and professional backgrounds (see Table 104), as compared with 55 per cent of the business leaders from these backgrounds. At the other extreme, 17 per cent of the wives came from the laboring class, whereas 15 per cent of the business leaders originated at this level. Fifteen per cent had farm backgrounds compared with only 9 per cent of the business leaders. The column at the far right of Table 104 gives a further breakdown of the occupational categories showing that the laborers were largely skilled, that those in the white-collar category were principally salesmen rather than clerks, and that the farmers were owners and managers rather than workers or tenants.

A question arises as to how the men who originated from the differing levels married. Did the sons of laborers marry the daughters of

Table 104. Occupations of the Business Leaders' Fathers and Occupations of the Wives' Fathers

Occupation (8 Groupings)	Father	Wife's Father	Occupation (19 Groupings)	Wife's Father
Laborer	15%	17%	Unskilled or semiskilled laborer	5%
			Skilled laborer	12
White-collar worker..	8	7	Clerk or retail salesman	2
			Salesman	5
Minor executive	11	7	Foreman	2
			Minor executive	5
Major executive	15	8	Major executive	8
Business owner	26	28	Owner of small business	18
			Owner of medium business	8
			Owner of large business	2
Professional man	14	15	Doctor	4
			Engineer	2
			Lawyer	4
			Minister	2
			Other professional man	3
Farmer	9	15	Farm worker or tenant	1
			Farm owner or manager	14
Other	2	3	Military career	1
			Government service	2
Total	100	100	Total	100

laborers? And did the daughters and sons of white-collar men tend to marry within their own level or above themselves? Table 105, on occupational mobility and marriage, is arranged to aid in answering these and similar questions. The column to the left gives the wife's father's occupation. The other columns list the occupation of the husband's father. The percentages indicate to what extent the members of the elite, according to their backgrounds, marry into different levels.

All men of the elite tend to marry a higher proportion of women from the levels of their origin than from any other level, but men from every level, whether their fathers were from the business elite or laborers or farmers, marry women from all other levels in sizable percentages (see Tables 105 and 106). Both exogamy and endogamy operate and are vital factors in determining occupational succession. Men and women marry above and below themselves, but they mate more often with those from contiguous classes than with those at a greater distance.

The sons of fathers from the business elite were second (35 per cent) only to the sons of laborers (42 per cent) in marrying women from their own occupational origins (Table 105). The men of the business elite whose fathers were in the white-collar level married less within their own group (19 per cent) than those from all other origins. This is in conformity with most of their other activities, for they tend to be less contained than other groups. They are more likely than any other class, except laborers themselves, to marry the daughters of

Table 105. Occupational Mobility and Marriage: Occupation of Wives' Fathers by Occupation of 1952 Business Leaders' Fathers

Occupation of Wife's Father	Laborer	White-Collar Worker	Owner of Small Business	Major Executive or Owner of Large Business	Professional Man	Farmer
Laborer	42%	18%	16%	7%	9%	17%
White-collar worker	12	19	15	14	12	11
Owner of small business	15	18	26	16	20	16
Major executive or owner of large business	6	16	14	35	23	7
Professional man	8	14	14	19	23	15
Farmer	17	15	15	9	13	34
Total	100	100	100	100	100	100

The Marriages of the American Business Elite

laborers. They marry into each of the other levels with almost the same frequency as they do at their own level. Their marriages range from 19 per cent within their own class, through 18 per cent to the daughters of laborers and small business owners, down to 14 per cent to daughters of professional men.

Those who come from the laboring, farming, and business elite classes seem to respond most noticeably to status factors and to the influences of fathers' occupations. The following comparisons make this clear. These three groups led all others in the proportion of those who married at their own levels (42 per cent of laborers, 35 per cent of the elite, and 34 per cent of farmers); the laborers' and farmers' sons married the daughters of business executives in smaller proportions than any other occupational category, the first with but 6 per cent, the latter, 7 per cent. Only 7 per cent of the sons of businessmen married daughters of laborers, and 9 per cent married daughters of farmers, a sizable proportion of whom were of the well-to-do and gentleman-farmer class. When the sons of businessmen married out of their own occupational group, they married the daughters of professional men (lawyers, doctors, ministers, and teachers) — women of their own social level — or the daughters of small business men or white-collar workers, in that order. Such marriage percentages seem to be moderately accurate measurements of the social distance existing between the business elite and other occupational groups.

Certain other observations are worthy of closer examination. For in-

Table 106. Occupational Mobility and Marriage: Ratio of Marriage by Occupations of Business Leaders' Fathers to Marriage Unrelated to Occupational Origins of Wives

Occupation of Wife's Father	Occupation of Leader's Father					
	Laborer	White-Collar Worker	Owner of Small Business	Major Executive or Owner of Large Business	Professional Man	Farmer
Laborer	2.44	1.47	0.93	0.39	0.54	0.98
White-collar worker ...	0.87	1.32	1.08	1.00	0.79	0.73
Owner of small business	0.81	0.95	1.38	0.89	1.05	0.87
Major executive or owner of large business.	0.30	0.86	0.73	1.84	1.21	0.39
Professional man	0.49	0.89	0.90	1.20	1.51	0.97
Farmer	1.11	1.01	0.98	0.57	0.87	2.23

stance, the sons of laborers, showing the most endogamy, marry women from the same occupational group more than they do all others.

Perhaps an examination of the ratios (Table 106) is now in order. The survey of the percentages has indicated the general arrangement of in-marriages and out-marriages in the several occupational classes. The ratios provide a more precise statement of the actualities. Laborers, farmers, and the business elite still lead in amount of endogamy, but it will be seen that farmers (2.23) now lead the elite (1.84). The sons of small business owners and white-collar workers show the greatest amount of out-marriage, the white-collar sons marrying proportionately more daughters of laborers than women of their own occupational level. An examination of the vertical column for the two occupations demonstrates that they marry women from other classes in higher proportions than do all others.

In summary, the sons of fathers who belonged to the white-collar class married women from the small business and major executive classes at or beyond the expected level (1.00). Laborers' sons married into the farmer class and farmers' sons into the laboring and professional classes at a relatively high level of frequency. The sons of professional men married wives whose fathers were small business men and business elite. Although in general there is a tendency to marry within the level of origin, more marry outside their occupational class than within.

Another way to view marriage and occupational status is to think of it in terms of the occupational career not only of the man but of the married pair. Mobile men tend to marry at or near their own birth level, and they and their wives work their way up as a family pair. Since most of them have children moderately early, their children, too, experience some of the vicissitudes of climbing the social and economic ladder. For example, 71 per cent of all sons of laborers married at the laborer, white-collar, and farmer levels; 62 per cent of farmers' sons married at these three levels; and so did 52 per cent of the sons of white-collar men (see Table 105).

A re-categorization of the several occupational classes into but four types (see Table 107) brings the problem into more general focus. Laborers' sons marry farmers' daughters more than would be expected; the sons of white-collar workers (combined with small business men) marry the daughters of laborers and farmers at about the ex-

The Marriages of the American Business Elite

Table 107. Occupational Mobility and Marriage: Ratios for Four
Categories of Occupation

Occupation of Wife's Father	Occupation of Business Leader's Father			
	Laborer	White-Collar Worker or Owner of Small Business	Major Executive, Owner of Large Business, or Professional Man	Farmer
Laborer	2.44	0.98	0.45	0.98
White-collar worker or owner of small business ...	0.84	1.18	0.94	0.81
Major executive, owner of large business, or professional man	0.39	0.84	1.47	0.65
Farmer	1.11	0.99	0.68	2.23

pected level (0.98 and 0.99); farmers' sons marry laborers' daughters
near the expected level; only the elite do not marry women from any
class outside their own at or above the expected level. They do marry
the daughters of white-collar workers and small business men in considerable numbers (0.94).

In brief, mobile men from the several occupational classes more
often than not marry women from their own or adjacent classes. Men
of the birth elite do the same thing. But the members of each group
marry the sisters and daughters of the others in sufficient proportion
to maintain flexibility and fluidity in an open class system.

The Influence of Three Generations on Marriage

The problem, however, needs further examination. Until now we
have considered only two generations. We know about the marriages
of business leaders in relation to fathers' occupations only. What we
do not know is whether the sons of men whose fathers also belonged
to the business elite (the father's father) show the same evidence of
endogamy and exogamy. Do they marry out more or less? Do mobile
men whose paternal grandfathers were at the bottom show less tendency to marry up than those who had only fathers there? We need to
know about the effect of three generations on the marriage of the contemporary business leaders to be sure how descent and family influence marriage choices of both the birth elite and the mobile elite.
Table 108 shows what happens when the paternal grandfather was a

Table 108. Occupational Mobility in Three Generations and Marriage

Occupation of Wife's Father	Occupation of Business Leader's Father			
	Laborer	White-Collar Worker or Owner of Small Business	Major Executive, Owner of Large Business, or Professional Man	Farmer
Occupation of Paternal Grandfather: Laborer				
Laborer	54%	31%	23%	28%
White-collar worker or owner of small business..	26	39	30	25
Major executive, owner of large business, or professional man	11	20	39	19
Farmer	9	10	8	28
Total	100	100	100	100
Occupation of Paternal Grandfather: White-Collar Worker or Owner of Small Business				
Laborer	35	13	6	16
White-collar worker or owner of small business.	38	46	42	44
Major executive, owner of large business, or professional man	19	30	46	16
Farmer	8	11	6	24
Total	100	100	100	100
Occupation of Paternal Grandfather: Major Executive, Owner of Large Business, or Professional Man				
Laborer	36	9	4	8
White-collar worker or owner of small business..	38	41	27	28
Major executive, owner of large business, or professional man	24	40	61	47
Farmer	2	10	8	17
Total	100	100	100	100
Occupation of Paternal Grandfather: Farmer				
Laborer	28	16	9	17
White-collar worker or owner of small business..	23	31	28	25
Major executive, owner of large business, or professional man	13	27	44	21
Farmer	36	26	19	37
Total	100	100	100	100

The Marriages of the American Business Elite

laborer, when he belonged to the white-collar class or was a small business man, when he belonged to the business elite or professional class, and when he was a farmer. It is arranged according to the previous tables in the chapter.

Perhaps a review of these changes will prove helpful in enabling us to understand the influence of high- and low-status ancestry on the marriage of the business elite and how such influences operate. When the fathers' fathers were laborers, 54 per cent of the elite whose fathers were also laborers married women of this level and only 11 per cent married women from the elite. But if the father came from the laborer's level to white-collar work or small business, the percentage marrying into the elite almost doubles (20 per cent). Should the father have risen to the top level, 39 per cent — or almost double the previous figure — marry women of upper status.

This same type of analysis should be applied to the data for leaders whose paternal grandfathers started a notch above the laboring level. Thirty per cent of those with two generations of white-collar work and small-owner background married women from the top level, that is, 10 per cent more than sons of white-collar fathers and laborer grandfathers. The figure rises to 46 per cent for men whose fathers had risen from white-collar work or small business to large business and professional work.

When the father and father's father were top-level business or professional men, 61 per cent (almost two thirds) married at this same high level, only 4 per cent married the daughters of laborers, and 8 per cent married the daughters of farmers. Slightly more than a fourth married small business men's daughters or those from the white-collar class.

If the fathers had lost high position and dropped to the laboring class, the percentage of marriages at the highest level dropped to about a fourth (24 per cent). The sons of men who had dropped to the laboring class married up in far greater proportions than the sons of men whose fathers had been of that class. A comparison of the leaders whose fathers' fathers were major executives, etc., with leaders whose fathers' fathers were laborers shows that, whereas only 26 per cent whose father and grandfather were both laborers married into the white-collar group, 38 per cent did when the grandfathers belonged to the elite and over twice as many married back into the elite.

Occupational Mobility

The son of a small business man or white-collar worker who had dropped from the executive or professional class was most likely to marry a woman of his father's class (41 per cent) or a daughter of the top level (40 per cent). If a man's paternal grandfather was also a white-collar worker the figure went up to 46 per cent for marriage with a girl from the small business or white-collar group and dropped to but 30 per cent for marriage at the top level.

In general, if the paternal grandfather was of high status, the effect is to increase the likelihood of the grandson's marrying higher than he would if the paternal grandfather had been of low status. As the status of the grandfather rises, the marriage of the son's son is likely to be higher, and fewer marriages take place with women of laboring class origins.

Three generations of endogamy and the percentage of those who practice it are presented in Table 109. As we have seen, 61 per cent of those whose fathers and fathers' fathers were big business and professional men marry women whose fathers were also big business men or in professions. Those men of the elite coming from two generations of laborers are next most likely to marry women of the class of their origin. The white-collar men are least likely to marry at their own class level.

The Men Ambitious Women Marry

The problem of marriage at the different occupational levels has been examined on the basis of the proportions of men from the sev-

Table 109. Endogamy over Three Generations

Occupation of Father's Father	Occupation of Father	Occupation of Wife's Father	Percentage of Intermarriage to Total Possible
Laborer	Laborer	Laborer	54
White-collar worker	White-collar worker	White-collar worker	24
Owner of small business	Owner of small business	Owner of small business	37
Major executive or owner of large business	Major executive or owner of large business	Major executive or owner of large business	48
Professional man	Professional man	Professional man	31
Farmer	Farmer	Farmer	37
Big business and professional man	Big business and professional man	Big business and professional man	61

eral economic backgrounds marrying women of the same or different backgrounds. We have also learned how the factor of the preceding generations in the male line affected the choice of mate by these men. The wives of the men in our study are accorded a status equivalent to that of their husbands, not only economically but socially. Essentially, it is the wife who translates the *economic* success of the member of the business elite into *social* success. As the mother of his children, she is responsible for training the children to be *successful* members of *superior* social levels and to take their places as adequate members of this society.

Our analysis has already indicated that the wives come from all economic levels. Despite the seeming spread across all walks of life, these women, like their husbands, are a very select elite group. Many of them have used marriage, the oldest and most acceptable way available to women, to advance themselves to the top levels of American society. They, like their husbands, were economically and socially ambitious. Marriage was their way to success. They often married position. Others, equally ambitious, married men with "good prospects," and were pulled from economic and social obscurity into the elite. Many of them became active partners in the exciting game of improving the family fortunes and played positive and aggressive roles in their husbands' mobility.

Are the marriages of these women different in pattern from those of the men, or the same? Do women of top status tend to marry fewer men from lower levels than from the top level? Do the daughters of laborers more often marry up than the sons of these men? Do women in the white-collar and small business levels marry men who are above rather than below them? These are questions which the tables and discussion in this section will attempt to answer.

It will be noted that Table 110 gives the percentages of women from the several economic backgrounds who marry husbands with these same origins. Forty-four per cent of the daughters of the elite married men who were also born to this position. Sixty-two per cent born to this position married either at this level or into the professional class. Women who have inherited their position in the elite overwhelmingly marry men who by right of birth also occupy this top level. Although those from the professional classes score lower than any other group, except the farmers, for endogamy (22 per cent), actually this presents a distorted picture for they tend to marry *across* into the business elite and *within* the same social level. Twenty-nine per cent marry the sons of the business elite, making a total of 51 per cent who marry men born to the top levels. An examination of these same columns shows that neither group of women marries to any extent into the bottom level: only 5 per cent from the business elite and 7 per cent from the professional level. Such marriages usually mean that the men have already advanced themselves to higher levels.

The daughters of laborers who are now the wives of business leaders married men from the same origins more than from any other level (37 per cent), the second largest percentage in the table. This indicates that a sizable proportion, over a third, of such women share a mobile career from the bottom to the top with their husbands. The daughters of white-collar workers and small business men marry less within their own levels than do those from the laboring and top business classes. The daughters of farmers more often marry men from the lower levels than from higher ones (see the last column on the right).

The question now arises, how do these percentages of female marriages compare with those of the males? Do the daughters of laborers marry more often above or at their own levels? To find the answers we will compare Tables 106 and 111. Although these women marry up and out of their own levels more than the men do, the differences

Table 110. Marriage and Occupation: Occupation of 1952 Business Leaders' Fathers by Occupation of Wives' Fathers

Occupation of Fathers of 1952 Business Leaders	Occupation of Fathers of Wives of 1952 Business Leaders					
	Laborer	White-Collar Worker	Owner of Small Business	Major Executive or Owner of Large Business	Professional Man	Farmer
Laborer	37%	13%	12%	5%	7%	17%
White-collar worker ..	20	25	19	17	17	19
Owner of small business	17	19	25	13	16	17
Major executive or owner of large business	9	24	21	44	29	14
Professional man	8	12	15	18	22	13
Farmer	9	7	8	3	9	20
Total	100	100	100	100	100	100

The Marriages of the American Business Elite

Table 111. Marriage and Occupation: Ratio of Marriage by Wife's Father's Occupation to Marriage Unrelated to Occupational Origins of Business Leaders

Occupation of Fathers of 1952 Leaders	Occupation of Fathers of Wives of 1952 Leaders					
	Laborer	White-Collar Worker	Owner of Small Business	Major Executive or Owner of Large Business	Professional Man	Farmer
Laborer	2.45	0.87	0.82	0.30	0.49	1.11
White-collar worker ...	1.03	1.32	0.96	0.87	0.89	1.01
Owner of small business	0.93	1.02	1.69	0.73	0.91	0.98
Major executive or owner of large business.	0.40	1.00	0.88	1.84	1.20	0.57
Professional man	0.60	0.79	1.05	1.21	1.50	0.88
Farmer	0.98	0.73	0.87	0.38	0.97	2.21

are not great. The daughters of laborers marry into the business elite and professional classes as well as into the white-collar and small business classes in slightly larger proportions than do the sons of laborers. If we compare Tables 106 and 111, we see that while the sons of white-collar men marry down more often than the daughters do, the latter marry up more often than the sons. The daughters of small business men marry at their own level more than do the sons (1.69 to 1.38). They marry down less frequently and up more often. The sons and daughters of men of the business elite choose mates from their own levels in exactly the same proportions (1.84 for each). The men marry in the laboring class somewhat more than the women. In general there is slightly more tendency for women from the lower levels to marry above and less tendency to marry beneath themselves than for the men.

Education, Marriage, and Occupational Mobility

Previous discussion has clearly established the important role of education for the advancement of men into high position in the business world. Men born to high status tend to be college educated; men born to lower levels are likely to be college trained and to use this training as an important factor in their mobile careers. We now know that many men and women of low or moderate status marry at their own level and advance with their mates to higher levels; a large percentage of those of higher status marry at their own levels, and a smaller but important group marry down. How does education fit into

189

Occupational Mobility

this pattern of marriage? Do educated men marry higher more often than their less educated competitors? Do men of the elite who are of low educational attainment marry women from the lower occupational categories? In brief, how does a man's education affect his choice of a mate? Or perchance his being chosen?

Table 112 helps answer some of these questions. Men with college education married the daughters of the business elite more than they did the daughters at any other level (23 per cent), and they did so in larger percentage than did high school graduates (16 per cent) or those who had not graduated from high school (10 per cent). They married the daughters of laborers less than those at any other occupational level (12 per cent). Those men who did not graduate from high school married the daughters of laborers more than those from any other level (32 per cent). They married the daughters of professional men least frequently — only 7 out of every 100 marriages were of this type. Only 10 out of every 100 of them married daughters of business leaders.

More than twice as many college-educated men (42 per cent) as those with low educational attainment (17 per cent) married women of superior status. College-trained men are less likely to marry daughters of farmers (13 per cent) than less well educated men (18 per cent).

In summary, college-educated men are more likely than those with less education to marry women of higher levels. But perhaps education may affect the mating of men of different status quite differently. Table 113 tells us what kinds of marriages men of six occupational backgrounds made in terms of their educational achievement.

Do the sons of laborers, when they are college trained, marry women of higher status in the same way as the sons of small business men

Table 112. Education and Marriage: Education of 1952 Business Leaders by Occupation of Wives' Fathers

Occupation of Wife's Father	College Graduation	Some College or High School Graduation	Less Than High School Graduation
Laborer	12%	22%	32%
White-collar worker	15	14	14
Owner of small business	18	19	19
Major executive or owner of large business..	23	16	10
Professional man	19	11	7
Farmer	13	18	18
Total	100	100	100

The Marriages of the American Business Elite

who are also college trained? Are men who have risen from the level of laborers and who did not finish high school more likely to marry at their own or at higher levels than men of the same educational background but higher social status? Fully a third of the college-trained sons of laborers married daughters of laborers (34 per cent), double the next highest number at any other occupational level. They married the daughters of big business men less than those of all other levels (9 per cent). On first inspection, it would look as if education influenced them to marry within the class of their origin. A compari-

Table 113. Occupational Mobility, Education, and Marriage: Occupation of Wives' Fathers by Occupation of Fathers and Education of 1952 Business Leaders

Occupation of Wife's Father	Education of Leaders			All Leaders
	College Graduation	High School Graduation or Some College	Less Than High School Graduation	
Occupation of Father: Laborer				
Laborer	34%	41%	54%	42%
White-collar worker ...	16	11	11	12
Owner of small business.	14	17	13	15
Major executive or owner of large business	9	4	6	6
Professional man	10	7	4	8
Farmer	17	20	12	17
Total	100	100	100	100
Occupation of Father: White-Collar Worker				
Laborer	14	21	22	18
White-collar worker ...	18	21	18	19
Owner of small business.	17	19	19	18
Major executive or owner of large business	21	11	12	16
Professional man	16	12	10	14
Farmer	14	16	19	15
Total	100	100	100	100
Occupation of Father: Owner of Small Business				
Laborer	11	21	24	16
White-collar worker ...	16	15	13	15
Owner of small business.	24	25	34	26
Major executive or owner of large business	16	14	7	14
Professional man	18	9	6	14
Farmer	15	16	16	15
Total	100	100	100	100

Occupational Mobility

Table 113 *Continued*

Occupation of Wife's Father	Education of Leaders			All Leaders
	College Graduation	High School Graduation or Some College	Less Than High School Graduation	
Occupation of Father: Major Executive or Owner of Large Business				
Laborer	5	9	16	7
White-collar worker ...	14	14	19	14
Owner of small business.	16	18	21	16
Major executive or owner of large business	37	31	23	35
Professional man	21	14	6	19
Farmer	7	14	15	9
Total	100	100	100	100
Occupation of Father: Farmer				
Laborer	13	22	19	17
White-collar worker ...	12	11	5	11
Owner of small business.	20	10	14	16
Major executive or owner of large business	7	8	6	7
Professional man	20	11	6	15
Farmer	28	38	50	34
Total	100	100	100	100
Occupation of Father: Professional Man				
Laborer	8	13	16	9
White-collar worker ...	10	12	23	12
Owner of small business.	20	20	9	20
Major executive or owner of large business	22	27	19	23
Professional man	27	13	16	23
Farmer	13	15	17	13
Total	100	100	100	100

son of how they married with the marriages of the less well educated modifies this first impression. Forty-one per cent of high school graduates and 54 per cent of those who did not get that far married the daughters of laborers. On the other hand, only 4 per cent of the high school graduates and 6 per cent of those with less education married daughters of business leaders. College education decreases the likelihood that such men will marry at the level of their origin and increases the chance they will marry at higher levels.

The Marriages of the American Business Elite

Men who came from the white-collar class and achieved a college education married women from the elite more than women from any other level (21 per cent). They married daughters of farmers and laborers least (14 per cent each). But men from the white-collar class with less than a high school diploma were more likely to marry the daughters of laborers than any others (22 per cent), and those with a high school diploma married daughters of laborers (21 per cent) or those from the white-collar class (21 per cent) more than any other.

College education has a considerable effect on the choice of mates of men who have come from the white-collar class; they tend to marry up more often than do those less highly educated. Education seems to increase their chances of marrying into the elite and professional classes far more than it does the chances of the laborer: 37 per cent of the college-trained men originating from the white-collar class married daughters of the business elite or professional classes, compared with only 19 per cent of college-trained men of the laboring class. Another measurement helps to indicate the power of education: 22 per cent of the white-collar class of lower education married into the professional and business elite compared with about the same percentage (19 per cent) of men whose fathers were laborers but who had acquired a college education.

The marriages of the sons of small business men are in many ways similar to those of sons of the white-collar class. Thirty-four per cent of the college graduates married women from the professional and business elite categories, compared with only 13 per cent of those with less than a high school diploma. A comparison with the figures for sons of white-collar men indicates many similarities and certain differences, the principal difference being a greater tendency to marry at their own level for both college graduates and those without high school diplomas. Also, fewer college graduates here than in the white-collar group married into the business elite.

Although men born to the business elite do not show quite the extremes in their marriage behavior as the sons of laborers, the figures given in Table 113 for all three educational levels indicate that status and education play very important roles in their choice of mates. Only 7 per cent of the men born to the elite married daughters of laborers. However, education modified their behavior considerably, those with college education falling below the average (5 per cent married daughters of laborers), and those with less than a high school diploma going up to 16 per cent. At the other extreme, 35 per cent of all these men married women from their own level, but only 23 per cent of those who had not graduated from high school married women of this class, compared with 37 per cent of those who had graduated from college. The full effect of the educational factor becomes apparent in the figures for marriage to daughters of the professional class. The average of all marriages of the sons of the business elite into this class was 19 per cent, but only 6 per cent of those with less than a high school diploma married into this class, compared with 21 per cent of college graduates. Fifty-four per cent of all the marriages of the sons of the elite were to the daughters of the business and professional elites combined: 29 per cent of the least educated men and 58 per cent of those who had graduated from college made this type of marriage. College education reduces the likelihood of the marriage of these men to farmers' daughters — only 7 per cent of the college men compared with 15 per cent of those with only high school training.

In general, Table 113 indicates, the college-educated sons of professional men were more likely than those with less education to marry at their own level or to marry the daughters of business leaders. The principal exception to this was the greater percentage of high school graduates (27 per cent) than of college graduates (22 per cent) who married daughters of big business men.

Thirty-four per cent of the sons of farmers married within their own class, twice as many as married into any other class. But only 28 per cent of the college graduates in this group married women from their own occupational class, compared with 50 per cent of those who had not graduated from high school. Although education has little or no effect on the number of these men who marry into the business elite, it does affect marriage to daughters of the professional classes: 6 per cent of those with the lowest education and 20 per cent of those who graduated from college married daughters of professional men.

Higher education, particularly college, tends to lift the level of marriage from lower occupational levels and to increase the likelihood of those of higher levels marrying within their own class. Therefore, college education has, paradoxically, a double effect, the two tendencies opposing each other. On the one hand, it increases the likelihood of the complete social acceptance (marriage) of those from lower levels, but

The Marriages of the American Business Elite

Table 114. Education and Marriage of Business Leaders When Both Father and Father's Father Were Major Executives, Owners of Large Businesses, or Professional Men

Occupation of Wife's Father	Education of Business Leader		
	College Graduation	High School Graduation or Some College	Less Than High School Graduation *
Laborer	2	9	13
White-collar worker or owner of small business	27	27	38
Major executive, owner of large business, or professional man ..	64	53	39
Farmer	7	11	10
Total	100	100	100

* N = less than 100.

for those born to high position it tends to strengthen status discriminations in the choice of a mate. Table 114 sharpens the focus in the problem of status and marriage. It includes only men whose fathers and paternal grandfathers were in the professional and business elites. Almost two thirds (64 per cent) of all the marriages of this birth elite are with women from the same high position and only 2 per cent with the daughters of laborers. On the other hand, those with low educational training married women of the white-collar and small business classes (38 per cent) in almost the same proportion as they did women from their own levels (39 per cent). College-trained men married women of this class in considerable numbers but with less than half the frequency (27 per cent) with which they married women of their own level. Men of low education were six and a half times more likely than college men to marry daughters of laborers.

A glance back at the two tables on the relation of status, education, and marriage brings out the basic role of the high school, which seems to be intermediate between the two extremes of education. There are fewer large and small percentages; the differences, for the high school graduates, among the proportions of those who marry at the various levels are usually smaller than for those with less than a high school diploma or for the college graduates. Generally more college men marry up and fewer down, and more who are less than high school graduates marry down and fewer up, than those who have graduated from high school or had a year or so of college.

195

Occupational Mobility

With the exception of Table 114, the previous analysis of the effect of education, particularly college, on the marriages of the men of the business elite carried the reckoning of a man's socioeconomic heritage back one generation. It considered only the father's occupation. Previous studies have indicated that the differential effects of recent arrival to high position or the long time occupancy of such a position by a family and its descendants have a considerable consequence in the lives of the members because of the choices they make and the values they place on objects and people.

For a better understanding of such matters as they apply to the business elite, particularly the effect of college education on marriage and the family, Table 115 should be scrutinized. It shows how college education is related to the choice of a mate. A glance across the column for college graduates with laborer backgrounds shows that college education decreased the likelihood of marrying lower and increased the chances of marrying higher. But the increase is minimal at the business leader level and only significant as part of a general configuration. On the other hand, those with less than a college education overwhelmingly married at their own level: 60 per cent of all marriages of the sons of laborers of lower education were with women of the laboring class.

The marriages of the grandsons and sons of white-collar men tell a similar story but in a different way. Those who are college graduates more often marry out of their class. They marry women from the laboring, white-collar, and small business classes less frequently and women from the business and professional elite more than do those with less education. A somewhat similar story is true for the grandsons of small business men.

For the grandsons of business leaders, the differences among them as to marriage to women of their own class in terms of college education are not great: 49 per cent for those who are college graduates, and 45 per cent for those who are not. Nor does the college factor count for much in the choice of mates from the small business and white-collar classes. There is, however, a sharp drop at the lowest level: only 2 per cent of the college graduates married the daughters of laborers, compared with 8 per cent of the others. Furthermore, even fewer married farmers' daughters (6 per cent to 11 per cent). The college-educated grandsons of the elite are more likely to marry women from the professional classes: 19 per cent compared with 12 per cent of the others.

A glance at the figures for the grandsons of professional men tells much the same story. Those without college education are eight and a half times more likely than college men to marry the daughters of laborers. They are likely to marry the daughters of small business or large business men in about the same proportions, but there is a considerable increase in the percentage of college men who marry women of their own levels: 37 per cent, compared with only 15 per cent of those with less education.

Table 115. Occupation over Three Generations, Education, and Marriage: Occupations of Wives' Fathers by Education of Business Leaders and Occupational Origins of Business Leaders

Education of Leader	Occupation of Wife's Father						Total
	Laborer	White-Collar Worker	Owner of Small Business	Major Executive or Owner of Large Business	Professional Man	Farmer	
Occupation of Father and Father's Father: Laborer							
College graduate ..	43%	18%	14%	5%	10%	10%	100%
Other	60	11	12	4	5	8	100
Occupation of Father and Father's Father: White-Collar Worker							
College graduate * .	13	23	13	19	19	13	100
Other *	22	26	14	16	10	12	100
Occupation of Father and Father's Father: Owner of Small Business							
College graduate ..	8	15	33	15	18	11	100
Other	13	11	43	14	8	11	100
Occupation of Father and Father's Father: Major Executive or Owner of Large Business							
College graduate ..	2	15	9	49	19	6	100
Other	8	14	10	45	12	11	100
Occupation of Father and Father's Father: Professional Man							
College graduate ..	2	9	23	22	37	7	100
Other	17	13	22	23	15	10	100
Occupation of Father and Father's Father: Farmer							
College graduate ..	13	11	20	6	19	31	100
Other	21	8	11	8	9	43	100

* N = less than 100.

Occupational Mobility

The grandsons of farmers present a somewhat different picture. The college graduates marry daughters of laborers less than do the others. But college education increases the likelihood of their marrying daughters of the small business and white-collar classes. There is a decrease in the percentage of those marrying daughters of business leaders, but more than twice as many (19 per cent) as those with less education marry women from the professional class.

The Prestige and Power of Big Business and Marriage

It seems possible that other status factors are influential in determining how the men of the elite marry. Possibly men of the highest occupational position, such as chief executive, marry women of higher status more often than men of lower position — vice president or lower — in the occupational hierarchy. The twin factors of prestige and increased power might be directly or indirectly related to the choice of a mate. Or possibly the mate chosen had some effect on achievement. Since most men have married before achieving high position, the latter reason has seemed plausible.

Still another factor is the size-category of the firm; the president of Du Pont's vast empire has more prestige and power than the head of one of the companies belonging to our smallest type. Do men in large enterprises more often marry women of superior or lesser status than those who are owners or managers of lesser enterprises? We shall attempt to answer these questions.

Table 116, on marriage and business position, is divided into two sections: the first examines the marriages of men who came from laboring backgrounds, and the second the marriages of those from the top business class. The business positions have been reduced to three levels: chief executive, vice president, and those below this status, who are classed as "other."

If the father of the leader also belonged to the business elite and if the leader was a chief executive, he was far more likely to marry a woman of this background (41 per cent) than if he were a vice president (34 per cent) or below that position in the managerial hierarchy (24 per cent). He was less likely to marry the daughter of a laborer (5 per cent) or a farmer (7 per cent) than those beneath him. The same general pattern holds true for the sons of laborers in the several managerial positions. The man with a laborer background who is a

The Marriages of the American Business Elite

Table 116. Marriage and Business Position

Occupation of Wife's Father	Business Position of Leader		
	Chief Executive	Vice President	Other
Father's Occupation: Laborer			
Laborer	40	39	48
White-collar worker	10	15	10
Owner of small business	11	17	15
Major executive or owner of large business	10	5	4
Professional man	10	7	7
Farmer	19	17	16
Total	100	100	100
Father's Occupation: Major Executive or Owner of Large Business			
Laborer	5	7	9
White-collar worker	13	15	16
Owner of small business	15	17	20
Major executive or owner of large business	41	34	24
Professional man	19	17	20
Farmer	7	10	11
Total	100	100	100

chief executive is twice as likely as one who is a vice president to marry the daughter of a business leader. If he is a chief executive or vice president, he is less likely to marry the daughter of a laborer (40 per cent) than are those below the position of vice president (48 per cent). It is difficult to interpret the real significance of the figures. Most, if not all, of these men who are chief executives were married long before they attained this position. Did such marriages help them to advance or were personality or other social factors operating which influenced both choice of mate and degree of advance? Evidence from our schedule is insufficient to determine what is involved.

Table 117, on marriage and the size of the business firm the leader was in at the time of the study, is also divided into two parts, again giving the two extremes of occupational origin. In each the leaders are grouped according to the size of business (gross income per year), the column on the left giving the smallest (less than 10 million dollars), the one on the right, the largest (250 million dollars or more). With few exceptions there appears to be little or no difference among the three groups. Exactly 6 per cent of the sons of laborers in all the cate-

Occupational Mobility

Table 117. Marriage and the Size of the Leader's Business Firm
(Gross Income per Annum in Millions of Dollars)

Occupation of Wife's Father	Size of Leader's Business		
	Less Than 10	10–250	250 or More
Father's Occupation: Laborer			
Laborer	40	42	42
White-collar worker	11	12	15
Owner of small business	10	16	17
Major executive or owner of large business	6	6	6
Professional man	10	8	4
Farmer	23	16	16
Total	100	100	100
Father's Occupation: Major Executive or Owner of Large Business			
Laborer	5	8	6
White-collar worker	15	14	19
Owner of small business	17	16	17
Major executive or owner of large business	34	35	34
Professional man	20	19	15
Farmer	9	8	9
Total	100	100	100

gories of size of business married women from the business elite. They married the daughters of laborers in about the same proportion. Men in the smaller enterprises were more likely to marry daughters of farmers (23 per cent) and professional men (10 per cent) than were those in the 250-million-dollar class (16 per cent and 4 per cent). Very similar proportions hold for the sons of the business elite, most percentages signifying little or no difference among the several categories.

Table 118 combines the three job categories of the hierarchy — chief executive, vice president, and other — with the size of the enterprise, and relates these categories to the occupational origin of the wife. It inquires into the occupational origins of the wives of leaders in the several levels of power and prestige in both larger and smaller enterprises, regardless of the origin of the leader. In general, men of higher status in both position and the size of the firm tended to have wives from a higher occupational background, and those in lower status, according to rank and size of the business, tended to marry women from a lower position. For example, it will be noted that only 7 per cent of the chief executives of enterprises with an income of more

The Marriages of the American Business Elite

Table 118. The Business Hierarchy and Marriage: Occupations of Wives' Fathers by Size of Business Firm and Business Position of 1952 Leaders

Business Position and Size of Business of Leaders	Occupation of Wife's Father						Total
	Laborer	White-Collar Worker	Owner of Small Business	Major Executive or Owner of Large Business	Professional Man	Farmer	
Chief executive							
Under $50 million	11%	13%	16%	27%	18%	15%	100%
$50–$250 million.	12	12	18	27	19	12	100
Over $250 million	7	14	17	28	18	16	100
Vice president							
Under $50 million	14	17	16	20	19	14	100
$50–$250 million.	18	15	19	18	15	15	100
Over $250 million	16	16	19	17	14	18	100
Other							
Under $50 million	26	14	17	15	10	18	100
$50–$250 million.	25	15	21	11	12	16	100
Over $250 million	21	14	20	14	16	15	100

than 250 million dollars married daughters of laborers, compared with 16 per cent of vice presidents from this size of enterprise and 21 per cent of those below the latter position (see top horizontal column).

Men of the chief executive class in all categories of size of enterprise were more likely than men from the lower levels to marry daughters of the business elite. What these differences signify, as we said earlier, is very difficult to determine. Larger cultural and unstudied personality factors may influence these results. Possibly the high social and economic position of a wife who was a daughter of a business leader may help the husband climb higher into the top management levels. Such inferences need to be further scrutinized. Possibly our detailed study of the family life of a selected sample of the cases may provide the answers now sought.

The Boss's Daughter

The man who married the boss's daughter is a symbolic figure in American life. Around him surge many strong, conflicting feelings and beliefs. He is envied by many, despised by others. In a society where individual achievement is stressed, particularly economic and occupational, a man who marries place is often under attack and more often than not feels the need to defend himself. In fiction and fact, this defense takes the form of proving himself by doing his job a little better or by insisting that advancement is more difficult for him.

No one test of advantage or disadvantage is satisfactory as a measurement of what happens to a man when he marries above his class, particularly into the top levels, but a fairly reliable indicator lies in the determination of how long it took him to achieve *entrance* into the business elite from the time he became self-supporting. Table 119 is designed to supply some of the answers. If he is advantaged and promotions come rapidly, it would be expected that the time would be shorter; if he is not advantaged, or is disadvantaged, the time should be longer.

The occupation of the wife's father is in its usual place on the left; the columns to the right give the occupation of the business leader's father. The figures themselves are the means of the number of years it took for each type to reach the *first* position he had in the elite. For example, the son of a laborer who married the daughter of a laborer spent a mean of 26.1 years in achieving his first position in the elite. At the bottom of the table we find the mean for each background. It took the sons of businessmen only 21 years to achieve their leadership, compared with 26 years for the sons of laborers. The sons of profes-

Table 119. Marriage and Achievement Time: Mean Number of Years to Achieve Business Position for Leaders by Occupation of Father and Wife's Father

Occupation of Wife's Father	Occupation of Business Leader's Father					
	Laborer	White-Collar Worker	Owner of Small Business	Major Executive or Owner of Large Business	Professional Man	Farmer
Laborer	26.1	25.1	26.1	22.8	22.4*	25.7*
White-collar worker ...	25.2	25.7	25.3	20.5	24.1	24.0*
Owner of small business	26.9	26.0	25.3	21.0	22.8	25.4*
Major executive or owner of large business	25.9*	24.6	24.7	24.9	22.3	29.4*
Professional man	24.8*	24.8	22.9	20.3	21.9	24.5*
Farmer	24.8	24.9	24.7	22.7	23.4	24.5
Mean for background ..	26.0	24.9	22.6	20.8	22.5	25.1

* N = less than 100.

sional and small business men took about 23 years, and of white-collar workers and farmers, about 25. The sons of big business men are advantaged from 2 to 5 years over the others.

A comparison of these figures for each level tells a most significant story. Let us contrast laborers and the sons of big business men. The sons of the elite who married daughters of laborers took 23 years, and those who married women of their own level, 25 years, about two years longer. If there is any advantage it is in favor of out-marriage for the sons of the elite, for all other periods are shorter than for marriage at their own level. The range of time, however, is only 5 years.

The time it takes a laborer is almost exactly the same whether he marries a woman from the top or someone of his own class — 25.9 years for the former and 26.1 for the latter. Marrying the boss's daughter or someone of equivalent status does not shorten his climb to the top, nor does any other marriage seem to help. The range here is about two years. The story for each occupation is very similar to this; a narrow range of difference among all levels of marriage characterizes each. If the number of cases is reliable for generalization, the fact that it takes the sons of farmers 29.4 years to advance to the business elite when they marry women of the elite level and only 24.5 when they marry women of their own level is another indicator that marriage up does not give an advantage. Another test is to compare the difference in achievement time for all occupational levels between those who marry into the laboring class and those who marry into the big business class. For the laboring, white-collar, and professional classes, there was almost no difference: the white-collar man who married up was advantaged by a year; the sons of businessmen and farmers who married the daughters of laborers took two and three years less than those who married into the business elite.

Clearly, if there are any advantages in the shortening of time, they do not lie with the man who marries the boss's daughter or someone in the superior economic group. What gains such marriages bring lie in the *social* rather than in the economic area. These men seem to advance on their merit or through *social* advantages which are part of the total business situation. American businessmen "do not get places" in business by upward marriage; they get there by "doing things."

Occupational Mobility

Careers of the Business Leaders' Sons

It would be extremely helpful, for predictive purposes and for an understanding of how the flow of the past moves through the present and into future generations, to learn about the careers of the sons of the men in the elite. To provide this information we asked each leader the following question:

What career has he (they) entered? If more than one son is self-supporting, please enter the number in each career.

Not entered a career as yet...................... ————
Business owner or partner......................... ————
Businessman (not owner or partner)............... ————
Profession .... ————
Military career.................................. ————
Government service............................... ————
Other (please specify)........................... ————

Table 120, on the careers of the sons of the present leaders, gives the evidence this question evoked. Unfortunately, it can tell us only in very broad terms what we need to know. The answers are not yet recorded in the careers of these young men. Either they are too young to have started earning a living or their careers are not sufficiently advanced to indicate the outcomes. At all levels, whether the occupations of the business leader's father and the wife's (mother of the boy) father were high or low, the sons are pursuing business or professional careers. Obviously most of them are directly or indirectly following in the general paths set by their fathers rather than in those set by their paternal and maternal grandfathers. It seems likely that the next generation will continue in the same general style as the fathers. If the trend to more flexibility holds, fewer will achieve business leadership; if the system becomes tighter, more will stay at the top.

Geographic Origin and Marriage

It is commonly assumed that the ethnic members of American society are at a disadvantage. Previous sections of this volume show that, generally speaking, the ethnic competitor of the old American does exceedingly well and often excels men whose fathers have been here for many generations. Perhaps the most crucial test of how much ethnic status interferes with those ambitious ones who seek high status in the larger American society is to be made by examining the kind

The Marriages of the American Business Elite

Table 120. Careers of Sons of Business Leaders in Relation to Occupations of Sons'
Paternal and Maternal Grandfathers

Occupation of Wife's Father	Career of Son						Total
	Business Owner or Partner	Businessman (Not Owner or Partner)	Professional Man	Military Career	Government Service	Other	
Occupation of Father: Laborer							
Laborer	7%	43%	40%	8%	2%	0%	100%
White-collar worker or small business man ..	8	42	33	9	3	5	100
Big business man or professional man ..	15	36	34	6	5	4	100
Farmer	12	38	40	6	0	4	100
Occupation of Father: White-Collar Worker or Owner of Small Business							
Laborer	10	44	37	6	2	1	100
White-collar worker or small business man ..	12	41	35	8	3	1	100
Big business man or professional man ..	14	44	28	8	3	3	100
Farmer	14	42	34	4	3	3	100
Occupation of Father: Major Executive, Owner of Large Business, or Professional Man							
Laborer	10	42	34	6	4	4	100
White-collar worker or small business man ..	16	46	26	7	1	4	100
Big business man or professional man ..	13	49	28	6	1	3	100
Farmer	17	45	23	10	2	3	100
Occupation of Father: Farmer							
Laborer	20	32	34	12	2	0	100
White-collar worker or small business man ..	12	41	32	8	4	3	100
Big business man or professional man ..	23	46	23	2	4	2	100
Farmer	14	38	39	6	2	1	100

of women they marry and by comparing the results with those for old Americans. Table 121, on nativity and marriage, helps answer this important question. The occupational origin of the wife is listed in its usual place on the left, and the nativity of the business leader to the right of it. From these one can learn about the marriages of the mem-

Occupational Mobility

bers of the elite who were foreign-born ("business leader foreign-born"), who were born in the United States of foreign parentage ("business leader U.S.-born"), or whose father and father's father were U.S.-born.

Table 121. Nativity and Marriage of Business Leader

Occupation of Wife's Father	Father's Father U.S.-Born	Father U.S.-Born	Business Leader U.S.-Born	Business Leader Foreign-Born	Total
Laborer	12%	20%	26%	22%	17%
White-collar worker ...	15	15	14	14	14
Owner of small business	17	19	21	23	19
Major executive or owner of large business	21	20	14	14	19
Professional man	18	14	11	11	16
Farmer	17	12	14	16	15
Total	100	100	100	100	100

In general those men whose grandfathers and fathers were American-born tend more to marry women from the higher levels and less to marry those from the lower levels than the men who were foreign-born or first-generation Americans. For example, 26 per cent and 22 per cent of those who were either first-generation Americans or foreign-born married the daughters of laborers, only 14 per cent of each married daughters of business leaders, and only 11 per cent of each married women from the professional classes. One fifth of the men (21 per cent) with paternal grandfathers born in the United States and 20 per cent of those with fathers born here married women of the elite. Eighteen per cent of those with paternal grandfathers born here married women from the professional classes, and only 12 per cent married daughters of laborers. The business leaders who were foreign-born and those born here whose fathers were foreign-born married the daughters of small business men more often than did old Americans.

In general, a comparison with the percentage for the total shows that while old Americans are advantaged the differences are not drastic and do not indicate that ethnic status is necessarily a deterrent to marriage at any higher levels.

The problem of in-marriage and out-marriage among the occupational groups may be viewed territorially in terms of the region of origin and the size of the birthplace. Any such reckoning has its difficulties, since the family of origin might have moved early from a small to a large city or from one region to another. However, inspection of the returns indicates that a considerable reliance can be placed on the data about birthplace as the environment which was most likely to have been of greatest influence in the formative years. Furthermore, a considerable number are still in the region of origin, and of course those born in cities are most likely to have had their careers in similar communities.

Let us first ask whether there are differences in the marriages of the men from the several regions. Do more men in New England and the Deep South, for example, marry at their own levels than do those in the Mountain states? Many believe that this is so. The table on endogamy and geographic origins, Table 122, supplies us with some of the evidence. The column on the left listing the occupational levels is for marriages to women with the same occupational backgrounds. The columns following give the percentages for each of the nine regions for endogamic marriage in each occupation. (Since this table accounts only for in-marriage, the percentages are not supposed to add to a hundred.) At the bottom of each column is given the mean of occupational endogamy for the region. The averages for each occupational background are listed in the far right-hand column.

The average for all occupations and all regions for the whole country is 29 per cent, or about three marriages out of every ten. There is more *out-marriage* in the Far West, including the Mountain and Pacific Coast regions, than elsewhere in the United States. There is a greater tendency in the East, including New England and the Middle and South Atlantic regions, for men to marry within their occupational group than there is in the other regions (about a third of the marriages).

The combination of regional and occupational endogamy shows several patterns of behavior that are not easily interpreted. The mean percentage for in-marriage of farmers is about 34 per cent for the whole country, the mean for all in-marriages in the Mountain states is 23 per cent, yet 55 per cent of all the marriages of the business elite in the Mountain states who came from the farmer class were with women from that background. But in that same region only 6 per cent of the men from white-collar backgrounds married women from the

Table 122. Endogamy and Geographic Origins

Occupation of Father and Wife's Father (the Same)	New England	Middle Atlantic	East North Central	West North Central	South Atlantic	East South Central	West South Central	Mountain	Pacific	Occupational Endogamy
Laborer	53%	46%	41%	35%	42%	33%	25%	16%	33%	42%
White-collar worker	13	16	19	17	21	17	21	6	17	19
Owner of small business	23	32	24	22	26	27	24	13	20	26
Major executive or owner of large business	37	39	31	33	37	37	32	34	28	35
Professional man	29	26	16	20	31	13	32	24	29	23
Farmer	16	28	30	34	35	48	40	55	22	34
Regional endogamy	31	31	27	27	32	29	29	23	25	29

The Marriages of the American Business Elite

same backgrounds, compared with 19 per cent for the country; and 13 per cent of the marriages of sons of small business men took place within that group, compared with 26 per cent for the whole country. Perhaps the clue lies in a comparison between the two contiguous regions which rank first in out-marriages, the Pacific and the Mountain.

Only 22 per cent of Pacific Coast men of the elite who came from farms married farming women. Why the difference between the two regions? It seems possible that the nature of farming in the two regions and of the culture surrounding farm life are partly responsible. A large percentage of the sons of farmers on the Pacific Coast came from small farms which are often as urban as they are rural, the sons and daughters going to urban schools where children of all levels grow up together. Farmers' children are likely to be far less isolated on the Coast than in the Mountain states where large ranch and rural life are accentuated. The other occupations (largely urban) of the Mountain region approach the mean for the country or fall far below it, indicating at least for some that status factors operate *less* there than elsewhere in the choice of a mate.

The mean percentage for endogamy in the labor group is 42 per cent for the whole country. Only two regions are above it: New England (53 per cent) and the Middle Atlantic (46 per cent). The Mountain states rank last (16 per cent). Throughout the United States the mean percentage for in-marriage of the big business group was 35 per cent, second only to labor. Four regions were above it: the Middle Atlantic (39 per cent), and New England, the South Atlantic, and the East South Central (each 37 per cent). The Pacific Coast ranked last (28 per cent).

Many other comparisons can be made. We will content ourselves with one. As we said, the mean for endogamy of the farm group for the United States was 34. Four regions were above it: the Mountain states (55 per cent), the East South Central (48 per cent), the West South Central (40 per cent), and the South Atlantic (35 per cent). In general, those states have large numbers of farmers who are culturally and physically isolated. The lowest percentages for endogamy among farmers came from the two extreme regions of America, New England (16 per cent) and the Pacific Coast (22 per cent). Each has a farming class that is closely interrelated with city and town life.

Occupational Mobility

The Size of the Community

The man who goes to college must usually leave home. Since a large proportion of the business elite are college men, many of them will have at least two social spheres, in addition to the one at the job, where they may meet the women they will marry — the home town and the college campus. Those with less than a college education are more likely to be confined to home-town girls, the office, or the social

Table 123. Marriage and the Size of the Business Leader's Birthplace

Occupation of Wife's Father	Size of Birthplace			All Sizes
	Over 100,000	2500 to 100,000	Under 2500	
Laborer	18%	16%	16%	17%
White-collar worker	16	15	12	14
Owner of small business	18	19	19	19
Major executive or owner of large business	23	21	11	19
Professional man	16	16	15	16
Farmer	9	13	27	15
Total	100	100	100	100

worlds surrounding their jobs. Table 123 implicitly reflects these factors. It lists the birthplace by three sizes of community, from metropolitan to rural, and presents the percentages of marriage to women of the different occupational backgrounds. There is little or no difference in the percentage of marriage to laborers' daughters among the three types of community of origin; the same holds true for marriage into the professional, white-collar, and small business classes. The real differences are in marriages to daughters of farmers and big business men. Business leaders are about twice as likely to marry women from business backgrounds if they come from rural areas. Business leaders born in rural areas are three times as likely to marry women who are daughters of farmers as leaders born in urban areas.

Since 73 per cent of the leaders of rural origins marry women from occupational backgrounds other than farming, it seems probable that these men marry women they meet at college or elsewhere in their careers. It also seems probable that the 9 per cent from metropolitan areas who marry women of farm background marry women who have left the country and fashioned careers at college or elsewhere.

The Marriages of the American Business Elite

The difference between men from metropolitan and small cities for marriages to daughters of the elite is not great (23 per cent to 21 per cent), as compared with only 11 per cent for rural areas. Urban environments of all sizes produce more marriages with that class than the rural area does. However, they represent only about a fifth of the marriages of the business leaders in each type of urban community.

Methods and Techniques of the Study

Present Use of the 1928 Techniques and Procedures

A DISCUSSION of the methods of the present study of occupational mobility must begin with an acknowledgment of the indebtedness of this research to that conducted by F. W. Taussig and C. S. Joslyn, reported in *American Business Leaders*. The meticulous execution of the earlier project, and its authors' careful and admirable reporting, provided a basis for the construction of the 1952 letter and questionnaire and for the selection of the sample to be studied. The full presentation of the 1928 methods substantially reduced the problems of comparing the two time periods and also increased the accuracy of the comparison.

The 1928 questionnaire is reproduced below (p. 241). This questionnaire, along with a thorough discussion of the rationale for its construction and the shortcomings revealed by its administration, is given in *American Business Leaders* (pp. 13–27). The 1952 questionnaire was constructed to provide data comparable to those of the 1928 questionnaire, to correct items where the authors indicated advantageous change, and to expand the scope of the questionnaire in the light of current understanding of occupational mobility in business and industry.

With these criteria for a revision of the study's basic technique, a preliminary 1952 questionnaire was drafted. This draft was reproduced and mailed to a sample of business leaders, so that experience with the instrument might be obtained. The men included in this pilot study were executives of a range of large firms in the Chicago area, men at the level of (and later included among) the business elite studied in the total research. A preliminary draft of the 1952 covering letter accompanied the questionnaire.

Methods and Techniques of the Study

Upon receipt of returns from this experimental mailing, interviews were conducted with the respondents. The interviews were focused on three problems: (1) the accuracy of the questionnaire responses — their reliability and validity as revealed through a lengthy discussion of the man's career and background; (2) the adequacy of the items employed in setting forth the outlines of the career and background of a business leader, and the possible areas of additional questionnaire items; and (3) the reaction of the business leader to the mode of presentation of the letter and questionnaire, and the effectiveness of their communication.

Interviews were also conducted with the men who did not return this draft of the questionnaire. A methodological problem throughout the study was the significance of failure to respond. It was clearly of the utmost importance to explore to the maximum possible extent the reasons for non-response, and to examine whether those men who did not respond differed systematically in career or background from the men who did. The results of this aspect of the pilot study were most reassuring and will be discussed below in connection with the question of the reliability of the data.

The 1952 Questionnaire

The questionnaire employed in the total study (reproduced below, pp. 242–45) consists of four pages of items, which were constructed to meet several criteria: First, it was necessary to duplicate the items included in the 1928 questionnaire, to provide accurate data for the comparison of 1928 and 1952. Second, it was necessary that the items communicate an unequivocal meaning, with each response comparable to all other responses. Further, it was desirable for maximum response that minimum demands be made on the respondent, preferably that he be able to respond by a simple check mark in categories of possible answers previously arranged. Finally, the overriding importance of a high rate of return to the questionnaire required brief items to keep the total questionnaire as short as possible.

The first questions asked, under item 1, relate to present age and the age of first entering business. They provide a familiar introduction to the questionnaire and are of intrinsic importance to the study. Some difficulties were experienced with the phrasing of the second part of item 1, "age entered business." The data needed concern the age at which the business career was begun. There are many ways of phrasing this question; none was found to be totally satisfactory, for all permitted some range of interpretation. While the great majority of responses clearly conformed to the intended meaning of the item, some few, especially in the case of professional and military careers, were in terms of entrance into the business hierarchy rather than the beginning of the individual's career. From comments by respondents, it was usually possible to correct such cases; others were rejected. The comparison of the two parts of this first item provides a third time factor, the length of the business career to date.

Item 2, concerning the present business position, presented no problems in construction or coding. Experience indicates, however, that the separation of senior and junior partner is not usually a meaningful one in large businesses today, and the separation was not made in the analysis of the data. The position of controller was added to the 1928 list since it has emerged in the interval as an executive position. The category "other" included a wide range of positions, from chairman of the finance committee and vice chairman of the board through assistant to the president (where this is ranked by the firm as an executive position).

Item 3 asked for the age of assuming this position. The difference between this age and the age of entering business provided an important datum, the length of time required to achieve the business position. Subtraction of the age at which the present position was assumed from the present age provided the length of time in present position.

On item 4, volume of sales or gross income was used as the criterion of size of business. While this criterion is subject to question, it appears that no single criterion of business size is totally satisfactory; it is no less satisfactory, when all types of business are considered, than total assets, total wages paid, number of employees, or some other measure of business size. Gross income has the further advantage, important in the present study, of being consistent with the criterion used in 1928.

Nine categories were used for indicating size of business. The category "none" was added to the 1952 categories, on the advice of the earlier study, for those cases where the company was founded by the respondent, or where he joined the firm at its founding. The 1928 category "$100,000,000 or over" was further divided into three categories for the 1952 study.

The size of the business at two points in time was asked for — "when you entered this organization," and "at present." The comparison of these two responses made possible the study of the influence of the company's growth on the business career. The item presents two major difficulties in terms of analysis. First, some businessmen consider this information about their firm confidential, and so indicated when failing to respond to this item. It was possible in most of these cases to complete the questionnaire by referring to the response of another man in the same firm. Thus many "no answers" to the question about size of firm were completed. Also many men filling out the questionnaire did not have this information at the time. In the interviews during the pilot study, the respondent occasionally asked that the information be obtained. In any case, the size of the categories employed makes it likely that substantial error in responses did not occur. Further, as will have been noted, when this datum was analyzed, the categories were further combined into very broad groupings. A misplacement of respondents by more than one category appears unlikely.

Item 5 asked for the age at which the respondent entered his present organization. The differences between this age item and items 1 and 3 were coded as additional age factors. The age of the company was the subject of item 6. The period 1928–29 was selected as the differentiating point, in item 6, between newer and older business firms because it marked the end of an era in American business, and because firms formed at that time would not have been included in the 1928 research.

Item 7 of the questionnaire concerns the number of business affiliations of the businessman during his career. The total number of firms with which he was associated was asked for in the first question of item 7, and the number with which he was associated as an executive in the second question. Again, the difference between the items provided an additional datum, the number of firms associated with as a non-executive. The third question in item 7 asked for the number of directorships held. The size of the businesses studied and the positions held by these men made for an unforeseen underestimation of the number of directorships, since many men indicated in comments that they did not include in their responses to this item directorships held in affiliated or subsidiary companies.

Item 8 was included in both the 1928 questionnaire and, with some changes in structure, the 1952 questionnaire. The question deals with the presence or absence of influential connections in the first firm, and in the firm with which the respondent is now associated.

The study of influence and connections in the careers of men can hardly be undertaken through a questionnaire, much less through a single questionnaire item. Since data in this area were collected in 1928, however, it was useful to include item 8 in the 1952 questionnaire, both to provide an indication of the role of connections and influence and to make possible a comparison with the 1928 data on the question. Item 8 represented the best construction of the question consistent both with the 1928 data and with the needs of the present study.

In 1928, "connections" were restricted to owners or executives, and firms were limited to first business and present business. In the 1928 form, relatives and friends were grouped together, and the 1952 phrase "business acquaintances" was not employed. The preliminary discussion of the 1952 form led to the separation of relatives and friends, as two quite different aspects of the question, and the results of the analysis fully justified this separation. However, in considering friends it was felt important to separate personal and social relationships from those who were friends only in a business and economic relationship. Since the primary question in the study of occupational mobility is the role of the family in the mobility process, the term "friends" may be taken by the respondent to include close friends of the family, associates of the father or of other relatives. It may also include friendships established through the peer group, in college and in the community. It may, however, also include men whose acquaintance has been made in the course of the business career, and on the whole these acquaintances may be little related to questions of birth status or family position. Because of the broad range of meanings included in the term "friends" as employed in the 1928 item, an attempt was made in the 1952 form to achieve at least a partial separation among the wide variety of meanings, by setting off the term "business acquaintances" from "friends."

A further difficulty with item 8 concerns that of limiting the item to the first and last firms worked for, with no inquiry about firms associated with at some intermediate point in the career. There was also no inquiry about the role of family and friends who may not be in the firm but are well placed in the business world to further career ambitions no less directly. This, as well as the other limitations of item 8, serves to restrict analysis and inferences from the data provided by the item. Essentially, the kind of information needed to study the role of family and friends in furthering the career can only be derived from intensive study of the total career. Item 8 may be used only as an index to over-all influence and connections, and differences between response to the 1952 item and the 1928 response can serve only as an approximation of changes occurring in this area over time.

Item 9, dealing with sources of financial aid early in the career, was phrased so that data comparable to those of 1928 might be obtained. Relatives and friends, combined on the earlier questionnaire, were listed separately in the 1952 form. As with the previous item, item 9 serves only as an indication of the whole range of kinds of financial aid possible and does not provide a full or complete statement of financial assistance in the business leader's career.

In item 10, concerning the occupational sequence of the business leader's career, the listing of occupations used throughout the questionnaire is first employed. The listing in item 10 is essentially the same as that used in later items concerning occupational background, in order to present to the respondent a consistent and familiar series of occupational categories. The basis for categorization will be discussed in connection with item 11. It should be noted in item 10, on the business career, that the category "formal training program in a business" is added to the 1928 listing, to include the increasing number of men whose first occupation is in connection with an executive development program in business.

The time points selected in item 10 are arbitrary. The maximum number possible in the space limits of the questionnaire were included. A "twenty years later" category was not included, for preliminary testing indicated that a substantial majority of the men studied become major executives within twenty years of their first self-supporting job.

Item 11 provides a critical datum for the study — the occupation of the father of the business leader. The occupation of the father was requested for a specific point in the business leader's lifetime so that comparable data among respondents might be ensured and the range of interpretation of the item minimized. Two indications of occupation were requested: when the respondent was in grammar school and when the respondent became self-supporting. This breakdown was employed to provide data on mobility within the father's career, as well as to make allowance for those cases where the father might later in his career have lost a relatively high business position held when the son was younger and which may have been important in the son's career.

The categorization of occupations has long been a problem for students of American society. The problem was complicated in the case of this research by the necessity of adjusting the occupational listing for father's occupation to the categories employed in the earlier research (see the 1928 questionnaire). Since an important element of analysis involves continued comparison with census data, the occupational categories used must also be comparable to those employed in census publications.[1] The listing of occupations employed in the questionnaire represents a compromise of the several demands of the research design.

The first two categories, dealing with laborers, were retained unchanged from the 1928 wording. The occupation of farmer includes an extensive hierarchy of occupations; and four categories of farmers, based on studies of occupational stratification within the farm population, were cited. The two categories dealing with lower level white-collar occupations presented some difficulties in phrasing. The term "salesman" includes both the clerk in a shop and an engineer selling machine tools. The significance of the range of sales occupations made it important to differentiate in the questionnaire between these extremes of white-collar work. Unfortunately, no term differentiating the two in all types of business is in general circulation. The device employed, that of including clerk and retail salesman in the first category and salesman alone in the second, was found in the pilot study to communicate the difference to the respondents and to differentiate the responses to the item.

[1] Alba M. Edwards, *Comparative Occupational Statistics for the United States, 1870–1940* (Washington, D.C.: U.S. Government Printing Office, 1943).

Methods and Techniques of the Study

A similar difficulty was encountered in the categorization of occupations below the executive level in the managerial hierarchy. While the term "foreman" includes a range of statuses and responsibilities, it does differentiate, on the whole, one level of management. The next level of management, intermediate between foreman and major executive, while most diverse in the ranks and types of occupation included, does not lend itself to further division, although such division of this broad category would be desirable for the purposes of this study. No terminology common to all business and effectively communicating to all businessmen was developed to further differentiate this category, and the term "minor executive" as used in the 1928 form was retained in the 1952 study.

The occupational category of major executive was made precise by reference back to the positions included under item 2 of the questionnaire. The business-owner group was divided into three categories by size of business. Two of the categories, under $50,000 sales and over $50,000 sales, had been used in 1928. To this was added an additional group, over $100,000 sales, to compensate for trends to business consolidation and inflation in the interval between the two studies.

In separating out the professions in the 1952 form, the four professions of doctor, engineer, lawyer, and minister were listed individually because of their presumed importance as occupational backgrounds for mobility by the son into top business positions, and because they communicate a fairly specific occupational position. Other professions that might have been separately cited did not meet these qualifications. "Teacher" is an example. It was not listed separately since the range of meanings and occupational statuses included under that general title is extremely wide. Further, as the questionnaire returns indicated, this profession does not play a role in mobility into business leadership comparable to that of the four professions listed separately. The request that responses to "other profession" be specified by name made it possible to recategorize responses where the respondent erred in including an occupation in professional status.

The two categories of military career and government service were added to the 1952 form to make possible the examination of careers in these areas apart from other career backgrounds. The "other" category again asked that the occupation be specified, and here too it was possible to recategorize responses where the respondent was in doubt or in error as to the appropriate category in which the occupation should be placed.

The asterisks at the executive and owner categories of item 11 were intended to draw the particular attention of respondents whose fathers held these positions to item 11a. Data on continuity of firm from father to son were obtained in 1928 by a supplementary mailing; these items were incorporated into the questionnaire used in 1952.

Items 12, 13, and 14 deal with the education of the business leader and of his father. The categories used to estimate formal education in item 12 are comparable both to census data and to the 1928 categories. The data obtained from item 13, on colleges attended and degrees taken, have not been analyzed for the current study; they will be included in other publications. Item 14, relating to formal business training, used fewer categories than the earlier study, but comparability of data was retained.

Item 15 concerns the occupation of the father's father and of the wife's father, and uses the same listing of occupations as item 11. Item 16 concerns the place of birth of the 1952 business elite. Data in this area were not included in the earlier study. The categories included under size of place of birth were established as the result of the preliminary interviewing and examination of census data. For the largest size category it was possible to list by name the seven cities included. The remaining categories of birthplace by population provide meaningful sociological distinctions between size groups, and at the same time they were found to be sufficiently broad to minimize error. The categories provide a wide margin of error; it does not appear likely that a response would be misplaced by more than one category in either direction.

Item 17 is addressed to the problem of birth rate as a factor in occupational mobility, and it requests, first, the number of sons of the business leader and, second, an indication of their career choice. The latter information, given the probable age of the sons and changes from one group of occupations to another, was expected to provide only an indication of the direction of career choice made by the sons. In fact, after administration of the questionnaire it was found that a large proportion of the sons had not entered careers as yet.

With reference to item 18, only six tenths of 1 per cent of the men studied indicated that they recalled filling out the 1928 questionnaire.

Methods and Techniques of the Study

The two business elites do then represent two different generations of business leaders.

These questionnaire items, along with the data available on the type of business and geographic location of business of the 1952 business leaders, made up the basic data for the study.

The covering letter that accompanied the 1928 questionnaire provided the basis for the drafting of the 1952 covering letter, which is here reproduced (p. 246). The requirements for this letter, in its phrasing, its length, and the extent to which it communicated the desired meaning to the men studied, were no less exacting than these requirements for the questionnaire.

The Organization of the Study

The authors of the 1928 study credited the organization of the project with an important role in the results achieved. The study's organization included an advisory committee of the following business leaders:

Julius H. Barnes
James F. Bell
Walter S. Gifford
Alexander Legge
Paul M. Warburg
Clarence Woolley
Owen D. Young

The present project was fortunate in being able to enlist the services, in a like capacity, of a group of men of equal stature and prominence. At the invitation of Chancellor Lawrence A. Kimpton of the University of Chicago, the following business leaders accepted membership on the 1952 Sponsoring Committee:

Lawrence A. Appley, New York City
John Cowles, Minneapolis
Clarence B. Randall, Chicago
Frank Stanton, New York City
General Robert E. Wood, Chicago

The support of these men was undoubtedly a major factor in the positive reception accorded the project by the businessmen studied. In addition, the Sponsoring Committee's members provided valuable comment on and criticism of the methods and techniques of the study and gave generously of their time and attention at critical points in the project's development.

A further group of business leaders played a central role in the project. In the formulation of the research, in obtaining financial support for the project, and in the execution of the study, a large measure of the success enjoyed must be attributed to the study's Steering Committee. The membership of this committee included the following men:

W. G. Caples, Chicago
L. H. Fisher, St. Paul
Howard Goodman, Chicago
James C. Worthy, Washington, D.C.

The Questionnaire Returns and Their Accuracy

The 1952 letter and questionnaire were submitted to a total of 17,546 businessmen. Each questionnaire was coded with an identifying number. Each return was read by the authors and only by the authors. In those cases where the questionnaire was not suitable for inclusion in the study, because of inadequate responses, it was rejected. Comments that had been solicited from the respondents enabled us to make adjustments in many returns which had not been filled out correctly or completely. The returns were categorized by type of business and location of business from information previously obtained on each respondent in the original selection of the sample.

A total of 8562 questionnaires were returned. Of these responses 262 were rejected after the preliminary screening, the majority because of incomplete or unclear answers to the question concerning the occupation of the respondent's father. A few businessmen refused to fill out the questionnaire and indicated their reasons. For the most part these were men who, because their careers were primarily in the professions, did not feel that they should be included in a study of business leaders.

The total number of usable responses to the 1952 questionnaire was 8300. This is a return of 47.6 per cent from the total mailing, comparing favorably with the 48.8 per cent return in the 1928 analysis. (The total response in 1928 was more than 57 per cent, including refusals, incomplete returns, and all other types of response to the mailing.)

This return of almost 48 per cent usable responses is high. When it is considered that the 1952 questionnaire was four times the length of that employed in 1928, and that an enormous volume of questionnaires of all kinds cross the desks of key businessmen, this proportion is surprising. It is substantially higher than that obtained in most questionnaire mailings. Certainly the interest in the subject on the part of businessmen helped to account for the results. The prestige of the University of Chicago was also a factor. During the interviews, businessmen also reacted positively to the idea of studying changes in mobility over a period of time. With all this, a major reason for the very substantial return of the questionnaire is without doubt the prestige and respect accorded the members of the project's Sponsoring Committee.

A major methodological problem throughout this study of occupational mobility is the extent to which the responses to the questionnaire accurately reflect the backgrounds and careers of 1952 business leaders. This question has two parts: One, are the men who returned the questionnaire representative of all the businessmen included in the mailing or are there systematic differences between the men who returned the questionnaire and the men who did not, in terms of career or background? Two, are the responses accurate? Do the replies received accurately portray the backgrounds and careers of the men studied?

Several types of evidence were obtained to answer these questions about the study's methods. The first problem concerns the extent to which the return from the mailing is representative of the entire population selected for study. In regard to this, the size of the return reduces considerably the probability of substantial differences. Further evidence is available, however. As pointed out above, following the experimental mailing in the Chicago area, interviews were obtained with men who failed to return the questionnaire. The answers of these men covered a range of reasons. Some had been out of the office when the questionnaire was received, and it had not come to their attention. In some cases, there was objection to questionnaires in general, and this one along with all others not demanding replies was consigned to the wastebasket. A few men objected to all forms of academic research and indicated that they would seldom if ever trouble themselves to cooperate in such an undertaking. In no case was there evidence that the questions were considered too personal or as dealing with private matters inappropriate to such inquiry.

All these reasons may rightly be considered by the critic to be insufficient evidence on the point in question, as they may well be convenient rationalizations appropriate for answering such inquiry. However, it should also be noted that in these follow-up interviews the career and background of the businessman were discussed, and no consistent differences between the backgrounds of the men who did not return the preliminary questionnaire and those who did were established.

At the present time the authors are undertaking a further research on occupational mobility — an intensive study of a selected sample of business leaders. This study employs interviewing and projective techniques to examine the process of mobility, and the meaning of mobility to the individual and his society. The results of this project are reported in another publication.[2] The selection of the population for study in this research is based on the questionnaire data obtained for the study here reported. These interviews provide a further check on the accuracy of the questionnaire returns. As with the interviews conducted following the pilot questionnaire study, the interview responses of the businessmen entirely support the thesis that the questionnaires were accurately and validly filled out.

Further data bearing on the representativeness of the returns of the questionnaire are available. It is possible to compare the returns with the total mailing on three factors: (1) type of business, (2) geographical location, and (3) the business positions held.

Table 124 compares the type of business of the entire mailing with that of the men who returned the questionnaire. The distribution by

Table 124. Distribution of Total Mailing and of Returns by Type of Business

Type of Business	Number		Percentage	
	Mailings	Returns	Mailings	Returns
Mining	410	170	2.34	2.05
Construction	1,066	492	6.08	5.93
Manufacturing	6,424	3,289	36.61	39.62
Trade	3,417	1,393	19.47	16.78
Finance	3,955	1,879	22.54	22.64
Transportation	1,043	468	5.94	5.64
Public utilities and communications ...	623	385	3.55	4.64
Services	608	224	3.47	2.70
Total	17,546	8,300	100.00	100.00

[2] W. Lloyd Warner and James Abegglen, *Big Business Leaders in America*.

Methods and Techniques of the Study

type of business of men who returned the questionnaire reflects closely the distribution by type of business of the entire mailing. Some differences were observed. Proportionately more men in manufacturing and public utilities returned questionnaires than were included in the total mailing. Proportionately fewer business leaders in the areas of retail and wholesale trade and in the service industries returned the questionnaire. These are the business areas where the size of business firms tends to be largest and smallest respectively. That is, it would appear from Table 124 that there was some tendency for men with the larger business firms to respond in higher proportion to the questionnaire, a result not inconsistent with the purposes of the study. On the whole, insofar as type of business is an indication, the conclusion must be that the return reflects accurately the nature of the total mailing.

Table 125. Distribution of Total Mailing and of Returns by Geographical Location

Region	Number		Percentage	
	Mailings	Returns	Mailings	Returns
New England	1,238	642	7.06	7.73
Middle Atlantic	7,174	3,228	40.89	38.89
East North Central	3,911	2,030	22.29	24.46
West North Central	1,381	694	7.87	8.36
South Atlantic	1,270	549	7.24	6.61
East South Central	350	146	1.99	1.76
West South Central	600	263	3.42	3.17
Mountain	141	69	0.80	0.83
Pacific	1,459	666	8.32	8.03
Territories	22	13	0.12	0.16
Total	17,546	8,300	100.00	100.00

A second characteristic on which a comparison of the entire mailing with the returns is possible is the geographical location of present business. This comparison is given in Table 125. The greatest differences in the two sets of proportions involve the East North Central states, the geographical region in which the University of Chicago is located. This difference is balanced by a somewhat smaller proportion than expected of returns from the Middle Atlantic states. The differences in this regard are not large, but must be kept in mind when the over-all study is being viewed. This factor is partially corrected for in the selection of the group included in the analysis of data.

Occupational Mobility

Table 126. Distribution of Total Mailing and of Returns by Business Position

Position	Number		Percentage	
	Mailings *	Returns	Mailings	Returns
Owner or partner	573	415	3.36	5.00
Chairman of the board	1,006	473	5.89	5.70
President	1,939	1,206	11.36	14.53
Vice president	9,857	4,492	57.74	54.12
Secretary	1,625	698	9.52	8.41
Treasurer	948	491	5.55	5.92
Controller	661	364	3.87	4.38
Other	463	161	2.71	1.94
Total	17,072	8,300	100.00	100.00

* The "mailings" columns do not include the business leaders in the real estate category on whom information as to business position was not available prior to the mailing; 474 mailings were in this category.

A third comparison of the total mailing with the returns is possible with respect to business position. The distributions are given in Table 126. The differences in proportion are not great; the largest are in the categories of "owner or partner" and "president." To the extent that the proportions in the return differ somewhat from those in the entire mailing, the difference tends to be in the direction of an increased proportion of respondents in the more important business positions.

Examination of the factors in which the total mailing may be compared with the returns indicates only minor differences between the total group and the respondents. The returns to the questionnaire on the basis of this evidence may be taken as an accurate and representative return to the mailing.

Since the range of factors available for this comparison was limited, and questions as to the reliability of the return remained, we decided to obtain further evidence on the representativeness of the return by undertaking a second mailing of the questionnaire. It was resubmitted to the men holding the positions of president and chairman of the board who had not replied to the first mailing. The returns from this second request for a completed questionnaire were then compared with the returns from men holding the same positions who replied to the first request. The thirty-eight response areas on the questionnaire were then compared by means of chi-square. Significant differences (beyond the .05 level of significance) between the two sets of responses

Methods and Techniques of the Study

were found in only three areas of the thirty-eight. The questions on which significant differences appeared, as phrased on the questionnaire, included (1) How many firms are you associated with at present as a member of the board of directors? (2) The extent of schooling of your father? (3) Do you recall filling out the questionnaire of Messrs. Taussig and Joslyn in 1928–29?

A detailed breakdown of the two sets of responses to these questionnaire items appears in Table 127. As an examination of the distributions will indicate, the differences are not in systematic directions, and, while real, they do not occur in critical areas of the questionnaire (e.g., occupation of the father, education of self, and the like).

To conclude this discussion of the degree to which the returns are representative of the total mailing to 1952 business leaders, an evaluation of these several data may be summarized. A final and irrefutable

Table 127. Returns to First and Second Mailing of Questionnaire on Three Items

Questionnaire Item	First Mailing	Second Mailing
I. Number of firms associated with as member of board of directors		
0	1.49%	3.21%
1	22.84	19.24
2	17.11	16.91
3	13.47	14.28
4	12.35	12.82
5	9.08	11.07
6	6.18	3.21
7	3.35	3.79
8	3.50	1.17
9 or more	8.63	12.24
No answer	2.01	2.04
II. Father's education		
Less than high school	34.59	33.23
Some high school	13.91	15.16
High school graduation	16.81	21.57
Some college	10.86	12.82
College graduation	12.64	11.37
Postgraduate study	7.37	3.50
No answer	3.79	2.33
III. "Do you recall filling out the questionnaire of Messrs. Taussig and Joslyn?"		
Yes	0.60	1.75
No	97.54	95.72
No answer	1.87	2.54

demonstration of the accuracy or inaccuracy of the returns in representing all 1952 business leadership is not possible short of a complete usable return to the mailing. Several kinds of evidence are available, however. Insofar as can be determined, there is no evidence to support the view that the questionnaires analyzed are not representative of the total selection of business leaders.

The question of the validity of the responses, the extent to which the questionnaires were honestly answered by the men who completed and returned them, does not lend itself to the varieties of study undertaken to examine reliability. As an example of the kind of question involved, and the most critical one in terms of the study's objectives, it may be asked whether there would be any tendency for the businessmen studied to shift systematically the occupational category assigned for father's occupation. In the past, it has commonly been held that there would be a tendency for a business leader whose position is the same as, or parallel to, that of his father to reject the silver spoon and portray himself as a "self-made man," and therefore to indicate an occupational status for his father different from the one he in fact occupied. Conversely, in the preparation of this study, a leading sociologist offering critical advice argued that, given the current values of businessmen, there would be a tendency for the men studied to cite for their fathers an occupation higher in the occupational hierarchy than they in fact occupied, and to deny and conceal, for example, the fact that the father was a laborer.

The point is debatable and hardly to be settled by speculation. For evidence, the present study has drawn on intensive interviews with samples of the men who returned the questionnaire. In the course of these interviews the entire family background of the business leader was explored in detail. Since the interviewed men were selected on the basis of their fathers' occupations, the issue of accurate response to the questionnaire received special attention. No cases of error or deliberate changes in the questionnaire response have yet been encountered in the detailed discussion carried on during these searching interviews.

Again, as with the question of the extent to which the return accurately reflects the composition of the total 1952 business elite, conclusions as to the validity of the questionnaire responses must rest with the summary statement that, so far as evidence is available, the questionnaires were honestly and accurately completed by the men studied.

The Selection of Men to Be Studied

In selecting the men to be included in the listing of 1952 business leaders, it was necessary to establish a population that would meet two basic criteria: One, the men studied must represent the 1952 business elite and provide an accurate sampling of the top-level business positions in American business and industry in 1952. Two, the men studied must be comparable to the group studied in 1928, for valid comparison of mobility in the two time periods. As will be seen, the two criteria are not identical.

The authors of the 1928 study explained that "for the purposes of this inquiry . . . a 'business leader' is regarded as a person occupying a position as major executive, partner, or sole owner in a business of such size as to be of more than local importance in its field." Discussing the source used as a basis for selection, they went on to say that "it was at just this time that the first (1928) edition of Poor's Register of Directors was published. An examination of this volume showed that it provided an excellent source, probably the best single source, from which a representative sample of business leaders, covering the nation at large, might be drawn." [3]

The authors considered a further definition of the 1928 selection necessary. "A random sample of the names appearing in the Register would probably have given us an undue proportion of small businessmen. Clearly some kind of selection was necessary . . ." [4] In the selection for the 1928 study, the criteria employed were those given in the following quotation:

(1) In order to get an adequate sample for the study, it is desirable to select only executive officers, partners, or men who are directors in a sufficiently large number of companies to indicate that they are probably on executive committees, or hold other positions which may not be stated in the directory.

(2) Since there have been marked changes in the various industries in the last few years, workers should make certain that an adequate sample is obtained from each of the industries listed on the attached

[3] F. W. Taussig and C. S. Joslyn, *American Business Leaders* (New York: The Macmillan Company, 1932), p. 6.
[4] *Ibid.*, p. 7.

sheet. This will insure that an adequate cross-section of American businessmen is included in the sample.

(3) Wherever possible, the executives in the leading companies in each industry should be included rather than those having positions in minor companies. This is important because the men in the leading companies are undoubtedly capable executives and are more likely to be in a position to furnish information that will be of value in this study than are men who occupy positions in minor companies, where they are often placed as subordinates by the leaders who really control the company and its activities.

(4) In most instances it should be clear from the importance of a man's connections that the companies with which he is associated are likely to be leaders. It should not be difficult, for example, to know that if a man is connected with or is an officer of the Radio Corporation of America, his name is a desirable one to include on the list.

(5) Where there is question as to whether or not a company is important, it is suggested that reference be made to the lists of companies on the New York Stock Exchange and on the New York Curb. Each worker will, of course, bear in mind that there are many companies which are not listed. Where there is some question on a strategic company, more adequate information can be obtained from Poor's or Moody's Manuals, where the number of shares outstanding or similar information will give an idea of the company's relative importance.[5]

When this definition of business leaders used by the 1928 authors in selecting their sample is reviewed in terms of the 1952 study, three basic criteria emerge. The first criterion listed above defines, for both 1928 and 1952, the kinds of business positions relevant to the study as executive positions in business firms, from sole owner to general manager (where this latter is included as an executive position). With respect to the second criterion, the type of business in which the position is held, a comparable sample may be selected by matching type of business in 1928 and type of business in 1952. The third, fourth, and fifth criteria employed in selecting the 1928 sample may be reduced to a single common factor — the size of the business. In 1928, and therefore in 1952, the men studied are to be drawn from the largest business firms in a given type of business. These criteria formed the basis for the selection of the sample of men to be compared to the group studied in 1928.

The selection procedure thus defined did not resolve the problems of selecting the 1952 sample. A major point of criticism of the 1928

[5] *Ibid.*, p. 8.

study was that the selection by type of business was skewed in the direction of an overrepresentation especially in the sample of men from financial firms and an underrepresentation of men in the distribution businesses.[6] Thus, for an accurate study of occupational mobility in present-day business, both the changes in the economy by type of business and industry since 1928 and the skewed distribution of the 1928 sample made necessary a separate selection of business leaders.

At this point, it may be well to review the problem of selection of the sample as it developed. The sample is composed of business leaders, defined as men occupying the highest positions in the largest business firms. In respect to these two criteria the 1928 and 1952 samples may be made directly comparable. Further, the sample is to include a representation of all types of business and industry. In this respect the 1928 and 1952 selection procedures diverge, and a sample must be selected that is comparable to the 1928 group and yet adequate for the 1952 study.

To meet these needs in the 1952 selection process, the following procedure was adopted. To provide the basis for selection by type of business, use was made of the data on national income produced by type of business as given in *National Income and Product of the United States, 1929–1950*.[7] The proportion of national income produced by type of business may be taken as an index to the relative proportions of business leaders by type of business in the population. The distribution of national income produced and the distribution by type of business of business leaders studied should be the same to ensure an adequate cross section of American business leadership.

Given this distribution of proportions, it was necessary to establish the largest firms in each type of business. In making this selection, the present format of Poor's Register of Directors and Executives (1952) provides an important aid, for listings are provided alphabetically by business leader, and business firms are also listed alphabetically by type of business; the business firms are further listed alphabetically with the executive officers of each firm given. To determine

---

[6] See, for example, Paul D. Converse's review of F. W. Taussig and C. S. Joslyn, *American Business Leaders*, in *Journal of Business*, Vol. 6 (1933), pp. 270–73.

[7] U.S. Department of Commerce, National Income Division, National Income and Product of the United States, 1929–1950 (Washington, D.C.: Government Printing Office, 1951).

the relative size of firms, a wide variety of resources was drawn upon. They are listed in the Bibliography at the end of this volume. Given this rank ordering of the largest firms in each type of business, it was possible to determine the executive officers of these firms, and to include in the sample a proportion that, if we assume equal returns by type of business, would provide a representative cross section of the total business structure.

The size of the desired study population was fixed at 7500 men. It was assumed that somewhat less than 50 per cent would reply to the questionnaire; therefore, more than 15,000 mailings were considered necessary.

On the basis of this selection process, the three critical criteria for the selection of the 1952 business elite were met. The men studied are executives, are with the largest firms in the country, and are a representative cross section by type of business of American industrial and business leaders. It is recognized that the sample, as selected, did not include all American business leaders; but it may be assumed that it included only business leaders.

Returning now to the problem of adjusting the population studied in 1952 to the 1928 sample by type of business, we can say that the problem was relatively simple in this approach to selection. It was necessary to include in the sample additional men from certain types of business, to increase the size of the return from these types and match the proportions used in the 1928 study. This increased the total mailing to approximately 17,500. The extent to which this matching of 1928 and 1952 by type of business was accomplished is discussed in detail below. It is clear that, in terms of the other criteria employed in 1928, the size of the business and business position, the bases for selection in 1928 and 1952 were identical.

The Selection of a Comparison Sample

In order to compare the results of the 1928 study with those of the 1952 study, the samples of the two studies must be comparable and we have seen that the sample selected in 1952 meets the criteria employed in the earlier research in two of the three critical respects. The men studied are from the same level of business position and from the same categories by size of business. The third criterion concerned the type of business. In order to compare the results for the two time periods, it was necessary to match the 1928 sample with a 1952 sample drawn from similar types of business in approximately the same proportions.

The distribution of the 1928 sample by the type of business did not represent a complete cross section of the business community. To adjust for this fact when comparisons were made, it was necessary to select from the total 1952 returns a group of business leaders whose career backgrounds with respect to types of business most closely resembled the group studied in 1928. To facilitate the comparisons further, it was desirable to duplicate the total number of men involved in the 1928 study.

The report on the earlier study employed categories for the types of business somewhat different from those in current use. From the subcategories used, however, a reclassification of responses into the currently used categories was possible. A further modification of the 1928 distribution was made necessary before the final selection of the comparison sample could be made. In the earlier study, a category of "farming and unclassified" was employed. This category included 2.2 per cent of the total men studied. Through the approach to selection of the sample used in the 1952 research, it was possible to avoid such a "miscellaneous" category, and to categorize all respondents precisely in terms of a type of business. To adjust for this difference, the best distribution of the "other" category in the 1928 sample would appear to be an equal distribution of this proportion through all types of business. The adjusted figures for 1928 then provide the basis for selection of the most nearly comparable group from the total 1952 returns. Table 128 presents the distribution by types of business of the 1928 sample, and of the comparison sample used in the 1952 analysis, with the difference of proportions noted.

The maximum difference between the two samples is in the proportion of men from the financial area, a difference of 2.3 per cent between the two samples, with the larger proportion of men in finance included in the 1928 sample. In other words, despite the inclusion of an additional number of mailings from this area, the overrepresentation in the 1928 study of leaders in the financial field was not entirely corrected for. The difference is not great, however, and on the whole a rather high degree of congruity exists between the two distributions. On the basis of this examination of the extent to which the sample criteria in 1928 were met in the construction of the 1952 sample, the analysis of the comparison sample was undertaken and the comparisons of the two time periods made.

It should be noted that on analysis of the data the issue of type of business became somewhat academic because of the limited relationship of the type of business to occupational mobility when broad categories of types of business are employed. The "comparison sample" on which all 1928-1952 comparisons were based did not differ appreciably in its characteristics from the "1952 business leaders," from which sample the 1952 distributions were derived.

A further note on the 1928 and 1952 samples is necessary. In the analysis of the data in the 1928 study, use was made of five categories

Table 128. Adjusted Distribution of Returns by Type of Business of Respondents for 1928 and 1952

Type of Business	1928 Adjusted Returns		1952 Comparison Sample		Difference between Percentages
	Number	Percentage	Number	Percentage	
Mining	182	2.5%	170	2.3%	—0.2%
Construction	190	2.6	200	2.7	+0.1
Manufacturing	3,185	43.2	3,289	44.6	+1.4
Wholesale and retail trade	922	12.5	955	13.0	+0.5
Finance, insurance, and real estate	2,044	27.7	1,879	25.4	—2.3
Transportation	352	4.8	365	5.0	+0.2
Communication and public utilities	305	4.1	315	4.3	+0.2
Services	191	2.6	198	2.7	+0.1
Total	7,371	100.0	7,371	100.0	0.0

Table 129. Distribution of Respondents by Size of Business Classes (1928 Classification)

Size Class (Gross Income per Annum)	Grade	Percentage of 1928 Sample	Percentage of 1952 Comparison Sample
$50,000,000 and over	A	13.4	54.5
$5,000,000–49,999,000	B	30.2	35.5
$1,000,000–4,999,000	C	29.5	7.8
$500,000–999,000	D	12.4	1.2
Less than $500,000	E	14.5	1.0
Total		100.0	100.0

of respondents by size of business. Table 129 presents the consolidation of responses by size of business as used in the 1928 analysis, along with the distribution of the 1928 and 1952 samples according to these size categories. The size classes were designated A through E, with A referring to the largest businesses with gross incomes exceeding 50 million dollars per annum. As would be expected, these size categories are not appropriate to the 1952 sample. Only 2 per cent of the 1952 respondents are included in the two smaller categories as defined for 1928, compared with 27 per cent of the 1928 respondents.[8] More than half of the 1952 respondents are with businesses whose gross income exceeds 50 million dollars.

Table 130. Distribution of 1952 Comparison Sample by Size of Business Classes (1952 Classification)

Size Class (Gross Income per Annum)	Grade	Percentage of 1952 Comparison Sample
$500,000,000 and over	A	13.2
$100,000,000–499,999,000 ..	B	27.8
$50,000,000–99,999,000	C	15.4
$10,000,000–49,999,000	D	26.8
Less than $10,000,000	E	16.8
Total		100.0

Since the size categories simply represent a scale of business size, the consolidation of size groups was changed for the 1952 sample to conform to the 1928 distribution. The results of the change are given in Table 130. Again, the designation A refers to the largest businesses studied. These are, in this changed distribution, businesses with a gross income exceeding 500 million dollars. The smallest size category, E, includes those businesses with a gross income of less than 10 million dollars. In the analyses of data by size of business employed in the study, comparisons of the 1928 and 1952 samples are based on these two different size groupings. Thus, size category A refers to men in the largest businesses — in terms of the 1928 sample 50 million dollars or over, in terms of the 1952 sample 500 million dollars and over. The

[8] It should be noted that those 1952 respondents with smaller businesses are drawn primarily from the fields of real estate and retail trade, business areas where concentration of firms has not proceeded as far as in manufacturing and other areas.

comparative rank of the men has not been changed; the change is only in terms of the criteria employed in making the ranking.

The 1952 Sample

For the analysis of the data for 1952, the basic criteria employed in deriving the comparison sample remain. The men included are the men in the highest positions in the largest firms in each type of business. Two changes were made between the 1952 comparison sample and the 1952 sample on which the separate 1952 analyses are based. It was decided in the original design of the study that 7500 cases would provide the optimal number for the research. Additionally, as noted, corrections in the distribution by type of business were required before proceeding from the comparison analysis to the full analysis of present-day occupational mobility.

Table 131 presents the distribution of national income by type of business and the distribution of the 7500 business leaders included in the 1952 study by type of business. The categories dominated by smaller business firms are somewhat underrepresented. These are the retail and wholesale trade group and the service businesses. In addition, the mining category is slightly underrepresented. The central groups in the American business structure, manufacturing and the financial enterprises, are both slightly overrepresented in this study.

The men studied in this research may be taken as an accurate sampling of the leaders of America's business and industry, and as providing a cross section of the total economy.

Table 131. Contribution to National Income by Type of Business and Type of Business of 1952 Business Leaders

Type of Business	Percentage of National Income	Percentage of Returns Included in Analysis
Mining	3	2
Construction	7	7
Manufacturing	41	44
Trade	23	19
Finance	11	14
Transportation	7	6
Communication	4	5
Services	4	3
Total	100	100

Methods and Techniques of the Study
The Use of Census Data in the Study

Information on the total U.S. population as derived from the national censuses played an important part in this study at many points. Since the application of census data to a study of this sort presents a number of problems, some separate consideration of the use of such data in the preceding analyses is necessary.

The most important census data for the purposes of this study deal with the distribution of the population by occupations. As has been noted earlier, categorization of the U.S. population by occupations is a hazardous procedure at best. The problem is not eased by the fact that each census defines occupational categories differently; especially when earlier censuses are dealt with, direct comparison of even similarly titled occupational groups is very difficult.

The first question with reference to the use of census data in this study had to do with the selection of the group to be studied. The problem is set forth in Chapter II. The questionnaire provided information on the occupation of the fathers of the business leaders at the time the business leaders became self-supporting. Inasmuch as the men studied were slightly over 50 years of age on the average, we may assume that in the questionnaire they gave the father's occupation for about 1920, on the average. Thus the comparison of the questionnaire data and census data involves the results of the 1920 census. The comparison is accurately made, however, not with the distribution of the entire population by occupation, but with a segment of it. The comparative group in the population should include only adults, and only males. Further, for examining the role of place of birth (U.S. or non-U.S.) and region of birth, the census data for 1920 on the occupations of adult males by state and region and by nativity were needed.

The importance of these qualifications of the basic definition of the comparison figures from census data should not be overlooked. All the factors — age, sex, and nativity — have an accumulative effect on occupational proportions in the population. Thus, younger workers, female workers, and foreign-born workers tend to be concentrated in the lower occupational statuses, which substantially alters the proportions in these occupations. An underestimation of occupational mobility would result if the comparison were made simply with the entire U.S. population by occupation. The effect of considering foreign-born and native-born populations separately may be seen in Chapter III.

Occupational Mobility

Since the kind of census data described is not available in the published presentations of census data for 1920, it was necessary to undertake in the course of this study an independent reorganization of census data. The results of this re-analysis of census data provide the basis for the comparisons made.

The census data for 1920 do not make possible a breakdown by occupation into the number of categories employed by the questionnaire. Thus the comparisons in the foregoing analysis are restricted to a more limited listing of occupations. Further, two central occupational groups essential to the present analysis — farmers and owners of small businesses — presented special problems in terms of the census material, and it was necessary to approximate their proportions in the population.

In the case of the 1920 farm population, there was an undercount of agricultural workers of some 500,000 persons as a result of the census being taken in January of that year, excluding thereby that number of seasonal farm laborers. Inasmuch as this study is concerned with permanent employees in each category, as nearly as can be determined, the figures have not been corrected for this undercount. It

Table 132. Census Data for 1920 on Distribution of Adult Male
Population by Occupation

Occupation	Total Male Adults		Foreign-Born Male Adults	
	Number	Percentage	Number	Percentage
Unskilled and semiskilled laborer	9,419,874	31.4	3,102,059	48.1
Skilled laborer	4,857,992	16.2	1,246,158	19.3
Farmer: worker	2,164,686	7.2	226,089	3.5
Farmer: tenant, owner, manager.	6,066,798	20.3	569,610	8.9
Clerk or salesman	2,880,443	9.6	354,441	5.5
Foreman	445,004	1.5	78,250	1.2
Minor executive, major executive, owner of small business, and owner of large business	2,649,024	8.8	671,083	10.4
Professional man	1,185,884	4.0	166,633	2.6
Doctor	(137,758)	(0.5)	(14,659)	(0.2)
Engineer	(136,080)	(0.5)	(15,938)	(0.3)
Lawyer	(120,781)	(0.4)	(7,517)	(0.1)
Minister	(125,483)	(0.4)	(26,720)	(0.4)
Other	(665,782)	(2.2)	(101,799)	(1.6)
Military career	172,681	0.6	20,295	0.3
Government service	118,596	0.4	10,667	0.2
Total for U.S.	29,960,982	100.0	6,445,285	100.0

should be noted further that the majority of the 500,000 not counted would in all probability be excluded from our estimates of total male adults by reason of age and/or sex.

A second occupational group, owners of small businesses, was most important in the analysis of occupational mobility. Unfortunately, the census data on occupations do not make possible an accurate separation of owners of small businesses from owners of large businesses. An estimate of the number of small businesses has been arrived at and is employed in Chapter II. In 1920 the total number of business enterprises, as given by census data, was 1,821,409. Studies indicate that no less than 80 per cent of these businesses would meet the criterion of a maximum volume of annual sales of $25,000. We may assume, then, that the minimum number of owners of small businesses in the population in 1920 was 1,460,000. Thus the total number of men in the executive or large-owner category would have been no more than 1,189,024. This estimate is the basis for the proportions employed in Table 2 of Chapter II.

The distribution of population by occupation in 1920 as derived for this study is given in Table 132. These proportions are applied to the analysis of data in Chapter II.

In the preparation of census data, the question of the inclusion of Negroes and other racial groups in the census data comes into focus. It might be argued that those groups notably discriminated against in American business might not properly be included in the distribution by occupation when mobility rates are being derived. There is no question that Negroes are concentrated in large proportions in the lower occupational levels. Further, Negroes tend to be concentrated in particular geographical areas. When the problem is viewed in terms of social structure, however, it will be seen that limiting the population data to white workers is unjustified. That is, in terms of occupational mobility, the general absence of the Negro from positions of business leadership is an element in the total recruitment process in the United States. Estimates of mobility based on the white population alone would be inaccurate. Further, in the social structure of the South particularly, the very presence of Negroes in large numbers in lower occupational statuses would presumably serve to accelerate the mobility of whites in the business structure. Thus, valid study of the representation of occupational groups in business leadership must include the Negro and other disadvantaged racial groups in the occupational distribution on which the mobility estimates are based.

The problems involved in applying 1900 census data to the analysis of the study's results were more difficult and less satisfactorily resolved than in the case of the 1920 census data. On review of the census materials for 1900, it was decided that the nature of the occupational information available did not justify the categorization of population by occupation beyond the basic categories of laborer, farmer, businessman, clerical or sales worker, professional, and other. By restricting the categories employed to these basic groupings, it was possible to derive, again by a re-examination of the census data for the purposes of this research, a satisfactorily reliable estimate of the population distribution. A further difference between the 1900 and 1920 census data concerns the definition of "adult" employed. For 1920, "adult" refers to those males in the laboring force who were 20 years of age or over; because of the age categories used in 1900, the definition of "adult" for that census year is males 16 years and over. The distribution of 1900 population by size of community and by census region was also developed by the authors, from the published data, for use in this research.

A further note about the use of census data concerns the somewhat awkward breakdown of the data on education of the U.S. population that was employed in Chapter IV. Previous to the 1940 census, data on education concerned only an inquiry on illiteracy. It was therefore necessary, in comparing the formal educational attainment of 1952 business leaders with that of the general population, to base the comparison on the age-by-education data available from the 1940 census.

In general summary of the use of census data in the study, it should be said that in estimating differences between the characteristics of business leaders and of the nation as a whole every effort was made to obtain accurate distributions of the appropriate comparison groups in the population. It should be noted, however, that all such comparisons are subject to the errors which must result from working with census data of past census years.

1928 Questionnaire

HARVARD UNIVERSITY
DEPARTMENT OF ECONOMICS
STUDY OF ORIGINS OF BUSINESS LEADERS

1. Your present age.

2. Age at which you first entered business.

3. Indicate by check the most important business position which you now hold.

Vice President	
Treasurer	
Secretary	
General Manager	
President	
Chairman of Board	
Junior Partner	
Senior Partner	
Sole Owner	
Other (please specify)	

4. Age at which you first assumed this position.

5. Approximate size of the business in which you hold this position:

Volume of Sales or Gross Income*	A When you assumed this position	B At the present time
Less than $500,000		
$500,000–999,000		
$1,000,000–4,999,000		
$5,000,000–9,999,000		
$10,000,000–49,999,000		
$50,000,000–99,999,000		
$100,000,000 or over		

*In case of banks and allied businesses, indicate instead amount of total assets.

6. Principal occupation of father and father's father:

Occupation	Father	Grand-father
Laborer—unskilled or semi-skilled		
Laborer—skilled		
Clerk or Salesman		
Farmer		
Minor Executive		
Major Executive*		
Owner Small Business (sales under $50,000)		
Owner Large Business (sales over $50,000)		
Professional Man		
Other (please specify)		

*Comprises executive positions listed in question 3.

7. Extent of schooling:

A. Non-business Training

Grammar School	
High or Preparatory School.	
College or Technical Institute— Graduated	
College or Technical Institute— Did not finish	

B. Business Training

Correspondence Course (if completed)	
Commercial Training in Public School	
Commercial Training in Private School	
Commercial Training in College or University	

8. Were any of your relatives or friends interested, as owners or executives:

	Yes	No
a. In the business which you first entered		
b. In your present organization when you entered it		

9. Did you, during the early stages of your business career (during the first five years or thereabouts), receive substantial aid (not less than $10,000) through the provision of capital from either of the following sources:

	Yes	No
Inheritance		
Relatives or friends		

Remarks (continue on other side if necessary)

November, 1928

241

1952 Questionnaire

THE UNIVERSITY OF CHICAGO
STUDY OF BUSINESS LEADERS

Strictly Confidential   1-5

1. What is your present age?............. .... ——   6-7

   At what age did you first enter business?... ..... ——   8-9
                                                                                                           10-11

2. What is your most important present business position?

Sole Owner	☐ 1
Senior Partner	☐ 2
Junior Partner	☐ 3
Chairman of the Board...	☐ 4
President	☐ 5
Vice President	☐ 6
Secretary	☐ 7
Treasurer	☐ 8
Controller	☐ 9
General Manager	☐ x
Other (please specify).....	☐ y

   12

3. At what age did you first assume your present business position?........................ .. ——   13-14

4. Approximate size of the business in which you now hold this position:

Volume of Sales or Gross Income	when you entered this organization	at present
None	☐ 0	
Less than $500,000	☐ 1	☐ 1
$500,000 - 999,000	☐ 2	☐ 2
$1,000,000 - 4,999,000	☐ 3	☐ 3
$5,000,000 - 9,999,000	☐ 4	☐ 4
$10,000,000 - 49,999,000	☐ 5 (15	☐ 5 (16
$50,000,000 - 99,999,000	☐ 6	☐ 6
$100,000,000 - 249,999,000	☐ 7	☐ 7
$250,000,000 - 499,999,000	☐ 8	☐ 8
$500,000,000 or over..............	☐ 9	☐ 9

5. At what age did you enter your present organization?.................................... ——   17-18

6. Was your present organization doing business in 1928-1929?......................Yes...... ☐ 1   19
                                                                                   No...... ☐ 2

7. How many firms have you been associated with during your business career
   (including your present firm)?... ——   20

   How many firms have you been associated with at the job level of minor
   executive or major executive (including your present firm)?............................. ——   21

   How many firms are you associated with at present as a member of the Board of Directors?... ——   22

8. Were any of the following interested as owners or executives

	in the business which you first entered		in your present firm when you entered it	
	Yes (1)	No (2)	Yes (1)	No (2)
Relatives	☐	☐ (23	☐	☐ (26
Friends	☐	☐ (24	☐	☐ (27
Business acquaintances	☐	☐ (25	☐	☐ (28

   (We would find any comments you might have on the above questions very helpful. If you
   have any further remarks, would you turn the page and enter them on the back of this page.)

242

9. Did you, during the first five years of your working career or thereabouts, receive substantial financial aid (not less than $10,000) from any of the following sources:

	Yes (1)	No (2)	
Inheritance	☐	☐	29
Relatives	☐	☐	30
Friends	☐	☐	31

10. After becoming self-supporting, what occupation did you engage in

Occupations	when you first became self-supporting (1)	5 years later (2)	10 years later (3)	15 years later (4)	
Worker—unskilled or semi-skilled	☐	☐	☐	☐	32
Skilled worker or mechanic	☐	☐	☐	☐	33
Farmer { farm worker or small tenant	☐	☐	☐	☐	34
farm tenant with paid help	☐	☐	☐	☐	35
farm owner without paid help	☐	☐	☐	☐	36
owner or manager with paid help	☐	☐	☐	☐	37
Clerk or retail salesman	☐	☐	☐	☐	38
Salesman	☐	☐	☐	☐	39
Foreman	☐	☐	☐	☐	40
Minor executive	☐	☐	☐	☐	41
Major executive (positions in question 3)	☐	☐	☐	☐	42
Owner small business (sales under $50,000)	☐	☐	☐	☐	43
Owner medium business (sales between $50,000-$100,000)	☐	☐	☐	☐	44
Owner large business (sales over $100,000)	☐	☐	☐	☐	45
Profession { Engineer	☐	☐	☐	☐	46
Lawyer	☐	☐	☐	☐	47
Other (please specify)	☐	☐	☐	☐	48
Military career	☐	☐	☐	☐	49
Government service	☐	☐	☐	☐	50
Formal training program in a business	☐	☐	☐	☐	51
Other (please specify)	☐	☐	☐	☐	52

11. Principal occupation of your father. (If father deceased, please indicate previous occupation.)

Occupations	when you were in grammar school	when you became self-supporting
Worker—unskilled or semi-skilled	☐ 1 (53	☐ 1 (55
Skilled worker or mechanic	☐ 2	☐ 2
Farmer { farm worker or small tenant	☐ 3	☐ 3
tenant with paid help	☐ 4	☐ 4
owner without paid help	☐ 5	☐ 5
owner or manager with paid help	☐ 6	☐ 6
Clerk or retail salesman	☐ 7	☐ 7
Salesman	☐ 8	☐ 8
Foreman	☐ 9	☐ 9
*Minor executive	☐ x	☐ x
*Major executive (positions in Item 3)	☐ y	☐ y
*Owner small business	☐ 1 (54	☐ 1 (56
*Owner medium business	☐ 2	☐ 2
*Owner large business	☐ 3	☐ 3
Profession { doctor	☐ 4	☐ 4
engineer	☐ 5	☐ 5
lawyer	☐ 6	☐ 6
minister	☐ 7	☐ 7
other (please specify)	☐ 8	☐ 8
Military career	☐ 9	☐ 9
Government service	☐ x	☐ x
Other (please specify)	☐ y	☐ y

(We would find any comments you might have on the above questions very helpful. If you have any further remarks, would you turn the page and enter them on the back of this page.)

*11-a. If your father was a business owner or executive, are you now connected with the same firm that your father was?

Yes...... ☐ 1
No...... ☐ 2

57

12. Extent of schooling of yourself and your father. (Please check only the highest correct category.)

	Self	Father
Less than high school.........	☐ 1	☐ 1
Some high school.............	☐ 2	☐ 2
High school graduate.........	☐ 3 (58	☐ 3 (59
Some college	☐ 4	☐ 4
College graduate	☐ 5	☐ 5
Post-graduate study	☐ 6	☐ 6

13. If you attended college, what was the name of the college or university at which you studied?

College or colleges attended   Degrees

_____   _____   60

_____   _____   61

_____   _____

14. How much formal business training have you had?

None .... ☐ 1
Correspondence courses, public school, or business college.... ☐ 2   62
Commercial training in college or university.............. ☐ 3

15. Principal occupation of your father's father and your wife's father:

Occupations	Your father's father	Your wife's father
Worker—unskilled or semi-skilled....................................	☐ 1 (63	☐ 1 (65
Skilled worker or mechanic...	☐ 2	☐ 2
Farmer { farm tenant or farm worker................................	☐ 3	☐ 3
tenant with paid help............................	☐ 4	☐ 4
farm owner without paid help............................	☐ 5	☐ 5
owner or manager with paid help............................	☐ 6	☐ 6
Clerk or retail salesman..	☐ 7	☐ 7
Salesman	☐ 8	☐ 8
Foreman	☐ 9	☐ 9
Minor executive	☐ x	☐ x
Major executive	☐ y	☐ y
Owner small business..	☐ 1 (64	☐ 1 (66
Owner medium business..	☐ 2	☐ 2
Owner large business..	☐ 3	☐ 3
Profession { doctor	☐ 4	☐ 4
engineer	☐ 5	☐ 5
lawyer	☐ 6	☐ 6
minister	☐ 7	☐ 7
other (please specify)......................................	☐ 8	☐ 8
Military career	☐ 9	☐ 9
Government service	☐ x	☐ x
Other (please specify)...	☐ y	☐ y

(We would find any comments you might have on the above questions very helpful. If you have any further remarks, would you turn the page and enter them on the back of this page.)

244

16. Place of birth:

		Self	Father	Father's Father
	U. S.	☐ 1 (67	☐ 1 (68	☐ 1 (69
	Non-U. S.	☐ 2	☐ 2	☐ 2

If your place of birth was non-U. S., please continue to question 17. (28

If born in the U. S., in which state were you born? _____ 70-71

What was the approximate population of your birthplace at the time of your birth?

New York, Chicago, Philadelphia, Baltimore, St. Louis, Boston or Pittsburgh (or a suburb of one of these cities which were 400,000 or over in 1900)............................ ☐ 1

Over 100,000 (or a suburb of a city this size).. ☐ 2
25,000 to 100,000........................... ☐ 3   72
2,500 to 25,000............................. ☐ 4
Rural or less than 2,500.................... ☐ 5

17. How many sons do you have?... ____ 73

If your answer is none, please continue to question 18.

What career has he (they) entered? *If more than one son is self-supporting, please enter the number in each career.*

Not entered a career as yet....................... ____ 1
Business owner or partner........................ ____ 2
Businessman (not owner or partner)............... ____ 3
Profession .... ____ 4   74
Military career .... ____ 5
Government service .... ____ 6
Other (please specify)........................... ____ 7

18. Do you recall filling out the questionnaire of Messrs. Taussig and Joslyn in 1928-9?

Yes...... ☐ 1
No...... ☐ 2   75

(If you have any further remarks about these matters, they would be most helpful. Would you use the space following and the reverse side of this page for any comments you would like to make.)

245

Letter to 1952 Business Leaders

THE UNIVERSITY OF CHICAGO
STUDY OF BUSINESS LEADERS

Sponsoring Committee

LAWRENCE A. APPLEY
New York City

JOHN COWLES
Minneapolis

CLARENCE B. RANDALL
Chicago

FRANK STANTON
New York City

GENERAL ROBERT E. WOOD
Chicago

Dear Sir:

With the sponsorship of a committee of American business leaders, The University of Chicago is undertaking the study of individual opportunity in American business and industry today.
By comparison with the earlier work of Professors Taussig and
Joslyn of Harvard University, "American Business Leaders," we
will study changes in the patterns of business opportunity in
this country since 1929. We will further determine what the
trends have been and what future developments might be predicted.
The results of the study will be made available for use by business men.

As in the earlier work, the data for this study will be based on
direct information from recognized business leaders throughout
the United States. We are, therefore, sending you the enclosed
schedule and asking your cooperation in filling it out. Almost
all of the questions can be answered by a simple check mark. (x)
Your replies will be held in strict confidence; they are keyed
so that only the two undersigned researchers will know your
identity. The inquiry is purely scientific in nature and is supported by grants from the Hill Family Foundation and individual
business leaders.

We believe you will find the few minutes of your time it takes
to fill out the schedule well repaid by the results of the inquiry which we hope to have ready for publication at an early
date. If, in filling out the schedule, questions and comments
come to mind, we would be grateful if you would send them on to
us. We want to maintain sufficient flexibility in our inquiry to
give our findings the significance they should have in determining
what has happened and is happening to individual opportunity in
America.

Sincerely yours,

246

APPENDIXES, REFERENCES, AND INDEX

Appendix I. FURTHER RESULTS OF THE STUDY

Male Reproduction and Occupational Mobility

Discussions of rates and trends in occupational mobility in America have frequently cited differential birth rates among the several social classes and socioeconomic levels as a factor in social and occupational mobility. In general it has been observed that birth rates vary inversely with socioeconomic status, and that lower status families have more children than do higher status families. From these data the conclusion has been drawn by some authors that occupational and social mobility in America is in part a function of the failure of higher status individuals to reproduce themselves biologically, thus in a sense "making room" at the top for the offspring of lower status families.

To examine this general issue in terms of mobility into the business elite we asked the business leaders replying to the 1952 questionnaire to indicate on the questionnaire the number of their surviving male children. Appendix Table 1 presents the results of the analysis of this questionnaire item. The column on the left lists the percentage of business leaders from the several occupational backgrounds who have no surviving male children. For the group as a whole, about one third of the men studied do not have male offspring. This percentage tends to vary with the general occupational background of the business leader, however. Thirty-eight per cent of the sons of laborers have no male children, while the proportion is only 27 per cent of the business leaders whose fathers were major business executives.

To allow examination of the data in another way, the column on the right presents the ratio of the total number of business leaders from each of the occupational backgrounds to the total number of sons of men from that occupational background. The ratio is then in a sense a measure of the "inheritance potential" of men from each of the occupational backgrounds. It is evident that the men from lower level occupational backgrounds have fewer male offspring than are necessary to match their numbers in the business elite. In other words, the men whose fathers were laborers, clerks, salesmen, foremen, or minor executives, do not quite reproduce themselves in terms of number of male offspring. The highest ratio of business leaders to male offspring obtains for men whose fathers were owners of large businesses or major executives. The number of sons that these men from higher level occupational backgrounds have had more than matches their own numbers in the business elite.

These data do not exhaust the inheritance potential of these groups of course, in the sense that daughters may marry men who function

Appendix Table 1. Occupational Mobility and Male Offspring

Occupation of Business Leader's Father	Percentage of Leaders with No Sons	Ratio of Total Number of Men to Total Number of Sons
Laborer	38	0.93
Clerk or salesman	33	0.94
Foreman or minor executive	31	0.99
Owner of small business	33	1.02
Owner of large business	30	1.13
Major executive	27	1.21
Professional man	31	1.08
Farmer	35	1.00
All occupations	32	1.01

in the role of sons and "inheritors." The results of this analysis do suggest, however, that insofar as biological reproduction is a factor in occupational mobility and inheritance, it is most likely to apply to the mobile men in the business elite. These men, who doubtless marry late and by choice or circumstance are less well able to assume the charge of large families, do not have a sufficient number of sons to fill the occupational positions they have come to occupy.

In some degree, then, to judge from this factor alone, the cycle of mobility is one of occupational inheritance by those men from higher status backgrounds, while the mobile men are not so frequently succeeded by their sons in their business positions. It is more often the mobile men of the business elite who leave room in the next generation for more mobility.

Mobility of the Fathers during the Fathers' Careers

In the design of the questionnaire for the study of mobility in business and industry, some consideration was given to the question of changes in the occupational positions of the fathers of business leaders during the careers of the fathers before the business careers of the present-day business leaders began. Thus the item relating to occupation of father provided for responses for two periods of time. The first was "when you [the responding business leader] were in grammar school"; the second, "when you became self-supporting." In preceding analyses, the responses used were those to the second part of this question, the occupation of the father at the time the business leader became self-supporting.

Appendix Table 2 presents the distributions of responses to both parts of this question about occupation of father. In general, the differences between the two time periods in occupation of father are not

Further Results of the Study

large. A somewhat higher proportion of fathers are indicated to have been laborers, white-collar workers, and farmers. The proportion of fathers in the positions of major business executives or owners of large businesses increased by about 4 per cent between the two periods. The mobility indicated as having taken place during the father's own career is then largely in the direction of movement out of lower status occupations into higher level business positions.

The patterning of this occupational movement by the fathers during the career of the fathers is shown in detail in Appendix Table 3, where the proportion of fathers moving from the several initial occupations to their terminal occupations is given. Thus, 85 per cent of the fathers who were laborers when their sons were in grammar school are shown to have been laborers still when their sons became self-

Appendix Table 2. Changes in Distribution of Occupations of Fathers of 1952 Business Leaders

Occupation of Father	When Son Was in Grammar School	When Son Became Self-Supporting
Laborer	17.0%	15.2%
Owner of small business	18.4	18.2
White-collar worker	20.6	19.4
Major executive or owner of large business.	19.9	24.0
Professional man	14.9	14.5
Farmer	9.2	8.7
Total	100.0	100.0

Appendix Table 3. Occupational Mobility of Fathers of Business Leaders during the Father's Career (Movement out of Earlier Occupation)

Occupation When Son Became Self-Supporting	Occupation When Son Was in Grammar School					
	Laborer	Owner of Small Business	White-Collar Worker	Major Executive and Owner of Large Business	Professional Man	Farmer
Laborer	85%	2%	1%	0%	0%	3%
Owner of small business	4	85	5	2	1	3
White-collar worker	8	5	78	2	2	3
Major executive and owner of large business	2	7	15	96	2	1
Professional man	0	0	0	0	95	0
Farmer	1	1	1	0	0	90
Total	100	100	100	100	100	100

supporting. Movement out of laboring occupations by the fathers was primarily into white-collar positions.

The least amount of occupational stability by fathers, and so maximum vertical mobility, is shown by the fathers who were white-collar workers when their sons were in grammar school. In these cases, 78 per cent remained in this occupational group, while a total of 15 per cent moved into the category of major executive and owner of large business.

On the whole, then, if we assume the reports to be complete, movement by the fathers during this period of their careers was limited, taking place generally in an upward direction through the business structure. Apparently about 10 per cent of the fathers who were farmers initially moved to urban occupations during this period, with little movement by men from other occupations into farming.

Appendix II. OCCUPATIONAL ORIGINS OF THE BUSINESS ELITE

Appendix Table 4. Occupation of Father for All 1952 Business Leaders and for Respondents to Item on Occupation of Father's Father

Occupation of Father	Distribution of Respondents to Item on Father's Occupation		Distribution by Father's Occupation of Respondents to Item on Father's Father's Occupation	
	Number	Percentage	Number	Percentage
Unskilled and semiskilled laborer.	338	4.5	301	4.4
Skilled laborer	773	10.3	694	10.1
Farmer				
1	23	0.3	22	0.3
2	27	0.4	25	0.4
3	275	3.7	259	3.8
4	314	4.2	304	4.4
Clerk	190	2.5	164	2.4
Salesman	446	5.9	383	5.6
Foreman	233	3.1	210	3.0
Minor executive	555	7.4	518	7.5
Major executive	1,097	14.6	1,037	15.0
Owner				
1	1,326	17.7	1,197	17.4
2	476	6.3	436	6.3
3	179	2.4	164	2.4
Doctor	165	2.2	158	2.3
Engineer	162	2.2	153	2.2
Lawyer	238	3.2	225	3.3
Minister	175	2.3	167	2.4
Other profession	314	4.2	293	4.2
Military career	21	0.3	20	0.3
Government service	139	1.9	129	1.9
Other	34	0.4	28	0.4
Total	7,500	100.0	6,887	100.0

Appendix Table 5. Occupation of Father and Occupation of Father's Father for 1928 Business Leaders

Occupation of Father's Father	Occupation of Father									
	Unskilled or Semi-skilled Laborer	Skilled Laborer	Farmer	Clerk or Salesman	Minor Executive	Owner of Small Business	Major Executive	Owner of Large Business	Professional Man	Other
Unskilled or semiskilled laborer	74	54	4	12	15	38	9	9	7	0
Skilled laborer	6	231	24	37	51	111	66	52	41	1
Farmer	41	175	720	127	144	467	264	232	290	17
Clerk or salesman	2	8	2	27	12	16	17	8	6	0
Minor executive	1	7	5	19	67	23	55	32	19	4
Owner of small business	11	49	23	69	72	435	182	203	95	13
Major executive	0	0	8	6	34	14	280	31	24	4
Owner of large business	1	6	6	17	21	54	85	272	59	8
Professional man	4	23	25	35	46	91	145	75	326	18
Other	0	3	9	4	5	10	23	15	15	12

Appendix Table 6. Occupation of Father and Occupation of Father's Father for 1952 Comparison Sample

Occupation of Father's Father	Occupation of Father									
	Unskilled or Semi-skilled Laborer	Skilled Laborer	Farmer	Clerk or Salesman	Minor Executive	Owner of Small Business	Major Executive	Owner of Large Business	Professional Man	Other
Unskilled or semiskilled laborer	138	23	89	0	1	9	1	9	11	4
Skilled laborer	96	236	220	7	10	54	8	9	26	10
Farmer	10	24	489	0	1	26	2	4	28	4
Clerk or salesman	31	65	165	39	15	112	17	35	38	14
Minor executive	62	117	206	28	59	122	23	44	61	24
Owner of small business	59	122	442	18	31	352	22	31	61	26
Major executive	24	88	196	29	46	218	185	115	122	25
Owner of large business	15	38	137	17	14	181	20	147	44	5
Professional man	21	70	332	15	28	113	37	81	263	31
Other	17	16	66	4	4	26	15	7	15	16

Appendix Table 7. Mobility Ratios from Occupation of Father's Father to Occupation of Father for 1928 Business Leaders *

Occupation of Father's Father	Occupation of Father										Mobility out of Occupation
	Unskilled or Semiskilled Laborer	Skilled Laborer	Owner of Small Business	Clerk or Salesman	Minor Executive	Major Executive	Owner of Large Business	Professional Man	Farmer	Other	
Unskilled or semiskilled laborer	17.67	3.33	1.00	1.00	1.00	0.33	0.33	0.33	0.00	0.00	0.81
Skilled laborer	0.44	4.67	1.00	1.11	1.22	0.67	0.67	0.44	0.33	0.11	0.67
Owner of small business	0.47	0.53	2.06	1.18	0.88	0.94	1.29	0.65	0.17	1.00	0.79
Clerk or salesman	0.50	0.50	0.50	4.00	1.50	0.50	0.50	0.50	0.00	0.00	0.50
Minor executive	0.25	0.25	0.50	1.25	3.50	1.25	0.75	0.50	0.25	1.25	0.69
Major executive	0.00	0.00	0.17	0.33	1.17	4.17	0.50	0.50	0.17	0.83	0.41
Owner of large business	0.12	0.13	0.50	0.68	0.62	1.00	3.63	0.87	0.12	1.88	0.60
Professional man	0.25	0.33	0.58	0.83	0.83	1.08	0.67	3.08	0.25	1.92	0.75
Farmer	0.78	0.86	1.00	0.97	0.84	0.62	0.68	0.89	2.35	0.59	0.80

* Average for all groups = 0.67; mean of diagonal = 5.01.

Appendix Table 8. Mobility Ratios from Occupation of Father's Father to Occupation of Father for 1952 Comparison Group *

Occupation of Father's Father	Occupation of Father										Mobility out of Occupation
	Unskilled or Semiskilled Laborer	Skilled Laborer	Owner of Small Business	Clerk or Salesman	Minor Executive	Major Executive	Owner of Large Business	Professional Man	Farmer	Other	
Unskilled or semiskilled laborer	7.29	2.00	0.86	0.86	1.14	0.29	0.43	0.29	0.29	1.14	0.81
Skilled laborer	0.83	2.83	0.92	1.00	1.33	0.75	0.58	0.58	0.33	0.83	0.79
Owner of small business	0.17	0.53	1.76	1.24	0.94	1.29	1.47	0.47	0.29	0.82	0.80
Clerk or salesman	0.00	0.50	0.50	3.50	2.00	1.50	1.50	0.50	0.00	1.00	0.83
Minor executive	0.33	0.33	0.67	1.00	2.67	1.33	0.67	1.00	0.00	0.67	0.67
Major executive	0.00	0.20	0.40	0.60	0.60	3.60	0.80	0.80	0.00	1.20	0.51
Owner of large business	0.29	0.14	0.43	1.00	0.86	1.57	3.43	1.71	0.14	0.71	0.76
Professional man	0.30	0.50	0.50	0.90	0.80	1.10	0.70	2.60	0.50	0.80	0.68
Farmer	0.83	0.94	1.09	0.83	0.83	0.51	0.71	0.94	2.34	1.06	0.86

* Average for all groups = 0.75; mean of diagonals = 3.75.

Appendix Table 9. Correlative Distribution by 22 Questionnaire Categories of Occupation of Father and Occupation of Father's Father for 1952 Business Leaders

Occupation of Father's Father	Unskilled or Semi-skilled Laborer	Skilled Laborer	Farmer — Farm Worker or Small Tenant	Farmer — Tenant with Paid Help	Farmer — Owner without Paid Help	Farmer — Owner or Manager with Paid Help	Clerk or Retail Salesman	Salesman	Foreman	Minor Executive	Major Executive	Owner of Small Business	Owner of Medium Business	Owner of Large Business	Prof. — Doctor	Prof. — Engineer	Prof. — Lawyer	Prof. — Minister	Prof. — Other	Military Career	Government Service	Other
Unskilled or semiskilled laborer	153	98	1	1	10	2	14	19	29	28	25	66	10	5	3	5	2	8	8	1	12	1
Skilled laborer	31	235	3	0	11	10	20	45	51	64	88	130	28	12	6	7	13	14	30	2	14	1
Farmer — Farm worker or small tenant	24	26	9	3	11	3	2	5	7	8	12	35	6	0	2	0	0	2	0	0	6	0
Farmer — Tenant with paid help	1	8	1	7	4	3	1	4	2	5	2	14	2	0	2	0	0	1	4	1	1	0
Farmer — Owner without paid help	57	152	4	5	178	77	25	67	42	74	90	272	66	13	32	15	29	46	52	1	28	8
Farmer — Owner or manager with paid help	6	45	1	5	20	166	16	40	16	55	87	134	47	16	30	14	36	24	46	3	11	5
Clerk or retail salesman	0	4	0	0	0	0	12	5	1	11	12	15	5	2	0	2	2	1	2	2	1	0
Salesman	1	1	0	0	0	0	6	17	1	14	15	3	6	6	0	1	2	2	1	0	1	0
Foreman	1	4	0	0	0	0	2	2	9	9	8	8	2	4	5	5	3	2	3	1	0	0
Minor executive	0	6	0	0	0	2	4	10	1	41	38	18	6	5	7	11	8	0	9	0	2	0
Major executive	0	6	0	0	0	0	29	10	3	17	185	21	19	37	11	26	24	3	12	0	1	4
Owner of small business	9	62	2	3	13	10	10	88	28	92	226	362	110	16	11	18	18	18	37	2	7	2
Owner of medium business	5	6	0	3	2	3	2	25	5	35	77	29	89	13	13	18	18	5	14	5	6	3
Owner of large business	1	1	0	0	0	1	2	2	0	3	33	2	7	32	3	0	1	2	4	0	0	0
Professional man — Doctor	3	5	0	0	2	7	2	8	1	8	23	10	6	4	18	4	11	6	7	1	2	0
Professional man — Engineer	1	2	0	0	1	0	1	1	0	4	18	5	2	1	3	15	4	1	8	0	0	1
Professional man — Lawyer	1	2	1	0	3	6	2	5	1	11	25	11	8	6	5	6	44	9	9	8	1	2
Professional man — Minister	3	8	0	0	3	3	5	13	4	9	28	24	7	3	8	4	11	27	11	3	3	0
Professional man — Other	1	14	0	0	1	1	6	6	4	14	27	12	5	8	4	6	8	7	30	0	0	0
Military career	0	6	0	0	0	0	1	3	2	1	8	9	2	0	4	2	4	0	4	0	9	2
Government service	3	1	0	0	1	1	1	5	1	9	11	10	2	0	1	6	3	3	2	1	9	1
Other	0	2	0	1	0	1	2	3	2	6	4	7	1	0	1	3	2	0	4	1	2	1

Appendix III. CIRCULATION OF THE ELITE

Appendix Table 10. Occupation of Father and Region of Leader's Birth: Correlative Distribution of 1952 Business Leaders

Occupation of Father	New England	Middle Atlantic	East North Central	West North Central	South Atlantic	East South Central	West South Central	Mountain	Pacific	Other
Unskilled or semiskilled laborer	45	102	83	39	15	8	7	8	8	0
Skilled laborer	76	223	197	86	42	14	18	15	25	1
Farmer	22	80	168	124	70	46	45	20	21	0
Clerk	20	46	40	21	21	7	13	2	8	0
Salesman	29	123	121	64	35	16	13	4	10	0
Foreman	26	56	69	27	13	7	4	3	9	0
Minor executive	53	178	119	61	35	24	9	18	24	1
Major executive	127	300	279	183	84	30	27	11	59	3
Owner of large business	131	359	306	192	88	33	47	27	53	1
Owner of medium-sized business	31	129	120	56	39	16	17	14	20	1
Owner of small business	19	60	35	21	10	2	5	2	12	1
Doctor	16	42	36	19	12	13	5	1	9	0
Engineer	12	52	34	3	13	4	5	7	11	0
Lawyer	22	57	45	32	31	11	15	5	15	0
Minister	16	33	27	36	19	10	7	3	5	1
Other profession	31	81	78	35	22	10	7	10	15	0
Military career, government service, other	22	40	38	22	33	4	8	4	9	0
Total	698	1,961	1,795	971	582	255	252	154	313	9

257

Appendix Table 11. Occupation of Father and Region of Leader's Present Business: Correlative Distribution of 1952 Business Leaders

Occupation of Father	New England	Middle Atlantic	East North Central	West North Central	South Atlantic	East South Central	West South Central	Mountain	Pacific	Other
Unskilled or semiskilled laborer	28	133	86	38	13	5	5	5	25	0
Skilled laborer	48	301	209	66	44	7	25	7	64	2
Farmer										
Farm worker or small tenant	0	5	6	2	4	0	2	3	1	0
Tenant with paid help	1	5	11	3	0	1	1	3	2	0
Owner without paid help	17	65	90	31	12	4	24	5	27	0
Owner or manager with paid help	18	90	62	31	36	20	23	9	24	1
Clerk or retail salesman	15	67	48	17	17	1	14	1	10	0
Salesman	22	177	117	46	32	6	16	1	28	1
Foreman	18	91	66	16	14	6	3	1	18	0
Minor executive	42	242	126	49	32	7	11	2	41	3
Major executive	95	419	279	102	71	19	21	3	88	0
Owner of small business	99	518	357	110	79	20	34	8	98	3
Owner of medium business	27	190	116	31	31	14	17	8	42	0
Owner of large business	18	73	38	16	10	1	5	2	16	0
Professional man										
Doctor	11	62	45	11	16	5	2	1	12	0
Engineer	14	72	43	7	7	1	4	1	13	0
Lawyer	19	101	59	13	12	5	6	2	20	1
Minister	8	73	34	14	19	4	8	0	15	0
Other	25	134	74	23	16	9	6	2	25	0
Military career	1	7	4	0	6	0	0	0	3	0
Government service	6	54	37	7	18	1	6	0	9	1
Other	3	7	7	6	5	1	1	1	2	1

Appendix Table 12. Occupation of Father and Region of Present Business for 1952 Comparison Sample

Occupation of Father	New England	Middle Atlantic	East North Central	West North Central	South Atlantic	East South Central	West South Central	Mountain	Pacific
Unskilled or semiskilled laborer	9.9%	36.7%	26.7%	9.9%	4.0%	1.2%	2.5%	1.6%	7.5%
Skilled laborer	7.4	40.0	26.4	7.8	5.3	0.9	3.2	0.7	8.3
Farmer	6.4	26.5	26.1	10.8	7.8	3.8	7.2	2.4	9.0
Clerk or salesman	7.2	38.6	25.3	8.5	8.3	1.0	4.7	0.3	6.1
Minor executive	8.0	43.1	23.5	8.2	5.8	1.4	1.9	0.1	8.0
Owner of small business	8.2	39.4	26.8	8.0	5.3	1.5	2.4	0.6	7.8
Major executive	9.3	40.0	24.6	8.8	6.2	1.6	2.0	0.3	7.2
Owner of large business	7.3	40.8	23.0	7.1	6.5	2.1	3.6	1.6	8.0
Professional man	8.6	43.7	22.2	7.3	6.1	1.8	2.0	0.3	8.0
All occupations	8.1	39.4	24.8	8.3	6.2	1.7	3.0	0.7	7.8

Appendix Table 13. Region of Birth by Region of Present Business: Correlative Distribution of 1952 Business Leaders

Region of Birth	Region of Present Business									
	New England	Middle Atlantic	East North Central	West North Central	South Atlantic	East South Central	West South Central	Mountain	Pacific	Other
New England	302	252	73	19	22	5	5	2	18	0
Middle Atlantic	86	1473	213	39	66	8	21	3	50	2
East North Central	45	376	1087	122	34	12	25	8	86	0
West North Central	24	220	214	346	29	5	27	13	91	2
South Atlantic	14	170	56	21	273	18	13	1	16	0
East South Central	8	45	53	15	30	74	19	1	10	0
West South Central	4	60	25	20	11	4	106	4	17	1
Mountain	7	41	29	8	4	0	2	27	36	0
Pacific	7	41	29	6	6	1	5	3	213	2
Other	0	1	0	1	0	1	1	0	4	1

259

Appendix Table 14. Occupation of Father and Size of Birthplace for
1952 Business Leaders

Occupation of Father	Over 400,000	100,000– 400,000	25,000– 100,000	2500– 25,000	Under 2500	All Commu- nities
Laborer	19%	15%	15%	15%	14%	16%
Owner of small business.	14	15	18	21	21	18
White-collar worker	24	20	21	20	14	20
Major executive and owner of large business	28	36	31	23	10	23
Professional man	13	12	12	16	15	14
Farmer	2	2	3	5	26	9
Total	100	100	100	100	100	100

Appendix Table 15. Occupation of Father and Nativity for 1952 Business Leaders *

Occupation of Father	Leader Foreign-Born	Leader U.S.-Born	Father and Leader U.S.-Born	Father's Father, Father, and Leader U.S.-Born
Unskilled or semiskilled laborer ..	19	134	77	107
Skilled laborer	65	221	194	292
Owner of small business	77	354	273	619
Clerk or salesman	34	115	136	351
Minor executive	36	155	173	424
Major executive	33	138	232	691
Owner of large business	35	132	139	348
Professional man	53	121	162	715
Farmer	33	67	92	442
Other	8	36	37	113
Total	393	1,473	1.515	4,102

* For the data on nativity, the following categories have been applied:

Paternal grandfather, father, and leader U.S.-born.

Men who have been born in the U.S. and whose fathers and paternal grandfathers were born in the U.S.; or

Men who were born abroad but whose fathers and grandfathers were born in the U.S.; or

Men who were born in the U.S., whose fathers were born abroad, and whose grandfathers were born in the U.S.

Father and leader U.S.-born.

Men who were born in the U.S., whose fathers were born in the U.S., and whose paternal grandfathers were born abroad; or

Men who were born in the U.S., whose fathers were born in the U.S., and who gave no answer to the question on birth of paternal grandfather.

Leader U.S.-born.

Men who were born in the U.S., whose fathers were born abroad, and whose paternal grandfathers were born abroad; or

Men who were born in the U.S., whose fathers were born abroad, and who gave no answer to the question on birth of paternal grandfather.

Men who were born in the U.S., who gave no answer to the question on birth of father, and who gave no answer to the question on birth of paternal grandfather.

Leader foreign-born.

Men who were born abroad, whose fathers were born abroad, and whose paternal grandfathers were born abroad; or

Men who were born abroad, whose fathers were born abroad, and who gave no answer to the question on birth of paternal grandfather.

Men who were born abroad and who gave no answer to the questions on birth of father and paternal grandfather.

(Men who failed to answer the question as to their own place of birth have been excluded from the analysis of this data.)

Appendix Table 16. Nativity and Territorial Mobility for U.S.-Born 1952
Business Leaders

Territorial Mobility	Leader U.S.-Born	Father U.S.-Born	Father's Father U.S.-Born	All Groups
Intrastate	28%	40%	43%	33%
Intrastate, rural to urban..	9	7	4	7
Interstate	15	14	14	15
Interregion	48	39	39	45
Total	100	100	100	100

Appendix Table 17. Distribution by State of Residence of 1928 Business Leaders
and by State of Present Business of 1952 Business Leaders

State	State of Residence of 1928 Leaders		State of Present Business of 1952 Leaders	
	Number	Percentage	Number	Percentage
Alabama	38	.5	28	.4
Arizona	5	.1	5	.1
Arkansas	26	.4	8	.1
California	406	5.5	442	6.0
Colorado	52	.7	34	.5
Connecticut	286	3.8	170	2.3
Delaware	25	.3	45	.6
District of Columbia	26	.4	45	.6
Florida	56	.8	36	.5
Georgia	50	.7	62	.8
Idaho	6	.1	3	.0
Illinois	376	5.1	822	11.2
Indiana	98	1.3	90	1.2
Iowa	50	.7	54	.7
Kansas	33	.4	25	.3
Kentucky	41	.5	40	.5
Louisiana	55	.8	28	.4
Maine	43	.7	18	.2
Maryland	57	.9	100	1.4
Massachusetts	863	11.7	359	4.9
Michigan	211	2.9	289	3.9
Minnesota	97	1.3	204	2.8
Mississippi	9	.1	1	.0
Missouri	153	2.1	288	3.9
Montana	3	.0	3	.0
Nebraska	36	.5	32	.4
Nevada	4	.1	0	.0
New Hampshire	21	.3	12	.2
New Jersey	149	2.0	177	2.4
New Mexico	0	.0	2	.0
New York	2,335	31.7	2,029	27.5

State	State of Residence of 1928 Leaders		State of Present Business of 1952 Leaders	
	Number	Percentage	Number	Percentage
North Carolina	54	.7	85	1.2
North Dakota	7	.1	1	.0
Ohio	331	4.5	472	6.4
Oklahoma	41	.6	41	.6
Oregon	18	.2	60	.8
Pennsylvania	697	9.4	696	9.4
Rhode Island	124	1.7	28	.4
South Carolina	26	.4	12	.2
South Dakota	2	.0	3	.0
Tennessee	50	.7	53	.7
Texas	85	1.2	146	2.0
Utah	32	.4	5	.1
Vermont	15	.2	7	.1
Virginia	67	.8	54	.7
Washington	55	.7	72	1.0
West Virginia	35	.5	27	.4
Wisconsin	82	1.1	146	2.0
Wyoming	3	.0	0	.0
Territories: Hawaii, Philippine Islands, Alaska, Puerto Rico, Canal Zone	27	.4	12	.2
Total	7,361	100.0	7,371	100.0

Appendix Table 18. Occupation of Father and Region of Residence for 1928 Business Leaders

Occupation of Father	New England	Middle Atlantic	East North Central	West North Central	South Atlantic	East South Central	West South Central	Mountain	Pacific
Unskilled or semiskilled laborer	21.7%	43.3%	16.6%	3.8%	3.2%	0.6%	1.3%	2.5%	7.0%
Skilled laborer	20.6	44.8	17.2	3.8	3.3	1.1	1.3	0.9	7.0
Farmer	12.3	33.6	15.8	8.2	9.5	3.5	5.1	2.9	9.1
Clerk or salesman	20.1	47.7	17.8	2.8	3.3	1.5	2.1	0.5	4.2
Minor executive	19.1	48.1	12.1	3.7	5.8	1.4	1.9	1.4	6.5
Owner of small business	16.8	44.9	16.3	5.0	4.8	2.2	2.6	1.3	6.1
Major executive	22.4	41.6	14.0	6.6	5.2	1.7	1.5	1.6	5.4
Owner of large business	19.4	46.7	14.2	3.6	4.5	1.3	2.8	0.9	6.6
Professional man	17.3	42.9	13.6	5.3	6.2	1.7	4.9	1.3	6.8
All occupations	18.4	43.3	15.1	5.2	5.4	1.9	2.8	1.4	6.5

Appendix Table 19. Region of Residence for 1928 Business
Leaders and Region of Present Business for 1952
Business Leaders

Region	1928 Leaders *	1952 Leaders *
New England	18.4%	8.1%
Middle Atlantic	43.1	39.4
East North Central	14.9	24.7
West North Central	5.1	8.2
South Atlantic	5.5	6.3
East South Central	1.8	1.7
West South Central	3.0	3.0
Mountain	1.4	0.7
Pacific	6.4	7.8
Total	99.6	99.9

* The total numbers on which these percentages are based
include, in addition to the United States proper, the following: Alaska, the Hawaiian Islands, the Philippine Islands,
Puerto Rico, and the Panama Canal Zone.

Appendix IV. THE EDUCATION OF THE BUSINESS ELITE

Appendix Table 20. Education of 1952 Business Leaders and Occupation of Fathers

Occupation of Father	Less Than High School	Some High School	High School Graduation	Some College	College Graduation	Post-graduate Work	No Answer	Total
Unskilled or semiskilled laborer ..	48	61	55	52	91	30	1	337
Skilled laborer	69	126	150	163	196	66	3	770
Farm worker or small tenant	1	6	3	4	5	3	1	22
Farm tenant, with paid help	0	2	5	9	8	3	0	27
Farm owner, without paid help	18	32	45	60	82	37	1	274
Farm owner or manager, with paid help	16	16	41	57	120	64	0	314
Clerk or retail salesman	13	31	30	32	56	27	1	189
Salesman	26	49	57	87	152	75	0	446
Foreman	21	31	43	51	57	30	0	233
Minor executive ...	15	48	61	116	208	104	3	552
Major executive	5	29	54	202	573	233	1	1,096
Owner of small business	49	122	159	238	507	249	2	1,324
Owner of medium business	7	26	50	92	198	102	1	475
Owner of large business	2	10	9	28	99	31	0	179
Doctor	5	7	8	36	69	39	1	164
Engineer	4	3	9	36	72	37	1	161
Lawyer	1	6	13	34	92	92	0	238
Minister	6	4	9	33	69	54	0	175
Other profession	4	12	24	39	134	101	0	314
Military career	3	2	1	7	5	3	0	21
Government service.	4	14	19	29	39	34	0	139
Other	1	3	3	6	15	6	0	34
Total	318	640	848	1,411	2,847	1,420	16	7,500

Appendix Table 21. Education of Father and Occupation of Father's Father for 1952 Business Leaders

Education of Father	Occupation of Father's Father						
	Unskilled or Semiskilled Laborer	Skilled Laborer	Owner of Small Business	White-Collar Worker	Major Executive or Owner of Large Business	Professional Man	Farmer	All Business Leaders
Less than high school ...	77%	55%	28%	26%	11%	14%	45%	37%
Some high school	13	20	18	17	10	9	16	15
High school graduation .	6	14	25	30	24	16	14	18
Some college	2	4	14	12	18	14	9	11
College graduation	1	4	11	12	26	27	10	13
Postgraduate work	1	3	4	3	11	20	6	6
Total	100	100	100	100	100	100	100	100

267

Appendix Table 22. Education of 1952 Business Leaders as Related to
Size of Place of Birth

Education	400,000 and Over	100,000– 400,000	25,000– 100,000	2500– 25,000	Under 2500
Less than high school ...	88	39	21	31	88
Some high school	164	74	64	98	164
High school graduation ..	159	106	99	188	229
Some college	333	194	156	260	376
College graduation	697	381	356	650	644
Postgraduate work	344	187	166	291	352
Total	1,785	981	862	1,518	1,853

Appendix Table 23. Education and Age at Time of Study of 1928 and 1952 Business Leaders

Highest Stage of Schooling Completed	All Business Leaders	Age at Time of Study for 1928 Leaders										
		Under 30	30-34	35-39	40-44	45-49	50-54	55-59	60-64	65-69	70-74	75 and Over
None	1.0%	0.0%	0.3%	0.7%	0.3%	0.7%	0.6%	1.4%	1.5%	2.1%	1.3%	1.8%
Grammar school	25.7	11.8	10.6	15.7	19.8	23.9	26.2	31.1	34.4	32.5	33.3	37.2
High or preparatory school.	28.0	22.4	21.2	23.8	25.5	27.8	27.2	29.9	30.9	33.1	32.0	34.5
Some college	13.4	23.7	24.2	17.3	14.5	13.5	13.4	10.7	11.0	11.5	7.4	11.5
College graduation	31.9	42.1	43.7	42.5	39.9	34.1	32.6	26.9	22.2	20.8	26.0	15.0
Total	100.0	100.0	100.0	100.0	100.0	100.0	100.0	100.0	100.0	100.0	100.0	100.0

Highest Stage of Schooling Completed	All Business Leaders	Age at Time of Study for 1952 Leaders										
		Under 35	35-39	40-44	45-49	50-54	55-59	60-64	65-69	70-74	75 and Over
Less than high school	4.3%	...	0.3%	0.3%	1.7%	2.8%	5.3%	7.8%	9.4%	12.0%	14.9%
High or preparatory school.	20.0	5.7%	4.1	9.4	12.0	19.7	26.6	26.0	31.1	30.4	26.3
Some college	18.5	28.6	15.9	18.8	20.1	20.7	17.7	16.1	14.5	16.8	20.2
College graduation	57.2	65.7	79.7	71.5	66.2	56.8	50.4	50.1	45.0	40.8	38.6
Total	100.0	100.0	100.0	100.0	100.0	100.0	100.0	100.0	100.0	100.0	100.0

Appendix Table 24. Formal Business Training and Age at Time of Study of 1928 and 1952 Leaders

Formal Business Training	All Business Leaders	Age at Time of Study for 1928 Leaders										
		Under 30	30–34	35–39	40–44	45–49	50–54	55–59	60–64	65–69	70–74	75 and Over
None	70.7%	52.6%	58.9%	60.7%	68.1%	69.8%	72.3%	72.5%	74.3%	79.3%	81.0%	85.7%
Business training in public school or business college ...	22.0	23.7	17.1	24.6	23.1	23.5	22.9	22.8	21.9	17.5	16.4	11.6
Commercial training in college or university	7.3	23.7	24.0	14.7	8.8	6.7	4.8	4.7	3.8	3.2	2.6	2.7
Total	100.0	100.0	100.0	100.0	100.0	100.0	100.0	100.0	100.0	100.0	100.0	100.0

Formal Business Training	All Business Leaders	Age at Time of Study for 1952 Leaders									
		Under 35	35–39	40–44	45–49	50–54	55–59	60–64	65–69	70–74	75 and Over
None	42.0%	26.1%	32.3%	34.8%	35.5%	38.2%	42.2%	48.4%	56.7%	74.4%	78.0%
Business training in public school or business college ..	24.9	14.5	11.9	14.2	18.0	25.5	33.2	32.6	30.5	18.8	16.0
Commercial training in college or university	33.1	59.4	55.8	51.0	46.5	36.3	24.6	19.0	12.8	6.8	6.0
Total	100.0	100.0	100.0	100.0	100.0	100.0	100.0	100.0	100.0	100.0	100.0

Appendix V. THE BUSINESS CAREER

Time Factors in the Career

Appendix Table 25. Age of 1952 Business Leaders at Time of Study

Age	Percentage of Respondents	Age	Percentage of Respondents
Under 30	0.2	52	4.6
30	0.1	53	4.1
31	0.1	54	3.8
32	0.1	55	4.0
33	0.3	56	3.7
34	0.4	57	4.1
35	0.7	58	4.1
36	1.0	59	3.6
37	1.0	60	3.5
38	1.1	61	3.0
39	1.2	62	3.0
40	1.8	63	2.6
41	1.7	64	2.3
42	2.2	65	1.9
43	2.3	66	1.5
44	2.7	67	1.2
45	3.1	68	1.1
46	3.5	69	1.1
47	3.5	70	0.7
48	3.9	71	0.7
49	4.1	72	0.6
50	4.0	73	0.4
51	3.6	74	0.3
		75 and over	1.5

Appendix Table 26. Age at Which 1952 Business Leaders Entered Business

Age	Percentage of Respondents
Under 14	2
14	4
15	3
16	6
17	7
18	9
19	6
20	8
21	15
22	15
23	11
24	6
25	4
26	2
Over 26	2
Total	100

Appendix Table 27. Number of Years 1952 Business Leaders Were in Business before Entering Present Organization

Number of Years	Percentage of Respondents
Less than 2	31
2–3	7
4–5	7
6–7	6
8–9	6
10–11	6
12–13	5
14–15	5
16–17	4
18–19	4
20–21	4
22–23	3
24–25	3
26–27	2
28–29	2
30–34	3
35 or more	2
Total	100

Appendix Table 28. Number of Years 1952 Business Leaders Have Been in Present Organization

Number of Years	Percentage of Respondents *
0–3	5
4–6	7
7–9	5
10–12	6
13–15	6
16–18	7
19–21	7
22–24	10
25–27	9
28–30	8
31–33	10
34–36	6
37–39	4
40–42	4
43–45	2
Over 45	4
Total	100

* No answer was made by 15 of 7500.

Appendix Table 29. Number of Years 1952 Business Leaders Took to Achieve Position

Number of Years	Percentage of Respondents
0–2	1
3–5	1
6–8	3
9–11	5
12–14	7
15–17	9
18–20	11
21–23	13
24–26	11
27–29	11
30–32	9
33–35	6
36–38	5
39–41	3
42–44	2
45 or more	3
Total	100

Appendix Table 30. Number of Years 1952 Business Leaders
Have Been in Present Position

Number of Years *	Percentage of Respondents †
0–3	28
4–6	24
7–9	14
10–12	10
13–15	6
16–18	5
19–21	4
22–24	3
25–27	2
28–30	2
Over 30	2
Total	100

* The median number of years is 6.7.
† No answer was made by 41 of 7500.

Appendix Table 31. Formal Business Training, Age at Time of Study, and Time
Required to Achieve Business Position for 1952 Business Leaders

Business Training	Present Age (Median)	Years to Achieve Business Position (Median)
None	55.4	23.0
Business training in public school or business college	56.4	27.0
Commercial training in college or university	49.5	21.4
All respondents	53.7	23.9

Appendix Table 32. Occupation of Father and Age at Time of Study for 1928 and 1952 Business Leaders

Age at Time of Study	Unskilled or Semi-skilled Laborer	Skilled Laborer	Farmer	Clerk or Salesman	Minor Executive	Owner of Small Business	Major Executive	Owner of Large Business	Professional Man	Total
Under 30										
1928	2.7%	8.2%	1.4%	5.5%	2.7%	15.1%	27.4%	21.9%	15.1%	100.0%
1952	...	...	...	...	12.5	12.5	25.0	50.0	...	100.0
30–34										
1928	2.3	6.6	5.0	5.2	7.3	18.6	27.5	16.9	10.6	100.0
1952	3.3	1.7	1.7	1.7	10.0	8.3	43.3	23.3	6.7	100.0
35–39										
1928	2.9	7.5	4.6	5.2	6.8	17.8	25.8	15.5	13.8	100.0
1952	3.3	6.8	3.3	7.1	9.4	12.3	31.5	13.6	12.7	100.0
40–44										
1928	2.5	6.9	8.1	6.9	9.0	18.1	21.1	16.1	11.3	100.0
1952	3.2	8.5	5.1	10.4	10.7	14.1	23.4	9.1	15.5	100.0
45–49										
1928	2.9	9.4	10.3	6.2	8.9	18.2	16.5	14.3	13.3	100.0
1952	4.3	11.4	6.1	7.8	11.2	17.7	17.7	7.4	16.4	100.0
50–54										
1928	1.5	8.6	12.9	6.0	6.1	20.4	17.6	13.3	13.6	100.0
1952	5.3	10.4	8.6	8.0	13.0	18.3	13.7	6.6	16.1	100.0
55–59										
1928	2.2	9.2	13.8	6.2	6.9	22.1	12.8	15.0	11.8	100.0
1952	5.1	12.0	9.6	9.9	12.1	19.6	10.8	7.8	13.1	100.0
60–64										
1928	2.0	10.6	16.4	3.1	7.2	20.6	11.4	13.5	15.2	100.0
1952	4.7	11.0	11.7	7.5	10.3	19.0	11.8	9.0	15.0	100.0
65–69										
1928	1.7	11.6	20.7	3.2	5.1	21.7	9.5	12.8	18.7	100.0
1952	3.7	11.3	10.1	10.5	9.9	17.7	12.2	12.0	12.6	100.0
70–74										
1928	0.9	5.7	20.9	3.1	4.8	25.3	11.8	13.5	14.0	100.0
1952	4.2	6.3	14.7	7.4	10.0	21.1	10.5	11.1	14.7	100.0
75 and over										
1928	0.0	11.7	23.5	0.9	1.8	24.3	8.1	9.9	19.8	100.0
1952	2.7	5.5	16.4	4.5	9.1	23.6	16.4	10.0	11.8	100.0

275

Appendix Table 33. Age of Business Leaders of 1928 and 1952 at Time of Study and Size of Business

Size of Business *	Average Age in Years	Age of Leaders										
		Under 30	30-34	35-39	40-44	45-49	50-54	55-59	60-64	65-69	70-74	75 and Over
Grade A												
1952	55.5	...	...	0.8%	5.7%	15.9%	21.0%	25.2%	22.1%	6.8%	1.8%	0.7%
1928	52.4	0.3%	2.7%	9.2	10.9	15.9	18.1	16.5	14.6	7.8	3.1	0.9
Grade B												
1952	54.0	0.1	0.3	3.2	11.0	16.9	20.6	21.6	16.5	6.3	2.1	1.4
1928	51.9	0.8	3.2	9.2	12.6	16.3	17.5	16.4	11.8	6.9	3.7	1.6
Grade C												
1952	53.8	...	0.7	4.1	10.8	16.7	21.1	21.6	13.8	7.0	2.2	2.0
1928	51.1	1.1	4.3	10.4	12.9	17.1	17.1	14.3	10.6	7.8	2.8	1.6
Grade D												
1952	52.8	0.1	1.4	6.1	10.6	20.0	20.0	18.7	12.2	6.2	3.1	1.6
1928	50.4	1.2	5.1	12.8	13.8	14.6	16.0	15.9	10.3	6.0	2.8	1.5
Grade E												
1952	53.0	0.4	1.7	6.1	10.6	19.2	19.5	17.7	11.9	7.2	3.8	1.9
1928	51.0	1.9	6.3	9.9	13.7	12.9	15.7	16.4	10.9	7.2	3.2	1.9
All grades												
1952	53.7	0.1	0.8	4.3	10.1	17.9	20.4	20.6	14.9	6.7	2.6	1.6
1928	51.4	1.1	4.1	10.1	12.8	15.7	17.1	15.7	11.5	7.2	3.2	1.5

* See pp. 234-35 for the annual income or sales of businesses here indicated by A, B, C, D, and E.

Appendix Table 34. Formal Business Training and First Occupation of
1952 Business Leaders

First Occupation	All Business Leaders	No Formal Business Training	Business Training in Public School or Business College	Commercial Training in College or University
Unskilled or semiskilled laborer ...	11%	12%	14%	8%
Skilled laborer	3	4	4	2
Clerk	34	23	51	36
Salesman	9	10	7	10
Foreman	1	1	1	1
Minor executive	9	10	5	12
Major executive	1	1	0	1
Business owner	1	2	1	1
Engineer	9	14	5	6
Lawyer	6	9	1	4
Other profession	9	8	6	12
Military career	2	2	1	1
Government service	1	0	1	1
Training program	3	3	2	4
Other occupation	1	1	1	1
Total	100	100	100	100

Appendix Table 35. Interfirm Mobility and First Occupation of 1952 Business Leaders

First Occupation	Number of Companies Leader Has Been Associated with			
	1	2	3	4 or More
Unskilled or semiskilled laborer ..	12%	9%	10%	12%
Skilled laborer	3	3	4	5
Clerk or retail salesman	33	32	33	36
Salesman	10	9	10	8
Foreman	1	1	1	1
Minor executive	10	8	10	9
Major executive	1	1	1	1
Business owner	1	2	1	1
Engineer	9	10	9	9
Lawyer	6	8	6	3
Other profession	6	9	9	10
Military career	2	2	1	1
Government service	0	1	1	1
Business training program	5	3	3	2
Other occupation	1	2	1	1
Total	100	100	100	100

Size of Business and Business Position

Appendix Table 36. Occupational Mobility of 1952 Business Leaders by Several Sizes of Businesses (in Millions of Dollars)

Occupation of Father	All Business Leaders	Size of Business				
		Less Than 10	10–49	50–99	100–249	250 or More
Laborer	15%	14%	16%	15%	15%	16%
Owner of small business	18	18	19	18	18	18
White-collar worker ..	20	15	19	20	21	21
Major executive and large owner	24	30	26	22	22	19
Professional man	14	14	13	16	15	16
Farmer	9	9	7	9	9	10
Total	100	100	100	100	100	100

Appendix Table 37. Occupational Mobility of 1952 Business Leaders into Several Business Positions

Occupation of Father	All Business Leaders	Position Held			
		Owner and Partner	Chairman or President	Vice President	Secretary, Treasurer, or Controller
Laborer	15%	10%	11%	15%	22%
Owner of small business ..	18	17	17	19	17
White-collar worker	20	14	16	21	21
Major executive or owner of large business	24	38	34	21	17
Professional man	14	16	13	15	13
Farmer	9	5	9	9	10
Total	100	100	100	100	100

Appendix Table 38. Size of Business in Millions of Dollars and Education of 1952 Business Leaders

Education	All Business Leaders	Size of Business				
		Less Than 10	10–49	50–99	100–249	250 or More
Less than high school	4%	4%	5%	4%	3%	4%
Some high school	9	9	9	8	8	9
High school graduation ...	11	11	13	10	11	10
Some college	19	20	21	19	16	17
College graduation	38	38	36	38	40	39
Postgraduate work	19	18	16	21	22	21
Total	100	100	100	100	100	100

Appendix Table 39. Business Position and Education of 1952 Business Leaders

Education	All Business Leaders	Owner and Partner	Chairman and President	Vice President	Other
Less than high school	4%	4%	6%	4%	4%
Some high school	9	8	9	8	9
High school graduation	11	6	11	10	14
Some college	19	19	17	19	21
College graduation	38	39	40	41	30
Postgraduate work	19	24	17	18	22
Total	100	100	100	100	100

(Position Held spans: Owner and Partner, Chairman and President, Vice President, Other)

Appendix Table 40. Education and Size of Business for 1928 and 1952 Business Leaders

Education	Grade A	Grade B	Grade C	Grade D	Grade E	All Sizes
Less than high school						
1928	21.2%	23.7%	27.4%	29.6%	34.1%	26.7%
1952	5.5	3.2	4.3	4.8	4.8	4.3
Some high school or high school graduation						
1928	25.0	28.4	28.7	30.7	25.9	28.0
1952	19.5	20.8	18.3	20.9	20.5	19.9
Some college						
1928	10.8	14.2	14.2	12.8	13.5	13.4
1952	16.0	17.5	19.5	20.6	19.0	18.5
College graduation						
1928	43.0	33.7	29.7	26.9	26.5	31.9
1952	59.0	58.5	57.9	53.7	55.7	57.3
Total						
1928	100.0	100.0	100.0	100.0	100.0	100.0
1952	100.0	100.0	100.0	100.0	100.0	100.0

(Size of Business spans: Grade A, Grade B, Grade C, Grade D, Grade E)

279

Appendix Table 41. Education and Business Position for 1928 and 1952 Business Leaders

| Education | Business Position of Leader | | | All Positions |
	Partner or Owner	Chief Executive	Subordinate Executive	
Less than high school				
1928	27.0%	27.4%	25.6%	26.7%
1952	4.1	5.7	3.9	4.3
Some high school or high school graduation				
1928	24.8	27.4	30.4	28.0
1952	15.6	20.0	20.3	19.9
Some college				
1928	15.5	13.8	11.9	13.4
1952	19.4	17.2	18.8	18.5
College graduation				
1928	32.7	31.4	32.1	31.9
1952	60.9	57.1	57.0	57.3
Total				
1928	100.0	100.0	100.0	100.0
1952	100.0	100.0	100.0	100.0

Appendix Table 42. Formal Business Training and Size of Business (in Millions of Dollars) for 1952 Business Leaders

| Formal Business Training | All Business Leaders | Size of Business | | |
		Less Than 10	10–249	250 and Over
None	42%	44%	40%	44%
Business training in public school or business college	25	24	25	26
Commercial training in college or university	33	32	35	30
Total	100	100	100	100

Appendix Table 43. Formal Business Training and Business Position for 1952 Business Leaders

| Formal Business Training | All Business Leaders | Position Held | | |
		Chief Executive	Vice President	Other Position
None	42%	55%	44%	21%
Business training in public school or business college	25	20	24	34
Commercial training in college or university	33	25	32	45
Total	100	100	100	100

Appendix Table 44. Formal Business Training and Levels of Business Leadership for 1952 Business Leaders

Position Held and Size of Company	Formal Business Training			Total
	None	Business Training in Public School or Business College	Commercial Training in College or University	
Chief executive				
Less than $10 million.	55%	18%	27%	100%
$10–$250 million	54	20	26	100
$250 million and over.	61	18	21	100
Vice president				
Less than $10 million.	46	23	31	100
$10–$250 million	43	24	33	100
$250 million and over.	46	26	28	100
Other position				
Less than $10 million.	21	37	42	100
$10–$250 million	20	34	46	100
$250 million and over.	24	31	45	100
All business leaders ...	42	25	33	100

Appendix Table 45. Formal Business Training and Size of Business for 1928 and 1952 Business Leaders

Formal Business Training	Size of Business					All Grades
	Grade A	Grade B	Grade C	Grade D	Grade E	
No business training						
1928	76.0%	71.3%	69.8%	68.3%	68.3%	70.7%
1952	43.4	43.3	39.3	38.7	46.5	42.0
Business training in public school or business college						
1928	16.1	21.4	22.2	25.0	26.1	22.0
1952	26.2	24.8	26.0	25.8	21.7	24.9
Commercial training in college or university						
1928	7.9	7.3	8.0	6.7	5.6	7.3
1952	30.4	31.9	34.7	35.5	31.8	33.1
Total						
1928	100.0	100.0	100.0	100.0	100.0	100.0
1952	100.0	100.0	100.0	100.0	100.0	100.0

Appendix Table 46. Formal Business Training and Business Position for
1928 and 1952 Business Leaders

| Formal Business Training | Business Position | | | All Positions |
	Partner or Owner	Chief Executive	Other Position	
No business training				
1928	75.0%	74.3%	64.3%	70.7%
1952	55.8	55.1	36.9	42.0
Business training in public school or business college				
1928	19.0	20.0	26.2	22.0
1952	14.0	20.3	27.2	24.9
Commercial training in college or university				
1928	6.0	5.7	9.5	7.3
1952	30.2	24.6	35.9	33.1
Total				
1928	100.0	100.0	100.0	100.0
1952	100.0	100.0	100.0	100.0

Appendix Table 47. Size of Business and Directorships for
1928 and 1952 Business Leaders

| Size of Business | Less Than 5 Directorships | | 5 or More Directorships | |
	1928	1952	1928	1952
Grade A	73%	86%	27%	14%
Grade B	86	84	14	16
Grade C	93	86	7	14
Grade D	95	88	5	12
Grade E	95	85	5	15

Interfirm Mobility

Appendix Table 48. Number of Companies 1952 Business Leaders Have
Been Associated with as Non-Executives (Total Number of
Companies Less Number Associated with as Executive)

Number of Companies	Percentage of Respondents *
0	47
1	25
2	15
3	7
4	3
5 or more	3
Total	100

* No answer was made by 75 of 7500.

Appendix Table 49. The Relationship between the Total Number of Companies 1952 Business Leaders Have Been Associated with and the Number of Companies Worked for as Non-Executives

Number of Companies Associated with as Non-Executive	Total Number of Companies Associated with								
	1	2	3	4	5	6	7	8	9 or More
1	100%	50%	30%	19%	16%	14%	11%	14%	27%
2		50	36	27	16	12	9	7	13
3			34	30	26	20	19	16	7
4				24	26	21	21	9	13
5					16	18	16	17	9
6						15	16	20	7
7							8	8	12
8								9	6
9 or more									6
Total	100	100	100	100	100	100	100	100	100

Appendix Table 50. Number of Companies 1952 Business Leaders Have Been Associated with as Non-Executives and Father's Occupation

Occupation of Father	All Business Leaders	Number of Companies Associated with as Non-Executive		
		None	1–2	3 or More
Laborer	15%	13%	16%	23%
White-collar worker	20	17	22	21
Owner of small business	18	18	19	17
Major executive or owner of large business.	24	30	19	16
Professional man	14	14	15	14
Farmer	9	8	9	9
Total	100	100	100	100

Appendix Table 51. Number of Companies 1952 Business Leaders Have Been Associated with as Executives and Father's Occupation

Occupation of Father	All Business Leaders	Number of Companies Associated with as Executive		
		None	1–2	3 or More
Laborer	15%	16%	14%	15%
White-collar worker	20	20	20	18
Owner of small business	18	17	19	21
Major executive or owner of large business.	24	24	24	21
Professional man	14	13	14	17
Farmer	9	10	9	8
Total	100	100	100	100

Appendix Table 52. Number of Companies 1952 Business Leaders Have
Been Associated with and Geographic Mobility

Geographic Mobility	All Business Leaders	Number of Companies			
		1	2–3	4–6	7 or More
Intrastate	41%	51%	40%	34%	31%
Interstate or interregion	59	49	60	66	69
Total	100	100	100	100	100

Appendix Table 53. Interfirm Mobility and Type of Business of 1952 Business Leaders

Type of Business	Number of Companies Associated with			Total
	1	2–3	4 or More	
Food and tobacco products	35	45	20	100
Stone, clay, and glass products	32	47	21	100
Textiles and apparel	30	46	24	100
Oil, gas, and their products	29	41	30	100
Machinery (except electrical)	29	42	29	100
Retail and wholesale trade	29	45	26	100
Railroads	29	38	33	100
Public utilities and communication	28	43	29	100
Wood and wood products	27	40	33	100
Chemical and allied products	27	45	28	100
Insurance	26	46	28	100
Other manufacturing	26	41	33	100
Paper and allied products	26	36	38	100
Metals and their products	25	45	30	100
Electrical machinery	24	49	27	100
Banking and finance	24	46	30	100
Printing and publishing	22	41	37	100
Real estate	21	43	36	100
Brokers and dealers	20	44	36	100
Construction	17	44	39	100
Transportation equipment	16	45	39	100
Mining	15	47	38	100
Miscellaneous transportation	14	42	44	100
Personal services	14	39	47	100
Business services	13	43	44	100
Highway transportation	9	47	44	100

Business Expansion

The effective analysis of business expansion as a factor in occupational mobility required grouping the business leaders studied into special, and somewhat arbitrary, categories. Two facets of business expansion are considered in Chapter V, the growth of the industry in which the businessman holds an executive position and the growth of the company with which he is associated.

To examine the influence of careers in expanding industry on opportunity to achieve business leadership, an examination of the expansion of the U.S. economy by industry was made for the period 1929 to 1950 (latest figures available at the time of the selection of the sample). As the index for size and expansion of industry, the national income by industrial origin has been utilized.[1] The comparison of 1929 to 1950 covers in large part the years in which the men studied have been engaged in their careers and, more important for purposes of the study, 1929 and 1950 are both years of high levels of industrial expansion, thus minimizing temporary increases or decreases in the size of an industry as a result of depression or temporary boom.

While income by industrial origin is not totally satisfactory as an index to the relative size of a given type of business or industry in the economy, all available indices are open to substantial question and this one seems at least as satisfactory as such other indices as number of men employed or salaries paid by types of business.

In order to hold such factors as inflation constant, the proportional contribution of each type of business during 1929 and 1950 was compared with the percentage increase in the contribution to national income for the United States, which provides a measure of the over-all expansion of the national economy and of inflationary trends in the data. The percentage increases for each type of industry in 1950 over its national income contribution for 1929 are shown below.

Type of Business	Percentage Increase in 1950 over 1929
Total United States	173
Mining, coal, and metal	96
Crude petroleum and natural gas	268
Nonmetallic mining	139
Contract construction and engineering	231
Food and kindred products	208
Tobacco manufactures	105
Textile mill products	156
Apparel and other finished fabric products	166
Lumber and timber basic products	161
Furniture and finished lumber products	177
Paper and allied products	372
Printing and publishing	126
Chemicals and allied products	342
Products of petroleum and coal	241
Rubber products	181

[1] Data are derived from U.S. Department of Commerce, *National Income and Product of the United States, 1929–1950* (Washington, D.C.: Government Printing Office, 1951).

Type of Business	Percentage Increase in 1950 over 1929
Leather and leather products	89
Stone, clay, and glass products	237
Metals and their products	236
Machinery (except electrical)	286
Electrical machinery	357
Transportation equipment	406
Miscellaneous manufacture	248
Wholesale and retail trade	231
Banking	44
Security and investment commodity brokers, dealers, and exchanges	46
Finance, n.e.c.	207
Insurance carriers, agents, and combination offices	167
Real estate	44
Railroads	67
Local railways and bus lines	6
Highway passenger transportation	219
Highway freight transportation and warehousing	480
Water transportation	196
Air transportation (common carriers)	(1929, zero contribution)
Pipe line transportation	59
Services allied to transportation	122
Telephone and telegraph, electric and gas utilities, and local public services, n.e.c.	143
Radio broadcasting and television	1,010
Hotels and lodging places	112
Personal services	113
Commercial and trade schools and employment agencies	330
Business services, n.e.c.	264
Motion pictures	102
Amusement and recreation, except motion pictures	100

To determine the relationship between industrial expansion and occupational mobility, the extremes of this distribution were compared and the occupational origins of business leaders in the industries showing most rapid and least rapid expansion were examined.

The results of this comparison were ambiguous. A comparison of the occupations of fathers of business leaders in these two groupings indicated that there was somewhat more mobility in *both* the most stable and the most rapidly expanding types of businesses. It appeared from these results that to adequately evaluate industrial expansion as a factor in mobility it would be necessary to study the full range of business expansion. The analysis in Chapter V is based on the following groupings of respondents:

I. *Industries which have expanded slowly since 1929 (33.9 per cent of the respondents)*
   Metal and coal mining
   Nonmetallic mining and quarrying
   Tobacco manufacturers

Textile-mill products
Lumber and timber basic products
Printing, publishing, and allied industries
Leather and leather products
Banking
Security and commodity brokers, dealers, and exchanges
Real estate
Railroads
Local railways and bus lines
Other transportation
Public utilities
Hotels and lodging places
Personal services
Motion pictures
Amusement and recreation

II. Industries which have expanded moderately since 1929 (33.4 per cent of the respondents)

Contract construction and engineering
Food and kindred products
Apparel and other finished fabric products
Furniture and finished lumber products
Rubber products
Trade
Insurance carriers, agents, and combination offices
Highway passenger transportation
Water transportation

III. Industries which have expanded rapidly since 1929 (31.8 per cent of the respondents)

Crude petroleum and natural gas
Paper and allied products
Chemicals and allied products
Products of petroleum and coal
Stone, clay, and glass products
Iron and steel and their products
Nonferrous metals and their products
Machinery, except electrical
Electrical machinery
Transportation equipment, including automobiles
Miscellaneous manufacture
Highway freight transportation and warehousing
Air transportation (common carriers)
Radio broadcasting and television
Commercial and trade schools and employment agencies
Business services, n.e.c.

In a few cases, inclusion of a type of business in one or another of these three categories is somewhat arbitrary. By this grouping, however, respondents were divided into three categories of nearly equal size which broadly represent three relative degrees of business expansion. The first group includes the respondents who are in types of businesses that have expanded less rapidly than business as a whole. The third of respondents in the intermediate group are with industries that have expanded at about the average rate of the national

287

economy, while the remaining third of the total number of respondents are with those industries whose expansion has been greater than the national average. The analysis of mobility by industrial expansion given in Chapter V is based on these three groupings.

A primary reason for the initial ambiguity of the results of studying the influence of industrial expansion on occupational mobility was the fact that industrial growth obviously does not occur merely on the level of a total industry. Within a stable industry a given firm may undergo rapid expansion, while a particular firm in a rapidly growing industry may suffer marked reverses. To consider business expansion as a factor in the business career, these two kinds of industrial expansion must be looked at jointly.

Data on the growth of the company with which the business leader is associated are available from the questionnaire. Question 4 of the 1952 questionnaire asked for the approximate size of the business leader's present business "when you entered this organization" and "at present." By comparing the two points in time a measure of the growth of the business leader's firm during his association with that firm is possible. The results of this comparison are shown in Appendix Table 54. On the basis of this distribution, four categories of respondents can be arranged. The first group includes those business leaders whose firm, during their association with it, has not increased beyond the limits of an interval as used in the questionnaire. Another group includes those respondents whose firms have increased beyond the limits of two intervals as used in the questionnaire. (Analysis indicated little difference between the two intermediate groups and the two groups are merged in the presentation in Chapter V.)

When evaluating these data, we must keep its limitations in mind. A precise analysis of expansion of firm as a factor in the business career was not possible. There are two reasons for this. First, the business leader may move up in a firm of one type and then obtain his

Appendix Table 54. Growth of the Business Leaders' Firms during Their Association with the Firms

Number of Intervals of Expansion	Percentage of Respondents *
0	23.4
1	29.8
2	25.1
3 or more	21.7
Total	100.0

* No answer was made by 15 of 7500.

executive position in a firm of another type. Thus, a man might move rapidly forward in his career through a rapidly expanding firm and after this background and training be selected by a stable firm for a position of leadership. The questionnaire does not make it possible to examine this aspect of company growth in the business leader's career.

There is an additional and more serious limitation involved in this analysis, a limitation which is a function of a weakness in the questionnaire. In order to permit a comparison with the questionnaire returns of the 1928 study, the number and kind of categories of company size used in the questionnaire were sharply limited and had to duplicate for the most part those employed in the earlier questionnaire. As a result, the intervals of size of firm as given in the questionnaire are not of equal or directly comparable size. Thus, for example, the smallest interval is that of a firm with a gross income of $500,000 to $999,000. The largest interval is $500,000,000 or over. Clearly, the larger firms may increase greatly in size and that increase not be indicated in the questionnaire response while a smaller increase in size by a smaller firm may make for an increase over one or more intervals.

These limitations of this aspect of the analysis should not be overlooked. The shortcomings are not totally disadvantageous, however. In summary of their implications for the analysis in Chapter V, it may be said that it is possible the category "slow expansion of firm" includes men who are or have been with firms that have expanded substantially. However, most of the men in this group are with firms whose expansion has been relatively slow. At the same time, all the men included in the category "rapid expansion of firm" are with firms whose expansion has been great. The total effect would be then to provide a conservative estimate of the relationship between growth of business firm and occupational mobility.

Classification of Respondents by Type of Business

The responses to the questionnaire were coded by type of business for analysis of the relationship between the area of business in which the business leader is engaged and his background and career. The categories in which the respondents were grouped are those used by the U.S. government in its publications on business activity, with certain closely overlapping groupings combined. A detailed listing of the total number of categories employed in the basic classification follows:

Mining
　Metal and coal mining
　Crude petroleum and natural gas
　Nonmetallic mining and quarrying

Contract construction and engineering
Manufacturing
  Food and kindred products
  Tobacco manufactures
  Textile-mill products
  Apparel and other finished fabric products
  Lumber and timber basic products
  Furniture and finished lumber products
  Paper and allied products
  Printing, publishing, and allied industries
  Chemicals and allied products
  Products of petroleum and coal
  Rubber products
  Leather and leather products
  Stone, clay, and glass products
  Iron and steel and their products
  Nonferrous metals and their products
  Machinery, except electrical
  Electrical machinery
  Transportation equipment, including automobiles
  Miscellaneous
Wholesale and retail trade
Finance, insurance, and real estate
  Banking
  Security and commodity brokers, dealers, and exchanges
  Finance, n.e.c.
  Insurance carriers, agents, and combination offices
  Real estate
Transportation
  Railroads
  Local railways and bus lines
  Highway passenger transportation, n.e.c.
  Highway freight transportation and warehousing
  Water transportation
  Air transportation (common carriers)
  Other transportation
Communications and public utilities
  Telephone, telegraph, and related services and utilities
  Radio broadcasting and television
Services
  Hotels and other lodging places
  Personal services
  Commercial and trade schools and employment agencies
  Business services, n.e.c.
  Motion pictures
  Amusement and recreation, except motion pictures

As indicated in the discussion of methodology (see Chapter VIII), the proportion of "national income by industrial origin"[2] for each of these categories formed the basis for the proportional selection of the sample of business leaders studied.

Eight broad categories by type of industry are used in this classifi-

[2] *National Income: A Supplement to the Survey of Current Business*, p. 159.

Appendix Table 55. Occupational Mobility and Expansion of Business Firm

Occupation of Father	Expansion of Firm			All Firms
	Slow	Moderate	Rapid	
Laborer	14%	15%	16%	15%
White-collar worker	20	19	21	20
Owner of small business	16	19	19	18
Major executive or owner of large business	26	25	19	24
Professional man	16	14	14	14
Farmer	8	8	11	9
Total	100	100	100	100

Appendix Table 56. Occupational Mobility and Expansion of Industry

Occupation of Father	Expansion of Industry			All Industries
	Slow	Moderate	Rapid	
Laborer	15%	15%	15%	15%
White-collar worker	20	18	21	20
Owner of small business	18	18	17	18
Major executive or owner of large business	23	27	22	24
Professional man	15	12	17	14
Farmer	9	10	8	9
Total	100	100	100	100

Appendix Table 57. Education and Expansion of Business Firm

Education	Expansion of Firm			All Firms
	Slow	Moderate	Rapid	
Less than high school graduation	8%	12%	19%	13%
High school graduation and some college	28	30	34	30
College graduation	64	58	47	57
Total	100	100	100	100

Appendix Table 58. Education and Expansion of Industry

Education	Expansion of Industry			All Industries
	Slow	Moderate	Rapid	
Less than high school graduation	11%	14%	14%	13%
High school graduation and some college	28	33	29	30
College graduation	61	53	57	57
Total	100	100	100	100

cation system: mining, construction, manufacturing, trade, finance, transportation, communications and public utilities, and services. The distributions of respondents within these categories are shown in Appendix Table 59.

Appendix Table 59. Distribution of 1952 Business
Leaders by Eight Types of Business

Type of Business	Percentage of Business Leaders
Mining	2
Construction	7
Manufacturing	44
Trade	19
Finance	14
Transportation	6
Communications	5
Services	3
Total	100

It was to be expected that these broad categories would not make a sociologically useful division of the types of business and industry in America, and preliminary analysis confirmed this. The categories include within themselves greatly diverse types of businesses. Thus, for example, transportation includes both a long-established type of business like railroads and a recently established type of business, air transport. Manufacturing, comprising much the largest single group, is extremely diverse and needs to be examined in detail for purposes of this research. Further, the size differences between the categories tend to obscure relationships.

For the analysis of the data by type of business, the types of business listed above were grouped into twenty-six categories. The grouping is such as to combine the similar categories and, at the same time, provide a statistically useful number of responses in each category. The results of this regrouping are shown in Appendix Table 60. In all categories, except that of "other transportation," the number of respondents exceeds 100. (Note that 33 respondents were not categorized by subtype of business.)

Appendix Table 60. Distribution of 1952 Business Leaders by Twenty-Six
Types of Business

Type of Business	Number of Respondents
Mining, coal, and metal	108
Oil, gas, and oil, gas, and coal products	237
Construction and engineering	489
Food and tobacco products	297
Textiles, apparel, and other finished fabric products	261
Wood and wood products	128
Paper and allied products	130
Printing and publishing	311
Chemicals and allied products	223
Stone, clay, and glass products	126
Metals and their products	558
Machinery (except electrical)	324
Electrical machinery	205
Transportation equipment	324
Other manufacturing (including rubber and leather products)	204
Retail and wholesale trade	1,391
Banking and finance	537
Security and commodity brokers and dealers	241
Insurance	162
Real estate	137
Railroads	255
Highway transportation	118
Other transportation (including air, water transportation)	92
Public utilities and communications	385
Personal services (including hotels, amusements)	105
Business services	119
Total	7,467

Age of Firm

Appendix Table 61. Business Leaders in Newer Business Firms
(Firms Established since 1928)

Type	Percentage of Leaders
Newer firms	6.0
Older firms	94.0

Appendix Table 62. Occupational Mobility in Newer Business Firms

Occupation of Father	Percentage of Leaders in Newer Business Firms
Farmer	7.1
Professional man	6.9
Owner of large business	6.7
Unskilled or semiskilled laborer	6.2
Minor executive	5.9
Owner of small business	5.8
Clerk or salesman	5.4
Skilled laborer	5.1
Major executive	5.1
All occupations	6.0

Appendix Table 63. Education of Business Leaders in Newer Business Firms

Education	Percentage in Newer Firms	Percentage in Older Firms
Less than high school	4	4
Some high school	7	9
High school graduation	10	11
Some college	23	19
College graduation	34	38
Postgraduate work	22	19
Total	100	100

Appendix Table 64. Number of Companies Leaders of Newer Business
Firms Have Worked for

Number of Companies	Percentage in Newer Firms	Percentage in Older Firms
1	7	27
2	20	23
3	27	21
4	18	13
5	9	7
6	8	4
7	4	2
8	2	1
9	5	2
Total	100	100

Appendix Table 65. Nativity of Business Leaders in Newer Business Firms

Nativity	Percentage in Newer Firms	Percentage in Older Firms
Leader foreign-born	4	5
Leader U.S.-born	19	20
Father U.S.-born	20	20
Father's father U.S.-born	57	55
Total	100	100

Appendix Table 66. Age of Business Leaders and Time Required to Achieve
Position in Newer Business Firms

Type	Age at Time of Study (Median)	Years to Achieve Position
Newer business firms	49.9	20.5
Older business firms	53.9	24.2

295

Appendix VI. A MAN'S FAMILY AND HIS CAREER

*Problems in Studying the Effects of "Influential Connections"
on the Business Career*

The questionnaire inquired into three types of influential connections at two points in the leader's career. The respondent was asked if relatives, friends, and/or business acquaintances were connected, as owners or executives, with either the firm he first entered or his present firm.

The question as phrased offers a wide variety of possible answers. It is first of all possible for the respondent to answer "yes" or "no" to the three types of connections, at the two career points. He may also fail to answer all or any part of the questions. Further, he may have been associated with only one firm during his career in which case his present firm will of course be his first firm, and thus he may or may not choose to answer both questions.

The analysis of responses to these questionnaire items required the preparation of special response categories. As the question stands, it is possible to answer in 729 separate ways. With respect to each of the categories — relatives, friends, and business acquaintances — the respondent may answer "yes," "no," or fail to answer. With respect to the firm he first entered he may make 27 different responses. He may do the same with the second question, relating to his present business firm, thus offering 729 possible combinations.

Two difficulties may rather readily be disposed of. First, inspection indicates that the pattern of "no answers," that is, where some part or all of the six possible check points are left blank, may be treated as "no" responses. The respondents appear, on the whole, to have adopted these as alternative ways of indicating no influence of a given type in a given company. Further, in those cases where the first business and the present business are the same business firm, this is indicated by the response to the question as to number of firms associated with during the business career. In our consideration of the responses to the question on present business firm, those men who have been with only one firm are separately categorized.

The alternatives for the remaining possibilities may be looked at in detail. When no answer and "no" are seen as alternatives, and only positive responses are considered, the business leaders responding may indicate any of the following with relation to influential connections in his first business firm: (1) Relatives, friends, and business acquaintances. (2) Relatives and friends. (3) Relatives only. (4) Friends and business acquaintances. (5) Friends only. (6) Relatives and business acquaintances. (7) Business acquaintances only. (8) No influential connections ("no" to all three, or no answer to any).

The same alternatives of responses are available for the question relating to present business firm. Inspection of the responses to the item on first business indicated that, for purposes of analysis, the eight categories may be reduced to six: (1) Relatives and friends and/or business acquaintances. (2) Relatives only. (3) Friends and business acquaintances. (4) Friends only. (5) Business acquaintances only. (6) No influential connections.

All six alternatives may obtain for both the first and present firm, either the first or present firm, or neither the first or present firm. In considering the forty-two remaining possibilities, the following frequency was obtained:

First Firm	First and Present Firm the Same	Present Business Firm					
		1	2	3	4	5	6
1	91	51	8	15	4	18	39
2	458	10	224	17	40	100	175
3	33	5	5	66	3	19	21
4	135	17	27	45	127	118	153
5	94	10	21	30	21	311	86
6	1,046	38	126	160	155	805	2,575

After inspection of the above tabulation, and the preceding analysis, the categories of response employed in Chapter VI, Table 89, were arrived at.

Appendix Table 67. Influential Connections and Occupational Mobility

Occupation of Father	Type I, No Connections	Type II, Friends	Type III, Relatives (in First Firm)	Type IV, Relatives (in Present Firm)
Laborer	20%	9%	6%	2%
Clerk or salesman	10	8	5	3
Owner of small business..	20	15	24	11
Minor executive	12	12	8	5
Major executive	8	17	19	46
Owner of large business..	5	9	19	22
Professional man	14	23	14	8
Farmer	11	7	5	3
Total	100	100	100	100

Appendix Table 68. Leadership in Same Firm as Father and the Business Hierarchy

Item	Leaders Who Are Sons of Executives or Owners		Other 1952 Leaders
	Same Firm as Father	Different Firm from Father	
Business position			
Owner or partner	7%	5%	4%
Chairman or president	44	22	18
Other	49	73	78
Total	100	100	100
Size of business (gross income per annum)			
Under $5 million	18	9	9
$5–9 million	12	7	7
$10–49 million	35	27	28
$50–99 million	13	17	17
$100–249 million	13	21	17
$250–499 million	4	9	10
$500 million and over	5	10	12
Total	100	100	100

Appendix Table 69. Leadership in Same Firm as Father and Occupation of Paternal Grandfather

Occupation of Paternal Grandfather	Leaders Who Are Sons of Executives or Owners of Businesses		Other 1952 Leaders
	Same Firm as Father	Different Firm from Father	
Laborer	12%	14%	25%
White-collar worker	7	7	4
Owner of small business	26	25	11
Major executive	16	5	2
Owner of large business	14	9	4
Professional man	9	8	12
Farmer	16	32	42
Total	100	100	100

Appendix Table 70. Leadership in Same Firm as Father and Territorial Origins

| Region of Birth | Leaders Who Are Sons of Executives or Owners | | Other 1952 Leaders |
	Same Firm as Father	Different Firm from Father	
New England	10%	11%	11%
Middle Atlantic	28	31	26
East North Central	27	25	26
West North Central	14	13	14
South Atlantic	9	7	9
East South Central	2	3	4
West South Central	3	3	4
Mountain	2	2	2
Pacific	5	5	4
Total	100	100	100

Appendix Table 71. Leadership in Same Firm as Father and Nativity

| Nativity | Leaders Who Are Sons of Executives or Owners | | Other 1952 Leaders |
	Same Firm as Father	Different Firm from Father	
Leader foreign-born	1%	6%	6%
Leader U.S.-born	15	20	20
Father U.S.-born	24	20	20
Father's father U.S.-born ...	60	54	54
Total	100	100	100

Appendix Table 72. Leadership in Same Firm as Father and Education

| Education | Leaders Who Are Sons of Executives or Owners | | Other 1952 Leaders |
	Same Firm as Father	Different Firm from Father	
Less than high school	0%	3%	6%
High school	9	17	24
Some college	21	18	19
College graduation	70	62	51
Total	100	100	100

Appendix Table 73. Leadership in Same Firm as Father and First Occupation

| First Occupation | Leaders Who Are Sons of Executives or Owners | | Other 1952 Leaders |
	Same Firm as Father	Different Firm from Father	
Laborer	13%	13%	16%
Clerk or salesman	38	42	44
Foreman or minor executive.	26	12	6
Major executive	3	1	1
Business owner	2	2	1
Engineer	5	10	9
Lawyer	3	6	6
Other profession	2	8	10
Business training program ..	6	3	3
Other occupation	2	3	4
Total	100	100	100

Appendix VII. THE MARRIAGES OF THE AMERICAN BUSINESS ELITE

Appendix Table 74. Leadership in Same Firm as Father and Marriage

Occupation of Wife's Father	Leaders Who Are Sons of Executives or Owners		Other 1952 Leaders
	Same Firm as Father	Different Firm from Father	
Laborer	6%	12%	23%
White-collar worker	15	16	13
Owner of small business	17	21	17
Major executive or owner of large business	34	23	13
Professional man	20	15	15
Farmer	8	13	19
Total	100	100	100

Appendix Table 75. Marriage and Occupation in Three Generations: Father and Paternal Grandfather of Business Leader and Father of Business Leader's Wife

Occupation of Leader's Father	Occupation of Leader's Paternal Grandfather				
	Laborer	White-Collar Worker or Owner of Small Business	Major-Executive, Owner of Large Business, or Professional Man	Farmer	Total
Occupation of Wife's Father: Laborer					
Laborer	66%	8%	4%	22%	100%
White-collar worker or owner of small business..	35	25	7	33	100
Owner of large business or professional man	30	18	20	32	100
Farmer	11	4	3	82	100
Occupation of Wife's Father: White-Collar Worker or Owner of Small Business					
Laborer	51	13	8	28	100
White-collar worker or owner of small business..	20	38	14	28	100
Owner of large business or professional man	10	33	33	24	100
Farmer	6	7	7	80	100
Occupation of Wife's Father: Major Executive, Owner of Large Business, or Professional Man					
Laborer	44	13	10	33	100
White-collar worker or owner of small business..	14	34	19	33	100
Owner of large business or professional man	8	23	46	23	100
Farmer	6	3	13	78	100
Occupation of Wife's Father: Farmer					
Laborer	27	4	1	68	100
White-collar worker or owner of small business..	13	21	9	57	100
Owner of large business or professional man	8	15	29	48	100
Farmer	2	1	1	96	100

Appendix Table 76. Occupational Mobility and the Careers of Sons of 1952 Business Leaders

Occupation of Leader's Father	Sons Who Have Not Yet Entered Career	Business Owner or Partner	Businessman (Not Owner or Partner)	Professional Man	Military Career	Government Service	Other	Total
Laborer	52%	10%	41%	36%	8%	2%	3%	100%
Farmer	43	16	40	33	6	3	2	100
White-collar worker	52	13	43	33	7	2	2	100
Executive and owner of large business	55	15	50	25	6	1	3	100
Owner of small business	49	13	41	33	8	3	2	100
Professional man	54	11	44	31	9	2	3	100
Other	42	21	42	23	8	2	4	100
Total	51	13	44	31	7	2	3	100

Appendix Table 77. Leadership in Same Firm as Father and Career of
Business Leader's Son

Career of Son	Leaders Who Are Sons of Executives or Owners		Other Leaders
	Same Firm as Father	Different Firm from Father	
Has not entered career	57%	52%	50%
Business owner or partner	18	13	13
Businessman (not owner or partner)	54	44	41
Professional man	17	31	33
Military career	5	7	8
Government service	2	2	2
Other	4	3	3
Total	100	100	100

SELECTED REFERENCES TO THE LITERATURE ON STATUS, OCCUPATIONS, AND OCCUPATIONAL MOBILITY

Concepts of Status and Class

Centers, Richard. *The Psychology of Social Classes*. Princeton, N.J.: Princeton University Press, 1949.

Davis, Allison, *et al. Deep South*. Chicago: University of Chicago Press, 1941.

Marshall, T. H. (ed.). *Class Conflict and Social Stratification*. London: LePlay House Press, 1938.

Marx, Karl. *Capital*. New York: Modern Library, 1936.

Parsons, Talcott. "An Analytical Approach to the Theory of Social Stratification," in *Essays in Sociological Theory Pure and Applied*. Glencoe, Ill.: Free Press, 1947.

Schumpeter, Joseph. *Imperialism and Social Classes*. New York: Augustus M. Kelley, Inc., 1951.

Sombart, Werner. *The Quintessence of Capitalism*. Translated by M. Epstein. London: T. F. Unwin, 1915.

Veblen, Thorstein. *The Theory of the Leisure Class*. New York: Viking Press, 1931.

Warner, W. Lloyd, *et al. Yankee City Series*. New Haven, Conn.: Yale University Press.

Warner, W. Lloyd, and associates. *Democracy in Jonesville*. New York: Harper and Brothers, 1949.

Warner, W. Lloyd, M. Meeker, and K. Eells. *Social Class in America*. Chicago: Science Research Associates, 1949.

Weber, Max. *Essays in Sociology*. Translated by H. H. Gerth and C. Wright Mills. New York: Oxford University Press, 1946.

————. *The Theory of Social and Economic Organization*. Translated by A. M. Henderson and Talcott Parsons. New York: Oxford University Press, 1947.

Occupations and Occupational Prestige

Anderson, H. Dewey, and Percy E. Davidson. *Occupational Trends in the United States*. Palo Alto, Calif.: Stanford University Press, 1940.

————. *Recent Occupational Trends in American Labor*. Palo Alto, Calif.: Stanford University Press, 1945.

————. "Are Edwards' Socio-Economic Levels Economic?" *School and Society*, 48, 1938.

Deeg, M. E., and D. G. Paterson, "Changes in Social Status of Occupations," *Occupations, 25*, 1947.

Edwards, Alba M. *A Social-Economic Grouping of the Gainful Workers of the United States*. Washington, D.C.: U.S. Department of Commerce, Bureau of the Census, 1938.

————. *Comparative Occupational Statistics for the United States, 1870–1940*. Washington, D. C.: Government Printing Office, 1943.

————. "Social-Economic Groups of the United States," *Publications of the American Statistical Association, 15*, 1918.

Hatt, P. K. "Occupation and Social Stratification," *American Journal of Sociology, 55*, 1950.

"Jobs and Occupations: A Popular Evaluation," *Opinion News*, 9, 1947.

Smith, Mapheus. "An Empirical Scale of Prestige Status of Occupations," *American Sociological Review*, 8, 1943.

U.S. Bureau of the Census. *Alphabetical Index of Occupations and Industries: 1950*. Washington, D.C.: Government Printing Office, 1950.

Welch, M. K. "The Ranking of Occupations on the Basis of Social Status," *Occupations*, 27, 1949.

Vertical Mobility and Occupational Mobility

Adams, Stuart. "Fact and Myth in Social Class Theory," *Ohio Journal of Science*, 6, 1951.

Centers, Richard. "Occupational Mobility of Urban Occupational Strata," *American Sociological Review*, 13, 1948.

Davidson, Percy E., and H. Dewey Anderson. *Occupational Mobility in an American Community*. Palo Alto, Calif.: Stanford University Press, 1937.

Dublin, Louis L., and Robert J. Vane, Jr. "Shifting of Occupations among Wage-Earners as Determined by Occupational History of Industrial Policyholders," *Monthly Labor Review*, 1924.

Foote, Nelson M., and Paul K. Hatt. "Social Mobility and Economic Advancement," *American Economic Review*, 43, 1953.

Form, W. H., and D. C. Miller. "Occupational Career Patterns as a Sociological Instrument," *American Journal of Sociology*, 54, 1949.

Havighurst, Robert J. "The Influence of Recent Social Changes on the Desire for Social Mobility in the United States," in Lyman Bryson, et al. (eds.), *Conflicts of Power in Modern Culture*. New York: Harper and Brothers, 1942.

Hertzler, J. O. "Some Tendencies toward a Closed Class System in the United States," *Social Forces*, 30, 1952.

Lasswell, Harold D., et al. *The Comparative Study of Elites*. Stanford, Calif.: Stanford University Press, 1952.

Lipset, Seymour, and Reinhard Bendix. *Social Mobility and Occupational Career Patterns*. Reprint No. 38. Berkeley, Calif.: Institute of Industrial Relations, University of California, 1952.

McGuire, Carson. "Social Stratification and Mobility Patterns," *American Sociological Review*, 15, 1950.

Merton, Robert K. "Social Structure and Anomie," in *Social Theory and Social Structure*. Glencoe, Ill.: Free Press, 1949.

Mills, C. Wright. "The Middle Classes in Middle-Sized Cities," *American Sociological Review*, 10, 1945.

Rogoff, Natalie. *Recent Trends in Occupational Mobility*. Glencoe, Ill.: Free Press, 1953.

Schneider, Joseph. "Social Class, Historical Circumstances and Fame," *American Journal of Sociology*, 43, 1937.

————. "Social Origin and Fame: The United States and England," *American Sociological Review*, 10, 1945.

Sibley, Elbridge. "Some Demographic Clues to Stratification," *American Sociological Review*, 7, 1942.

Sjoberg, Gideon. "Are Social Classes in America Becoming More Rigid?" *American Sociological Review*, 16, 1951.

Smith, Mapheus. "Occupational Mobility of Notable Persons," *Sociology and Social Research*, 23, 1930.

Sorokin, Pitirim A. *Social Mobility*. New York: Harper and Brothers, 1927.

Visher, S. S. "A Study of the Type of Place of Birth and of the Occupation of Fathers of Subjects of Sketches in Who's Who in America," *American Journal of Sociology*, 30, 1925.

Occupational Mobility in Particular Occupations

Adams, Stuart. "Business Differences in the Vertical Mobility of Business Leaders." Unpublished paper.

————. "Regional Differences in Vertical Mobility in a High Status Occupation," *American Sociological Review*, 15, 1950.

Anderson, W. A. *The Transmission of Farming as an Occupation.* Cornell University Agricultural Experiment Station, Bulletin 768, 1941.

Fortune. "The 30,000 Managers," 21, 1940.

————. "The Nine Hundred," 46, 1952.

Hill, George W., and Harold T. Christensen. "Some Cultural Factors Related to Occupational Mobility among Wisconsin Farmers," *Rural Sociology*, 7, 1942.

McMillan, Robert. "Farm Ownership Status of Parents as a Determinant of Socio-Economic Status of Farmers," *Rural Sociology*, 9, 1944.

Miller, William. "American Historians and the Business Elite," *Journal of Economic History*, 9, 1948.

————. "American Lawyers in Business and Politics," *Yale Law Review*, 60, 1951.

————. "The Recruitment of the American Business Elite," *Quarterly Journal of Economics*, 64, 1950.

Miller, William (ed.). *Men in Business: Essays in the History of Entrepreneurship.* Cambridge, Mass.: Harvard University Press, 1952.

Mills, C. Wright. "The American Business Elite: A Collective Portrait," *The Tasks of Economic History* (supplemental issue of the *Journal of Economic History*), 5, 1945.

————. *The New Men of Power, America's Labor Leaders.* New York: Harcourt, Brace and Company, 1948.

Oxenfeldt, Gertrude and Alfred R. "Determinants of Business Success in a Small Western City," *Social Forces*, 30, 1951.

Smith, Mapheus, and M. L. Brockway. "Mobility of American Congressmen," *Sociology and Social Research*, 24, 1940.

Sorokin, Pitirim. "American Millionaires and Multi-Millionaires," *Social Forces*, 4, 1925.

Stone, Robert C. "Factory Organization and Vertical Mobility," *American Sociological Review*, 18, 1953.

Suchman, Edward A. "Social Mobility in the Army," in *The American Soldier*, by Samuel A. Stouffer, *et al.* Princeton, N.J.: Princeton University Press, 1949.

Taussig, F. W., and C. S. Joslyn. *American Business Leaders.* New York: The Macmillan Company, 1932.

Wance, W., and R. Butler. "The Effect of Industrial Change on Occupational Inheritance in Four Pennsylvania Communities," *Social Forces*, 27, 1948.

American Business and Businessmen

Arnold, Thurman. *Folklore of Capitalism.* New Haven, Conn.: Yale University Press, 1937.

Barnard, Chester. *The Functions of the Executive.* Cambridge, Mass.: Harvard University Press, 1938.

Beard, Miriam. *A History of the Businessman.* New York: The Macmillan Company, 1938.

Berle, Adolf A., Jr., and Gardiner C. Means. *The Modern Corporation and Private Property.* New York: The Macmillan Company, 1933.

Brandeis, Louis D. *Business — A Profession.* Boston: Small, Maynard and Company, 1914.

Burnham, James. *The Managerial Revolution.* New York: John Day Company, 1941.

Cochran, Thomas C., and William Miller. *The Age of Enterprise: A Social History of Industrial America.* New York: The Macmillan Company, 1942.

Drucker, Peter F. *The Concept of the Corporation.* New York: John Day Company, 1946.

Gordon, Robert Aaron. *Business Leadership in the Large Corporation.* Washington, D.C., The Brookings Institution, 1945.

Harvard University Research Center in Entrepreneurial History. *Change and the Entrepreneur: Postulates and Patterns for Entrepreneurial History.* Cambridge, Mass.: Harvard University Press, 1949.

Lundberg, Ferdinand. *America's Sixty Families.* New York: Vanguard Press, 1937.

Myers, Gustavus. *History of the Great American Fortunes.* (2nd ed.) New York: Modern Library, 1937.

Redlich, Fritz. *History of American Business Leaders.* Ann Arbor, Mich.: Edwards Brothers, Inc., 1940.

Schumpeter, Joseph A. *Capitalism, Socialism, and Democracy.* New York: Harper and Brothers, 1947.

U.S. Temporary National Economic Committee. *Investigation of Concentration of Economic Power.* Number 21, Competition and Monopoly in American Industry. Washington, D.C.: Government Printing Office, 1940.

_____. *Investigation of Concentration of Economic Power.* Number 29, The Distribution of Ownership in the 200 Largest Nonfinancial Corporations. Washington, D.C.: Government Printing Office, 1940.

Veblen, Thorstein. *Engineers and the Price System.* New York: B. W. Huebsch, Inc., 1921.

_____. *The Theory of Business Enterprise.* New York: Charles Scribner's Sons, 1932.

Wector, Dixon. *The Saga of American Society.* New York: Charles Scribner's Sons, 1937.

Territorial Mobility and Vertical Mobility

Freedman, R., and A. H. Hawley. "Migration and Occupational Mobility in the Depression," *American Journal of Sociology,* 55, 1949.

Gibbard, H. A. "The Status Factor in Residential Succession," *American Journal of Sociology,* 46, 1941.

Gist, Noel P., C. T. Pihlblad, and C. L. Gregory. *Selective Factors in Migration and Occupation.* Columbia, Mo.: University of Missouri, 1943.

Handlin, Oscar. *The Uprooted.* Boston: Little, Brown and Company, 1951.

Landis, P. H. *The Territorial and Occupational Mobility of Washington Youth.* Bulletin No. 449, Youth Series No. 3, Agricultural Experiment Station, State College of Washington.

Nelson, L. "Distribution, Age, and Mobility of Minnesota Physicians," *American Sociological Review,* 7, 1942.

Punke, H. H. "Distribution and Migration of Persons Listed in Who's Who as Compared with the General Population," *Social Forces,* 14, 1935.

Schmid, Calvin F. "Migration within the State of Washington: 1935–1940," *American Sociological Review,* 7, 1942.

Thomas, Dorothy S. *Research Memorandum on Migration Differentials.* Social Science Research Council Bulletin No. 43, 1938.

Turner, F. J. *The Frontier in American History.* New York: H. Holt, 1921.

Education and Vertical Mobility

Anderson, H. Dewey. "The Educational and Occupational Attainments of Our National Rulers," *Scientific Monthly,* 40, 1935.

Havighurst, Robert J., and Mary Russell. "Promotion in the Armed Services in Relation to School Attainment and Social Status," *School Review,* 53, 1945.

Higher Education for Democracy. The Report of the President's Commission on Higher Education. New York: Harper and Brothers, 1947.

Hollingshead, August B. *Elmtown's Youth.* New York: John Wiley, 1947.

Kahl, Joseph A. "Education and Occupational Aspirations of 'Common Man' Boys," *Harvard Educational Review,* 23, 1953.

Mulligan, Raymond A. "Social Mobility and Higher Education," *Journal of Educational Sociology,* 15, 1952.

Shannon, J. R., and Maxine Shaw. "Education of Business and Professional Leaders," *American Sociological Review,* 5, 1940.

Warner, W. Lloyd. "Formal Education and the Social Structure," *Journal of Educational Sociology,* 9, 1936.

————, Robert J. Havighurst, and Martin B. Loeb. *Who Shall Be Educated?* New York: Harper and Brothers, 1944.

White, Clyde. *These Will Go to College.* Cleveland: Press of Western Reserve University, 1952.

Who Should Go to College? New York: Columbia University Press, 1952.

Marriage, Birth Rate, and Intelligence as Factors in Mobility

Anderson, C. Arnold, James C. Brown, and Mary Jean Bowman. "Intelligence and Occupational Mobility," *Journal of Political Economy,* 60, 1952.

Bossard, James H. S. "Marriage as a Status Achieving Device," *Sociology and Social Research,* 29, 1944.

Centers, Richard. "Marital Selection and Occupational Strata," *American Journal of Sociology,* 54, 1949.

Davis, Allison. *Social Class Influences upon Learning.* Cambridge, Mass.: Harvard University Press, 1952.

Dinkle, Robert M. "Occupations and Fertility in the United States," *American Sociological Review,* 17, 1952.

Eells, Kenneth W., *et al. Intelligence and Cultural Differences.* Chicago: University of Chicago Press, 1951.

Gough, Harrison G. "Relationship of Socio-Economic Status to Personality Inventory and Achievement Test Scores," *Journal of Educational Psychology,* 37, 1946.

Hatch, D. L. and M. A. "Criteria of Social Status as Derived from Marriage Announcements in the New York Times," *American Sociological Review,* 12, 1947.

Heberle, R. "Social Factors in Birth Control," *American Sociological Review,* 6, 1941.

Hollingshead, August B. "Class Differences in Family Stability," *Annals of the American Academy of Political and Social Science,* 1950.

Hunt, Thomas C. "Occupational Status and Marriage Selection," *American Sociological Review,* 5, 1940.

Janke, L. L., and Robert J. Havighurst. "Relations between Ability and Social Status in a Midwestern Community," *Journal of Educational Psychology,* 36, 1945.

Kiser, Clyde V. *Group Influences in Urban Fertility.* Baltimore: Williams and Wilkins Company, 1942.

———— and P. K. Whelpton. "Social and Psychological Factors Affecting Fertility, Fertility Planning and Fertility Rates by Socio-Economic Status," *Milbank Quarterly,* April 1949.

Notestein, Frank W. "Class Differences in Fertility," *Annals of the American Academy of Political and Social Science,* 1936.

Vertical Mobility in Other Nations

Ashby, A. W. "The Social Origins of Farmers in Wales," *Sociological Review,* 18, 1926.

Becker, Howard. "Changes in Social Stratification in Germany," *American Sociological Review,* 15, 1950.

Chapman, S. J., and W. Abbott. "The Tendency of Children to Enter Their Father's Trades," *Journal of the Royal Statistical Society*, 74, 1911.

Clarke, E. L. "The Recruitment of the Nation's Leaders," *Sociological Review*, 28, 1936.

Collier, A. "Social Origins of a Sample of Entrants to Glasgow University," *Sociological Review*, 30, 1938.

Doblin, E. M., and C. Pohly. "The Social Composition of the Nazi Leadership," *American Journal of Sociology*, 51, 1945.

Ginsberg, M. "Interchange between Social Classes," *Economic Journal*, 39, 1929.

——————. *Studies in Sociology*. London: Methuen and Company, 1932.

Glass, D. V. (ed.). *Social Mobility in Britain*. London: Routledge and Kegan Paul, Ltd., 1954.

Glick, Clarence. "The Relation between Position and Status in the Assimilation of Chinese in Hawaii," *American Journal of Sociology*, 52, 1946.

Hsu, F. L. K. "Social Mobility in China," *American Sociological Review*, 14, 1949.

Inkeles, Alex. "Social Stratification and Mobility in the Soviet Union," *American Sociological Review*, 15, 1950.

Japan Sociological Society. *Report of a Sample Survey of Social Stratification and Mobility in the Six Large Cities of Japan*. Mimeographed. Tokyo, 1952.

Jenkins, H., and D. Caradog Jones. "Social Class of Cambridge University Alumni of the 18th and 19th Centuries," *British Journal of Sociology*, 1, 1950.

Mannheim, Karl. *Man and Society in an Age of Reconstruction*. Translated by Edward A. Shils. New York: Harcourt, Brace and Company, 1934.

Rogoff, Natalie. "Social Stratification in France and the United States," *American Journal of Sociology*, 59, 1953.

Saunders, C. T. "A Study of Occupational Mobility," *Economics Journal*, 41, 1931.

Schneider, Joseph. "Class Origin and Fame: Eminent English Women," *American Sociological Review*, 5, 1940.

Sorokin, P. A. "War and Post-War Changes in Social Stratification of the Euro-American Population," *American Sociological Review*, 10, 1945.

"Social Stratification and Social Mobility," *Current Sociology*, 2, 1954.

Timasheff, N. S. "Vertical Social Mobility in Communist Society," *American Journal of Sociology*, 50, 1944.

Defining and Selecting the Study Sample

DEFINING THE SAMPLE

U.S. Bureau of the Budget, the Technical Committee of Industrial Classification, Division of Statistical Standards. *Standard Industrial Classification Manual*: Vol I. *Manufacturing Industries*. Vol. II. *Non-manufacturing Industries*. Washington, D.C.: Government Printing Office, 1942.

U.S. Bureau of the Census. *Alphabetical Index of Occupations and Industries: 1950*. Washington, D.C.: Government Printing Office, 1950.

U.S. Bureau of the Census. *Census of Manufacturers: 1947*. Vol. I, *General Summary*. Washington, D.C.: Government Printing Office, 1950.

U.S. Bureau of the Census. *Historical Statistics of the United States, 1789–1945*. Washington, D.C.: Government Printing Office, 1949.

U.S. Bureau of the Census. *Statistical Abstract of the United States, 1950*. Washington, D.C.: Government Printing Office, 1950.

U.S. Department of Commerce, Office of Business Economics. *Business Statistics: Statistical Supplement to the Survey of Current Business, 1951*. Washington, D.C.: Government Printing Office, 1951.

U.S. Department of Commerce, National Income Division. *National Income and Product of the United States, 1929–1950*. Washington, D.C.: Government Printing Office, 1951.

A. D. H. Kaplan. *Small Business: Its Place and Problems.* New York: McGraw-Hill Book Company, 1948.

SELECTING THE SAMPLE

Federal Power Commission. *Directory of Electric and Gas Utilities in the United States.* Washington, D.C.: Federal Power Commission, 1949.

Federal Trade Commission. *A List of 1,000 Large Manufacturing Companies, Their Subsidiaries and Affiliates, 1948.* Washington, D. C.: Federal Trade Commission, June, 1951.

Federal Trade Commission. *Report of the Federal Trade Commission on the Concentration of Productive Facilities.* Washington, D.C.: Government Printing Office, 1947.

Federal Trade Commission. *Report of the Federal Trade Commission on Interlocking Directorates.* Washington, D.C.: Government Printing Office, 1951.

Federal Trade Commission. *Report of the Federal Trade Commission on the Divergence between Plant and Company Concentration.* Washington, D.C.: Government Printing Office, 1950.

Hotel Management. Buyer's Directory Issue. 61 (No. 3), March 1952.

Industrial Marketing. 1952 Annual Market Data and Directory Number. 36 (No. 13). Chicago: Advertising Publications, Inc., 1951.

Interstate Commerce Commission, Bureau of Transport Economics and Statistics. *63rd Annual Report on the Statistics of Railways in the U.S. for the Year Ended December 31, 1949.* Washington, D.C.: Government Printing Office, 1951.

Moody's Manual of Investments, American and Foreign. Banks — Insurance Companies, Investment Trusts, Real Estate, Finance and Credit Companies. New York: Moody's Investor's Service, 1952.

Moody's Manual of Investments, American and Foreign. Industrials. New York: Moody's Investor's Service, 1951.

National Real Estate and Building Journal. Roster Issue. 53 (No. 4), April 1952.

The Petroleum Data Book, a one-volume library of the world's petroleum industry. (2nd ed.) Dallas, Texas: The Petroleum Engineer Publishing Co., 1948.

Poor's Register of Directors and Executives United States and Canada. 1952 edition. New York: Standard and Poor's Corporation, 1952.

Rand McNally Banker's Directory: The Banker's Blue Book. Final 1946 edition. Chicago: Rand McNally and Company, 1947.

Security Dealers of North America. Mid-Year 1949 edition. New York: Herbert D. Seibert and Company, Inc., 1949.

The Spectator. 1951 Annual Reports (Insurance in the U.S.). 160(No. 4): 26–77 (April 1952).

The Standard Advertising Register. 36, April 1951. New York: National Register Publishing Co., Inc., 1951.

Thomas' Register of American Manufacturers. (42nd ed.) Vol. I. Product Class A to L. Vol. II. Product Class M to Z. Vol. III. A to Z alphabetical list. New York: Thomas Publishing Company, 1951.

Who's Who in Commerce and Industry. (7th International ed.) Chicago: The A. N. Marquis Company, 1951.

INDEX

Abilities, class differences in, 21

Achieved status: defined, 9; role in occupational succession, 158–59

Achievement time, see Years to achieve position

Adams, Stuart, 19, 20

Age of business leaders

present age, 30, 129: and occupation of father, 130; and education, 131–32; *1952* compared with *1928*, 136

age of entering business, 30: and occupation of father, 129–30; and occupation of father, *1928* and *1952*, 136–37

age of entering firm, 129: and interfirm mobility, 134

age of entering position, 30, 129: *1928* and *1952* compared, 137; and occupation of father, *1928* and *1952*, 137

American Business Leaders, see Taussig, F. W.

Anderson, H. Dewey, and Percy E. Davidson, 14

Appley, Lawrence A., 221

Barnes, Julius H., 221

Bell, James F., 221

Birth cycle, 5

Birth elite, defined, 8–9

Birth rate, male reproduction of *1952* business leaders, 249–50. *See also* Differential fertility

Birth status: defined, 5–6; role in occupational succession, 158–59, 176

Birthplace of *1952* business leaders: size of, 26, 85–86; and region of birth, 69–70, 86–88; and U.S. population, 86; occupation of father and region of birth, 88–89; and marriage, 210–11

Business elite, types of, 8

Business expansion: and occupation of father, *1952*, 138–40; and education, 141–44; and region of birth, 144–45; in U.S., *1929–50*, 285–86; defined for analysis, 286–89

Business hierarchy: position in and occupational mobility, 31, 35; and occupation of father, 151, 153–54; and education, 153–55; and influential connections, 162–64; father and son in same firm, 164–66, 168; and financial aid, 173–74; and marriage, 198–201

Business position, categories employed in analysis, 151. *See also* Business hierarchy

Businessmen, history of recruitment in U.S., 16–17

Caples, W. G., 222

Career pattern, *1952* business leaders: and occupation of father, 30, 117–22; and education, 31, 122–23; method of study of, 115; and age, 123–26; and interfirm mobility, 127–28

Census data, as used in analysis, 39–40, 45–46, 237–40

Centers, Richard, 14, 21

Cowles, John, 221

Davidson, Percy E., and H. Dewey Anderson, 14

Differential fertility: effect on vertical mobility, 20; effect on mobility estimates, 40n

Directorships, *1952* business leaders, 155–56: and occupation of father, 156–67

Education, 20–21, 29

1952 business leaders, 95: and U.S. population, 28, 96–97; and occupation of father, 28, 97–98; and education of father, 28–29, 99–101, 105–8; and career pattern, 31, 122–23; and size of business, 31; and region of birth, 103–4; and nativity, 104–5; and geographical and occupational mobility, 105–8; and business training, 111–13; and interfirm mobility, 127; and present age, 131–32; and years to achieve position, 131–32; and business expansion, 141–44; and type of business, 147–49; and occupation of wife's father, 189–98; and occupation of father and wife's father, 190–98; and occupational succession over three generations and marriage, 196–98

1928 business leaders: compared with *1952*, 29, 108–11; formal business training, 111–14; and business hierarchy, 154–55; financial aid and influential connections, 174–76

Endogamy, 180–82: over three generations, 186; and region of birth, 209

312

Index

Entrepreneurship, and *1952* business leaders, 122

Exogamy, 180–82

Family, *see* Marriage; Occupational succession

Family structure, and occupational succession, 4–6

Farmers: as source of *1928* business leaders, 49; changes in U.S. population, 49–50; as source of *1952* business leaders, 56–67, 58–60; census undercount in *1920*, 238–39

Financial aid, 32–33: and occupation of father, 170–73; sources of, 172–73; compared with *1928*, 172; and position in business hierarchy, 173–74; and family, 174; and education and influential connections, 174–76

First occupation, *1952* business leaders, 117–19. *See also* Career pattern

Fisher, L. H., 221

Formal business training, *1928* and *1952*, 111–13

Fortune, 18, 70–71n

Frontier theory, and vertical mobility, 20

Geographical mobility: as factor in vertical mobility, 26–27, 82–83; and region of birth, 72–76; definition and method of study, 80–81; of *1952* business leaders, 81–83; of ministers' sons, 83; and education and occupation of father, 105–8; and years to achieve position, 132–33, 134. *See also* Region of birth; Nativity

Geographical sources of business leaders, *see* Region of birth

Geographical stability, 72–77

Gifford, Walter S., 221

Goodman, Howard, 222

Growth of industry and firm, *see* Business expansion

Immigration, 20. *See also* Nativity

Influential connections: and occupation of father, 32, 160–62; and position in business hierarchy, 162–64; and years to achieve position, *1928* and *1952*, 164; and financial aid, *1928* and *1952*, 174–76; and classification of questionnaire responses on, 296–97

Interfirm mobility: of *1952* business leaders, 30, 126; and occupation of father, 30, 126–27; and education, 127; career pattern, 127–28; and years to achieve position, 133–34; and age of entering firm, 134

Interviews with respondents: on response accuracy, 213, 224; for further study of mobility, 224

Joslyn, C. S., and F. W. Taussig, 10, 11, 19, 24, 49, 212

Legge, Alexander, 221

Lynd, R. S., and H. M. Lynd, 17

Marriage: and occupational succession, 7; and vertical mobility, 21; of *1952* business leaders, 33–34; role in occupational mobility, 177–78. *See also* Occupation of wife's father

Miller, William, 16

Mobile elite, definition, 8

"Mobility ratio," definition and method, 40–42, 47

Motivation, and mobility, 21–22

National income, by type of business, 231, 285–88

Nativity: related to vertical mobility, 20; factor in business mobility, 27, 92–94; of *1952* business leaders, 89–90; and occupation of father, 90–94; and education of *1952* business leaders, 104–5; and years to achieve *1952* business position, 133; and marriages of *1952* business leaders, 205–6

Negroes, and business leadership, 239–40

Nepotism, *1928* and *1952*, 168

Occupation of father
1952 business leaders, 24–25, 37–39: and U.S. population, 25, 39–42; and education, 28, 97–98; and years to achieve leadership, 30; professional man, 43; and region of birth, 77–80; and geographical mobility, 82–83; and size of birthplace, 88–89; and nativity, 90–94; and education of father, 101, 105–8; and career pattern of business leader, 117–22; and interfirm mobility, 126–27; and age at entering business, 129–30; and length of career, 130; and present age, 130; and business expansion, 138–40; and type of business, 147; and position in business hierarchy, 151, 157; and influential connections, 160–62; and financial aid, 170–72; and occupation of wife's father, 179–83, 187–89; and occupation of father's father and marriage, 183–86; and education and marriage, 190–98; and occupation of father's father, education, and marriage,

313

Index